1999 Best Newspaper Writing

WINNERS: THE AMERICAN SOCIETY OF NEWSPAPER EDITORS COMPETITION

EDITED BY CHRISTOPHER SCANLAN

The Poynter Institute
and
Bonus Books, Inc.

03   02   01   00   99   5   4   3   2   1

International Standard Book Number: 1-56625-138-9
International Standard Serial Number: 0195-895X

The Poynter Institute for Media Studies
801 Third Street South
St. Petersburg, Florida 33701

Bonus Books, Inc.
160 East Illinois Street
Chicago, Illinois 60611

Book design and production by Billie M. Keirstead
Cover illustration by Phillip Gary Design, St. Petersburg, Florida

Photos for the cover illustration were provided by the Associated
Press and are used with permission. Photo credits: AP photogra-
phers John Gaps III (Mark McGwire), Brian Hendler (Holocaust
Memorial, Jerusalem), Mark Humphrey (Carl Perkins), Arturo
Mari (Pope John Paul II in Cuba), and Rogelio Solis (school shoot-
ing). Photo of Pol Pot's coffin provided by the Thai Army to the
Associated Press. Photo of tornado is from the NOAA Photo
Library, NOAA Central Library. Photos of Tacoma, Wash., *News
Tribune* pages were provided by *The News Tribune.* Photos of
ASNE winners and finalists were provided by their newspapers.

Printed in the United States of America

This book is dedicated to the memory of the children killed in America's schools and to the future of their classmates who will be the country's next generation of journalists.

A few words about
Tony Berkshire

MAY 1999

Every time I get to meet one of journalism's celebrated writers it leads, inevitably, to the same discovery: Hey, this writer is just like the rest of us. Just like me.

Don't believe it? Look at this:

"Most of us are unbelievably insecure. I don't know about Dave, who's just been described as the funniest man on earth, but I bet you every time he starts [writing] he's saying, 'Oh God, is this funny or is this not funny?' There's terrible insecurity. You're out there. You've got your byline on whatever follows. There's always a feeling of, 'Did I get it right? Did I say it right? Does anybody understand?'"

That was Ellen Goodman talking. Talking about, among others, Dave Barry. They were on a panel at the 1998 convention of the American Society of Newspaper Editors. So were Donna Britt and Rick Bragg, along with the moderator, Roger Ebert. The panel was called "What Is Good Writing?"

Listening to those good writers talk about insecurity and about how they revered editors who played the roles of coach, supporter, abettor, shrink, I kept thinking about how long it took me as a writer to discover that the people whose work I'd idolized were every bit as shaky producing it as I was. As an editor, I resolved, but didn't always manage to maintain, a newsroom environment that would reflect how much nurturing even the best writers need.

That's what this book is all about. It's for those of you writers who haven't yet discovered that your idols are real people, that they are as bedeviled as you about style and cadence and technique, that they're not only willing but eager to talk about it if you give them a chance instead of gawking at them from a distance at the writing workshop or, worse, not even going to hear them speak about how they do for a living the same thing you do: sweat at the keyboard.

It's also for you editors who are going to too damned many meetings to have time to talk with your staff about stuff like writing. Skip a meeting. Send someone else. Talk about writing. It doesn't have to be elaborate.

"What editors can do most," Ellen Goodman said, "is praise you when you do it right and encourage you by saying not just, 'Hey, nice piece, kid,' but 'I really like the way you used that metaphor. I really liked the way your piece had a beginning, a middle, and an end,' which the copy editor didn't even take out. That can keep you going and keep you eager because we're all insecure enough that we're working for other people's praise just like when we were little and we were waiting for grades from our teacher. That's not as simplistic as it sounds. In this climate everybody's busy, everybody's overloaded, and we all have productivity problems. We're always on deadline, and it's easy to forget to tell people when what they've done is what you're really looking for. That's something that makes people feel more comfortable experimenting, too."

Ah, yes. Experimenting.

Great journalism is often experimental. Risk-taking. Bold. Rule-breaking. We follow the rules of the craft most of the time, and should. The trick comes in knowing when to violate them, not about fact but about form. The best editor is the one who pulls you back from the brink when the experiment didn't work, but who encourages you to try another experiment another time.

Tim Dwyer and Gene Foreman helped teach me that. Dwyer was a general assignment sportswriter when *The Philadelphia Inquirer* sent him to Atlanta to profile Jerry Glanville, the wacko who'd become coach of the pro football Falcons. Dwyer followed the coach around for several days and wrote down everything Glanville said—at practice, on his radio show, in interviews, driving around town, talking with Dwyer. Now this wasn't the first profile of Glanville, and Dwyer was determined to do something novel with it. So he sat down and figured out a way to assemble all those Glanville quotes in a sequence that let Glanville tell his own story. He showed his draft to a buddy who wrote for one of the Atlanta papers. "Are you nuts?" the buddy warned. "You send that to Philadelphia and they'll fire you."

Dwyer sent it. Assistant sports editor Gary Howard (now sports editor of the *Milwaukee Journal*) took one look and thought, "Oh, no. What am I going to do with this?" But he liked it, so he bucked it to the deputy sports editor, Nancy Cooney (now deputy foreign editor), who took one look and thought, "Oh, no. What am I going to do with this?" But she liked it and bucked it to the sports editor, David Tucker (now an enterprising bureau chief for *The Star-Ledger* in Newark), who did the same thing and bucked it to me, and I reacted the same way and took it to Gene Foreman, then *The Inquirer*'s number two editor, who said, "Don't put this in the paper tonight!" with such resoluteness the rest of us thought we'd hit the wall.

We hadn't. What Tim Dwyer had done was to arrange all those Glanville quotes in a single paragraph that was about 24 inches long. Gene Foreman realized that the paper had not prepared to publish the complete piece on the sports front and that a jump would destroy Dwyer's imaginative approach. So Foreman held it a day and cleared out space for the entire package, including a photo of the coach lounging on his Harley-Davidson, so that a reader could tell at a glance that this was a 24-inch one-graf story.

In an earlier number in this series, *Best Newspaper Writing 1996*, Ken Fuson, who's now at the Baltimore *Sun*, explained a similar venture at *The Des Moines Register*. He got one of those mundane assignments that many writers kiss off: Write a weather story to mark the first nice day of spring. Fuson reported what it looked, sounded, felt, and smelled like outdoors and then wrote it—as 290 words in a single sentence. Fuson described his editor's reaction:

"When I returned to the newsroom, I told Randy Essex, a deputy editor, that I wanted to try something different. He didn't roll his eyes. He read it and liked it. When it was time for the news meeting, he put the entire story on the budget. That's what they call 'closing the sale,' and I appreciated it."

That's how it should happen. The writer is inventive. The editors collaborate to show off the invention. The reader gets a nifty piece of writing—and another reason to want to keep taking the paper.

The editors who selected the stories in this book understand that is how it should happen. It isn't just being dutiful when they take three days out of their lives to assemble in St. Petersburg and immerse themselves in stories nominated for the ASNE Distinguished Writing Awards and the Jesse Laventhol Prizes for Deadline

News Reporting. They get to see, admire, learn from, and honor the work of writers who took risks to good effect. These editors deserve to be honored, too. The 1999 ASNE Writing Awards Board was led by Rena M. Pederson, editorial page editor of *The Dallas Morning News*. Her colleagues were:

Gilbert Bailon, *The Dallas Morning News*
Joann Byrd, *Seattle Post-Intelligencer*
Leonard Downie Jr., *The Washington Post*
Robert H. Giles, Media Studies Center, New York
Clark Hoyt, Knight Ridder Inc.
Maxwell King, *The Philadelphia Inquirer*
Craig Klugman, *The Journal Gazette,*
    Fort Wayne, Ind.
Forrest Landon, retired, Roanoke, Va.
David Laventhol, Times Mirror Co.
Carolyn Lee, *The New York Times*
Sandy Rowe, *The Oregonian,* Portland, Ore.
Paul Tash, *St. Petersburg* (Fla.) *Times*
Gil Thelen, *Tampa* (Fla.) *Tribune*
Cynthia Tucker, *The Atlanta Constitution*
Howard Tyner, *Chicago Tribune*

Which brings us to the occasional editor who needs guidance, not praise, and to Tony Berkshire. Donna Britt told this tale to the editors at that 1998 convention:

"My problem is when an editor thinks I'm just not that bright. I remember writing about the Berkshire Place Hotel in New York. I said, 'the tony Berkshire.' You know; it's tony, it's an elegant place. And someone uppercased it so that it read 'the Tony Berkshire Place Hotel.' Owned and operated by a lounge singer. When editors assume that maybe you made a little mistake and they're going to help you, it can make everybody look stupid. I just can't stress this enough. Go back to the writer. Most of us care so much about our writing that we will make the little changes you want so that it will flow, so that it will be beautiful."

We do care. Writers and editors can collaborate, must collaborate, to achieve what either cannot alone. You writers can learn from the achievers in this book. So can you editors. Take it from Tony Berkshire.

Cheers,
Jim Naughton, President
The Poynter Institute

Acknowledgments

This book reflects the efforts and contributions of many people and organizations, chief among them the American Society of Newspaper Editors, especially Lee Stinnett, former executive director, his successor, Scott Bosley, and Rena M. Pedersen of *The Dallas Morning News,* who chaired the writing awards committee. Chuck Zoeller and Grant Lamos of the Associated Press generously provided the news photos used on the cover.

Once again, the series has been especially enriched by my Poynter colleagues Roy Peter Clark, Aly Colón, Karen Brown Dunlap, and Keith Woods, who each interviewed a winning writer; and Kenny Irby and Monica Moses, who produced an illuminating section on the role played by visual journalists at one winning newspaper. Billie Keirstead, publications director, supervised the entire effort, assisted by Vicki Krueger, an experienced copy editor who wrote the Writers' Workshop sections, enabling us to produce this book on a journalism dead line. They were aided by Patty Cox, a skilled copy editor, and Joyce Barrett, Priscilla Ely, Martin Gregor, and Nancy Stewart of the Institute staff.

Readers benefit most of all from the stories and lessons about reporting and writing shared by the winners and finalists of this year's Distinguished Writing Awards and Jesse Laventhol Prizes. As always, *Best Newspaper Writing 1999* is their book.

Contents

Echoes of the writer's voice

Joe Distelheim sounded a little worried. Sitting at the annual convention of the American Society of Newspaper Editors in San Francisco last May, the editor of *The Huntsville* (Ala.) *Times* had just listened to excerpts from the winning entries in the annual writing contest. They included two first-person stories, as well as a column and an editorial that reflected the writer's obvious passion.

"What are we to read in this?" Distelheim wondered during question time for the session featuring this year's ASNE winners. "Is this coincidence?...Ought we to be worried about this or ought we to be celebrating that we're putting more of ourselves into this craft of reporting and writing?"

It's no coincidence, that's for sure. First person or not, the writer's voice, that unmistakable sense of one writer talking to one reader, is on display throughout the pages of this volume, the 21st edition of *Best Newspaper Writing.* As the winning writers responded to Distelheim's question, it became clear that they're convinced that the writer's voice has a place in every story.

"Good writing requires the writer to put himself or herself in the story, whether it be a first-person piece, a profile, or a long feature story," said DeNeen L. Brown of *The Washington Post,* who won the non-deadline writing prize for a story collection that tackles such emotionally charged topics as abortion, racial equality, juvenile injustice, and modern-day parenting with honest sensitivity and literary grace. "You can hear the writer's voice, even in hard news stories."

The first person appears nowhere in "Hanging by a Thread," the riveting reconstruction of a deadly avalanche on Washington's Mount Rainier that won the Jesse Laventhol Prize for deadline news reporting by a team. Written by Sandi Doughton based on reporting by a team of reporters and visual journalists at *The News Tribune* of Tacoma, Wash., the story evokes the rewards and risks that climbers face confronting the mountain's majestic and unforgiving power. That it does so with such dramatic power reflects the person behind the byline; within a month Doughton was set to make her first climb up Mount Rainier, she got the avalanche assignment.

"I was very nervous about what I would experience," she told the audience of editors. "I felt it very easy to connect and to put myself in the place of the people who were there and imagine what that might have been like. And I think that made it a richer and more emotionally evocative story."

Neither is there any first-person narrator in the stories by Bartholomew Sullivan of *The Commercial Appeal* in Memphis, who won the Jesse Laventhol Prize for deadline news reporting by an individual, about an Arkansas tornado, the funeral of rock legend Carl Perkins, and the trial of a Ku Klux Klansman. Yet, "I'm in the stories," Sullivan said. He's there, "...in the depth of experience I bring to asking the kinds of questions I ask...the kinds of people I talk to." Writing in the third person, Sullivan relies on the voices of the people he writes about: "What these people sound like and what they're saying...I hear voices and I try to bring them into the stories I write."

The only voice evident in many newspaper editorials is that distant institutional "we," an approach *Boston Globe* editorial writer Susan Trausch (an ASNE winner in 1995) aptly labeled "the traditional editorial scolding stance: 'It would be prudent if we all did this.'" Bailey Thomson of the *Mobile* (Ala.) *Register* won the editorial writing award for a blistering series of editorials about failures in education, environment, and political courage that also furnishes an effective catalog of solutions drawn from neighboring states. "I think in writing editorials there has to be a passion behind the work," Thomson said. "You have to feel deeply for your subject. Always being open to new ideas, always being open to new interpretations. But still something has to come from deep within you to write passionately about the wrongs you see and the future you want. And I think if you do those things, the work comes as naturally as it can for a writer."

When *The New York Times* sent Mirta Ojito to Cuba with a team covering Pope John Paul II's visit, she assumed she would visit a neighborhood to write an intimate account of life in Cuba today. She'd probably even visit the neighborhood where she and her family once lived. But she never thought she'd write about it, and never dreamed that her first-person account of that visit would appear on the front page, or win the "Covering the World" award given by ASNE to honor stories that best helped readers understand the impact of international news on their own lives.

Placing the reporter's experiences at the heart of a story is a gamble that pays off, Ojito said, "when you have something to say that's a lot broader" than your own experiences. The result: "You make it more personal and people pay attention."

J. Peder Zane, whose ASNE prize-winning commentary about books for *The News & Observer* of Raleigh, N.C., believes that newspaper writers are merely echoing a larger trend. "You've seen it in all other forms of writing. It has a lot to do with the desire of people for intimacy."

Writing about books, Zane often uses the first person "to bring readers in, then connect that experience that I've had or that observation I've had to something much larger." It's not always easy. "You need to find a way as journalists to use that first person to make people care, not about ourselves, but about other people," Zane said. "That's our job."

If newspaper writers can keep that in mind, editors need not worry when a writer's voice echoes in a story.

They can celebrate.

A NOTE ABOUT THIS EDITION

The discussions with the ASNE winners in this book are based on tape-recorded telephone interviews conducted by myself and my Poynter Institute colleagues Roy Peter Clark, Aly Colón, Karen Brown Dunlap, Kenny Irby, Monica Moses, and Keith Woods. For reasons of clarity or pacing, we reorganized some questions and answers, and in some cases, inserted additional questions. The edited transcripts were reviewed for accuracy and, in some cases, revised slightly by the subjects.

Christopher Scanlan
June 1999

1999 Best Newspaper Writing

DeNeen L. Brown
Non-Deadline Writing

DeNeen L. Brown is a general assignment reporter at *The Washington Post,* where she has worked since launching her career in 1986. She took the scenic route to becoming a metro reporter, beginning as a summer intern in 1986. She worked as a copy editor on the national, foreign, and metro desks during a time when crack cocaine and its accompanying murder rate were overtaking the District.

Because she had "too much energy and no life outside work," Brown says, she would often complete her duties on the metro copy desk, then go out to crime scenes with the night police reporter and write stories about victims. She switched to reporting full time in 1989, moving first to the newspaper's Fairfax bureau, then to the city staff, the Prince George's County bureau,

and—after a three-month "fellowship" in the Style section—back to the metro desk.

Along the way, she wrote about youth issues, including a story about children so traumatized by the violence around them that they had begun planning their own funerals. The story helped make her a finalist for the 1993 Livingston Award. Brown's work has also won awards in the Maryland-Delaware-D.C. Press Association writing contests.

Her winning stories combine the excellence of detail-rich reporting and lyrical writing with the insight she summons from being a minister's daughter, the offspring of black culture, and a mother.

—Keith Woods

Superintendent tries moving a mountain

JUNE 22, 1998

Prince George's County Superintendent Jerome Clark knew the call was coming before the phone rang. For months, there had been rumblings that the state would move to take over the county's lowest performing schools. Finally in January, State Superintendent Nancy S. Grasmick phoned midmorning: Nine schools were failing, and the state was dictating a strict timetable for improvement.

She summoned the Prince George's superintendent to a meeting in Baltimore. For Clark, the rest of the conversation remains a blur.

"She might have told me which schools," Clark recalls. "But I can't remember her saying anything else. I remember saying I would be there the next day. I just sat there," embarrassed that under his tenure the state would make that threat.

An ordained Baptist deacon, Clark falls back in moments of struggle and stress on a comfort his mother showed him long ago growing up in Indiana. He unlocks his desk and opens the left drawer. He finds the smooth, black, pocket-size leather Bible and unzips it. In the silence, he flips the gilded pages, lets the book fall open, looks down.

"If ye have faith as a grain of mustard seed, ye shall say unto this mountain, Remove hence to yonder place; and it shall remove."

For three years, Clark, 55, has been trying to move a mountain, the troubled Prince George's County school system. Instead, the mountain has moved him, changed him in ways that are irreversible. Curled his thick shoulders under the weight. Stopped the ink in the love sonnets he used to write. Robbed him of hours with his family. And directed an avalanche of blame toward him.

Clark started in the system in 1971 and to this day says he is a teacher at heart—an observation that may be revealing as he comes to terms with his stewardship. He's viewed by colleagues, teachers and parents as a scholarly visionary, but one who falters in getting programs running. He is known for his compassion, but some who have watched him think he may be too nice, as he has allowed poor principals and administrators to stay in the system. He despises politics, and as a consequence his big, booming voice has often been silent during debates in county and state politics.

Clark knows he is running out of time. His $125,000-a-year contract expires in July 1999.

By February, Clark and the board will make a decision, each about the other. Clark will decide whether to ask for another four-year contract. The board will decide whether he is the person to fix the schools in the five years before the deadline the state set for improvement. Whatever happens, Clark doesn't want anybody to say he coasted this last year.

"You can say I was ineffective, but don't ever say I was not trying.

"The question," he says, "is whether the mountain has become a hill or whether I've gone deeper into the valley. Because sometimes you think you've climbed the highest peak only to get to one point and realize you are halfway up the summit. I'm hoping the peak is in sight....The air is getting a little thin, though."

Three months after the Public School Superintendents Association of Maryland named him 1998 Superintendent of the Year, a majority of the school board rated him a 2 on a scale of 0 to 4 in an initial evaluation. His lowest marks were in management and operation of the school system.

Angered by leaks of the evaluation, Clark fired back a response.

"I *am* the Superintendent of this school system," he wrote. "I am not threatened by an evaluation that identifies areas for improvement. Any leader who does not recognize the constant need for growth and change does not have a vision for the future."

VISION AND POLITICS

Clark's announced vision when he took office was to improve the county schools by raising what he called "education outcomes," meaning student performance; restructuring the management teams that supervised schools; and drawing in the community to aid in the reforms.

He had made two unsuccessful attempts to become superintendent in 1984 and 1991. Finally, in 1995, the community and the board picked him over two outsiders. Clark described himself as a conciliator who could build bridges with parents, business people and elected leaders and spark changes in an already flagging system that ranked near the bottom statewide in academic performance. He asked for three years to scale the summit, and three years later, the reviews are rolling in.

Clark has had successes.

Scores on the Scholastic Assessment Test in 1996-97 rose six points, the first increase in eight years and the largest one-year gain in 15 years. Scores for minorities also rose, and more students took the college-entry test.

Clark also is credited with emphasizing intensive reading programs for students reading below grade level, structuring the overall budget to finance smaller class sizes and giving principals leeway to manage their schools' finances.

School board member Kenneth E. Johnson (Mitchell-ville), who was on the board that hired Clark, says he is impressed by Clark's achievements. "But we still have a ways to go."

Clark says he believes "I've done everything I told the board I would do. I haven't failed at anything."

Yet he acknowledges that several of his innovative concepts came up short because he did not execute them well.

Scores on the high-stakes test for third-, fifth- and eighth-graders known as the Maryland School Performance Assessment Program, fell slightly last year, putting the county further behind the statewide average.

Clark's breakdown of central management into smaller clusters failed to reach its potential because some team leaders "just sit back and don't do anything," says school board member Doyle Niemann (Mount Rainier). "If I was going to fault the superintendent, it would be that he has not acted aggressively enough to get rid of people not doing their jobs."

A special tutoring program Clark introduced foundered because volunteers were scant. Clark now says that to sustain that program, the positions should have been paid slots. Likewise, he says, after he personally reorganized the staffs of six schools, he got disruptions without improvements.

School board Vice Chairman Verna Teasdale (Bowie) continues to credit Clark as "genuinely a visionary. But sometimes a visionary can see the things that they want to accomplish so clearly, they don't recognize others don't see it as clearly and there needs to be a lot of planning that goes into creating the vision."

"I think he is a nice guy," says County Council member Isaac Gourdine (D-Fort Washington), who chairs the council's education committee. "But niceness doesn't get things done."

For Clark, who openly disdains politics, consensus building has become even more complicated as Prince George's continues to change socially and economically and the constituencies involved with the schools become more demanding.

The two superintendents who were his immediate predecessors, Edward Felegy and John Murphy, dealt with a longtime core of business and elected leaders, many of whom have been replaced as the county has both grown and become majority African-American.

In the midst of an increasingly politicized environment, Clark says, "I try to be as sophisticated as I can."

But it may not be enough. "Clark is no different from his predecessors. The climate is different," but Clark should adapt by becoming a tougher personality, says a board member, who asked not to be identified because of the pending evaluation of Clark. "In this environment, when they are besieged by the state, they need George Patton."

Clark was not that forceful during a recent session in Annapolis. In fact, he was overlooked.

In a packed hearing room, the Prince George's leaders involved with school funding had gathered to make their case. It was clear their testimony could make or break the request for school construction funds. Sen. Barbara A. Hoffman (D-Baltimore) called Prince George's leaders to the table: County Executive Wayne K. Curry (D), School board Chairman Alvin Thornton (Suitland), County Council Chairman Ronald V. Russell (D-Mitchellville). Clark was left waiting.

He went to the table anyway. When he was not recognized to speak, he stormed out.

"I raised my hand to speak, and the gavel fell," Clark says. "I thought it was disrespectful."

JOURNEY TO THE MOUNTAIN

Tall and imposing, with rich brown skin and a black-and-white beard, Clark has an easy smile, and when he talks in his deep Barry White voice, people listen. Conversations with staff are peppered with phrases like "this is high stakes," and "I need this now." The words are spoken more matter of factly, not with emphatic flashes of anger or angst.

In his office, the walls are decorated with a black-and-white picture of a segregated classroom, scales of justice, a painting of Martin Luther King Jr., a sketch titled "Tell the Truth" and prized paintings of black Buffalo soldiers.

The many plaques describing his achievements are in a box, and it is hard to tell whether the box is packed for coming or going. Lying on top is a stuffed monkey. Clark picks it up, explains with a smile that this is his symbol of management.

Ask his staff members and they can tell you about the monkey. When they come in, they know, "Don't bring me any monkeys. When you come in, don't tell me, 'We have a problem.' Say, 'I have a problem and this is how I think we ought to resolve it.'"

Clark puts down the monkey. "I have my own problems," he says.

The increasing presence of poverty in the schools, declining test scores, the drain of qualified teachers, the patchwork of struggling reforms—those are Clark's problems, many inherited, some created. He is concerned. He had promised himself that as long as he was sitting in the superintendent's chair, he would project a professional image, he would look the part, he would have the information. Becoming the county's first African-American school superintendent, Clark carried the accomplishments of a race on his shoulders. Nothing he would do would bring embarrassment upon that chair.

How did Clark get to this mountain?

Follow Interstate 70 west to Indianapolis. Turn down McCarty Street and come on a view of Eli Lilly, the giant pharmaceutical company. Drive west on Kenwood to what remains of Senate Avenue and Michael Park. The houses are gone, the parks disappeared, the schools vanished.

"It was as if we didn't exist," Clark says.

He was born Aug. 31, 1942, one of six children to Jesse Evans Clark, a secretary and bookkeeper, and Waymon Clark, a laborer in a steel mill.

Jerome was the second oldest, one of two boys. His mother never gave him a middle name.

He could read long before he started school, *Robinson Crusoe* and the children's version of the Greek classics. His mother taught him to read with phonics—a topic debated in her son's school system, although she is unaware of that. "I told them there is no way you can know words if you don't know how to pronounce them." recalls Jesse Clark, now 78 and living in Indianapolis.

Clark went to a hand-me-down school. When the district built a school for whites, Clark and his neighbors went to the building they left behind.

No matter their ambitions, by 10th grade, the system began weeding them out of the rigorous curriculum, encouraging students to learn trades, with the most promising steered toward barbering. "Nobody in my family had gone to college. I had not seen any examples of anyone going," Clark says. "My desire was to graduate—get myself a barbershop and enjoy life."

It was only by chance that Clark ended up at Indiana Central College. A group of friends dared each other to go to college "to see what it was like." But there, "I didn't think they wanted African-American students," he says. "I was rough around the edges. I used to wear brims, and I used to refuse to take them off."

He dropped out and worked at a warehouse and later, for Chrysler, where he assembled car starters at $3.20 an hour. The work was mind-numbing, and in a factory where heat rose to 110 degrees, "you quickly come to the realization there is something better to do."

He returned to the same college and graduated in 1966 with a degree in early childhood education.

He began teaching in Indianapolis. In 1969, he went to visit an uncle in the District and got a temporary job teaching sixth grade. When the job ran out, someone told him to check out Prince George's. He interviewed at Beltsville Elementary and was hired on the spot. He taught sixth grade for three years, and then took leave to work on his doctorate at the University of Massachusetts at Amherst. He returned to teaching and quickly rose through the administrative ranks.

It was as an elementary teacher that he recognized a type of teacher he now denounces. In the lounge, Clark could learn all the gossip, but he also often heard teachers disparaging students in a way he found repugnant.

He vowed never to go to a teachers' lounge again, and he decided he would someday write a book called *Hired Assassins,* about teachers killing off students one by one by assassinating their dreams, lowering their expectations.

"Basically, those teachers are there for a paycheck." They are found in Prince George's, too, he says. "We are doing everything we can to get them out." But he can act only on those referred to him by principals.

Clark pauses. "It's not easy."

TOUGHNESS AND POETRY

The superintendency is a lonely job. To find people who understand his job, Clark reaches across county lines. Of his colleagues across the region, Clark talks most regularly with Paul L. Vance, superintendent of the Montgomery County schools.

"He is a very thoughtful person," Vance says of Clark. "When there is data published that puts the school system in a bad light, he takes it very personally and becomes determined to do something about it. He accepts it. He handles it. His public face, his stoicism is remarkable."

But inside, Vance says, "there is a volcano raging."

That tough side of Clark is one many outside the system still have not glimpsed.

Don't read him wrong, Clark says of himself. He is no weak man.

"I don't mind a fight," he says sternly. But as superintendent, he believes he must maintain a professional image.

Jerome Clark the man is another story.

"As Jerome Clark, I'm a different person," he says. His face changes. His long fingers tap his gold wire-rimmed glasses. Living as an African-American man in this country for 55 years, he has learned never to back down.

He is thinking of a trip when he was 17, riding with a church group to a revival. They stopped in Nashville, got off at a restaurant. The owner served them on paper plates and told them, "You can't eat it here. You have to eat it on the bus."

Clark stepped forward. "We are not going to eat then. We got back on the bus and the owner called the police."

Clark wasn't afraid. "You have to stand up for what you believe. I'm quiet, but I'll look at you straight in the eyes. And my body language is multilingual. Folks know. I don't think I'm misread."

After three decades in the system, many people know about Clark. But they don't know him. He doesn't trust easily. A guarded person, he says, he never wanted anybody to get too close.

He talks openly about his 11-year-old son, Jared, a fifth-grader at Woodmore Elementary School, but doesn't want to reveal details about the rest of his family. A request for an interview with his wife, Karen, a 46-year-old resource teacher in the county, was declined. "I want to keep that part separate," Clark says.

Few people in his Cabinet have been to his home, where he collects antique cars. And he "holds pure" one weekend day each week for his family. On those days, he wakes them early. They know not to ask questions. It is his treat to pile them in a car and take them to surprise destinations.

He is a poet and a musician. His poetry says what he won't. His pen name is Jay Cei, and he writes of love—deep, sometimes unrequited love:

I walked with an arrogance that love afforded...my gait was haughty...my shoulders erect....Time was my slave and I was a hard task-master.

Now...I sit with voice mellowed by the strength of our love given over time. The cadence of my walk has slowed...my back now bends toward the earth...both signs that time, now free, reclaims what it so generously gave in my youth.

His three volumes, each bound, each poem dated, abruptly stops in 1995, the year he got this job. The last volume is titled *Just Before the Silence.*

PARKING LOT MEETINGS

There is no more time to write poetry. Clark squeezes time at both ends of his day, meeting as early as 6 a.m.

Sometimes, before he pulls into his parking space in his metallic rose Lincoln Continental, people already are waiting for him. On a recent day, a vice principal to whom Clark has been a mentor catches him. The man wants to become a principal, and for an hour, Clark stands in the lot talking about his aspirations. "Those parking lot meetings," as he calls them, "are the most important ones."

But for the rest of that day, Clark runs behind, late even to his staff meeting where senior managers await him in a conference room ringed with grids charting test scores for each school in the system. In many of the frames, the bar graphs fall short of the black line, the standard. They are reminders of the urgency of his job. The 17-hour days are taking a toll on Clark physically, emotionally and spiritually. Murphy, one of the prior superintendents, saw him recently at a conference in California. "He was tired. You could see he is tired," Murphy says.

He doesn't eat breakfast. He doesn't eat lunch. If he returns early to his house in the affluent gated community of Woodmore, he says his son asks: "'Are we going to be able to do anything together or do you have to go to another meeting?' Most times, I say I have to go to another meeting."

Men don't last in these jobs forever.

Clark watched Julius W. Becton Jr. retire after a year and a half trying to uproot the bureaucracy in D.C. schools. Becton gave in, saying he was tired. Clark empathizes with Becton, but says nobody would write that kind of ending to his tenure.

"I'll never quit anything," he says.

Clark won't say what he thinks the board will do about his contract. "People don't want to deal with the root causes of why kids fail," Clark says. Instead, "they throw out the superintendent. It's much easier."

Returning to teaching would not be a bad fate. "I always say, 'My name is Jerome Clark and I'm a teacher. I will always be a teacher.'" He is wistful only when he mulls his pension. "I only have 27 years in the state. Next year gives me 28. I need 30 to have a full pension."

If he leaves, Clark says, "they might say I wasn't hard-nosed as I might have been. But nobody can say I wasn't seriously compassionate about the kids." If he "can leave with my integrity intact, I don't care what else they try to take away."

Clark said he sees himself in the faces of little black boys in classrooms across the county. If he fails them, he fails himself.

"These are youngsters like the youngsters I played with in my neighborhood. And they keep you honest," Clark says. The Prince George's schools, Clark says, "will be turned around....I'm more determined than ever to make sure I don't lower my expectation and that no one in the organization will lower their expectations. I know what will happen to them if we do."

The risks are always there, a hard truth reinforced just last month.

One day when he was out of town, a former student who kept in touch with Clark called him. When Clark returned, his secretary handed him the pink "While you were out" slip.

While he was out, Clark then learned, the former student had been killed in an armed robbery attempt. "I wasn't here for him." He is shaken. "He may have needed some money. He might have needed to talk..."

The conference Clark attended may ultimately benefit many students, but Clark is haunted by the one who slipped away.

"I can't afford to fail these kids. And anybody who knows me knows I'm serious about that," Clark says. "I take it very seriously."

This time, his voice is steely.

Writers' Workshop

Talking Points

1) "Curled his thick shoulders under the weight. Stopped the ink in the love sonnets he used to write. Robbed him of hours with his family. And directed an avalanche of blame toward him." Note how the verbs give each sentence power. What makes this section effective? How do you guard against overwriting?

2) Trace the mountain metaphor through the story. How does the writer use it to frame the article?

3) The fact that Clark has stopped writing poetry is emblematic of the toll the superintendent's job has taken on him. What other details in the story are particularly telling? What techniques do you imagine Brown uses to learn such details?

Assignment Desk

1) Write a profile of the local school superintendent. Is there an image that would serve as a metaphor for that person? How would you incorporate it in the story?

2) Rewrite this story without the mountain metaphor. How does that affect the structure of the story?

A good whuppin'?

SEPTEMBER 13, 1998

She remembers the sting of the switch beating out the rhythm of her father's words against her bare legs. She prayed that the sentence would be short because with each word, with each syllable, the stick whipped the air and fell.

I (WHACK!) *told* (WHACK!) *you* (WHACK!) *to* (WHACK!) *stay* (WHACK!) *in* (WHACK!) *the* (WHACK!) *yard!* (WHACK!)

The stings swelled into welts that she nursed along with deeper hurts.

If I told you once, I told you a million times. When I tell you something, you better listen to me. Now stop all that cryin'. Stop! Do you want some more? Well, you better stop all that cryin'.

TuSheena Watson came of age in the 1970s, in a house where there was no debate about whether beatings were fair. The whuppin's were promised and always came. The infraction and its connection to the punishment were clear. Her father and mother never heard of such things as a "timeout." There was no talking, no talking back, no questioning authority and no analyzing disobedience. Going to your room meant nothing, because she had no room of her own. The beatings were plain and sufficient, and today the memories of them are seared in her mind, but "they were a good thing," she now declares as the parent of two children.

"My mother and my daddy would beat us, all 10 of us. The switch, they would pull the leaves off. You are crying before they come to you. And they used to give the neighborhood permission to whip you. They would whip you, then tell you to shut up. 'Shut up before I give you something to cry for.' You already did. You just beat me to death, now you're going to tell me to shut up. How can I shut up?"

She is living it again, sitting in a job-training classroom in Prince George's County. Hair pulled back from her face, clad in T-shirt and jeans, she looks young. Back in New Jersey she was the baby girl of the family, but now, at 32, she is on the other side of the switch. She knows the trials of controlling her daughters. She swears by spanking.

Go outside and pick me a switch. And don't pick a small one either.

That command, for many, is part of being black in America—part of a cultural tradition that sought to steel black children for the world, forge their characters, help prepare them for the pure meanness that waited out there, just because of the color of their skin. Many black parents who whipped felt more was at stake if they did not scourge their children.

Don't get it wrong. The wielding of the switch and the belt and the wooden spoon is not a practice unique to black people. Most races spank their children, especially Southern whites who are fundamentalist Christians. But the stories of beatings done in the name of love, beatings that were endured by many—not all—black parents, are like a familiar song. There are some bad associations with slavery. There are some good associations with survival.

Many black parents see what is happening now—the dope, the guns, the gangs—and they wonder what went wrong. When they came up, it didn't matter what socioeconomic class, a whuppin' was a whuppin'—and it seemed that adults were in control. Now, old people are locked in their houses even in the middle of the day, scared to go outside, scared of the young boys up the street. When did the old people, who would switch you all the way home if you did wrong, fold up their chairs and go inside? Maybe when the whuppin's stopped, the control stopped.

There was a ritual to whuppin's, and many of that generation talk with a kind of bravado about this rite of passage to adulthood. They tell tales of out-of-body experiences, of spiritual epiphanies, of praying to God, of the art of tearful fakery, of agonizing defiance against belts, of loyalty among siblings and not breaking rank, of the time so bad a parent broke a switch on a child's soft flesh. And they speak always of the wrong they committed and why they deserved it.

Spankings make up neighborhood legends and family folklore, comical and sincere. They connect folks, haunt them, set them up to wrestle over what they will do with their own children.

The questions are clear, the answers are not. Will the tradition continue? Will the law allow it? Should it continue? At what cost?

* * *

When she hung up from talking to the fifth-grade teacher, Armender Banks was sputtering with rage. For eight months, the tension had been building. Her 10-year-old daughter, Maria, had been "in a little rebellious mode." She had been grounded. Television had been forbidden. Her bicycle confiscated. Extra book reports assigned.

"I guess she thought she was grown," Banks remembers. "We kept asking her, 'What's wrong? Why are you acting this way?'"

On the afternoon of Feb. 9, Maria's teacher from Assumption Catholic School in Peekskill, N.Y., called. "Didn't you get the slips I sent home telling you about her behavior?"

There had been three—and neither Banks, a nurse, nor her husband, the Rev. Henry Banks, pastor of a small, nondenominational congregation, had seen any of them. Maria had forged her father's and mother's signatures. That evening, when Henry Banks came home, his wife was waiting in the kitchen to report Maria's latest infraction.

She pointed upstairs: "Get her!"

Henry Banks, who has a soft, caring face and graying hair, didn't like the idea of spanking his youngest daughter. But a God-fearing man has to do what a God-fearing man believes God tells him to do.

Proverbs 19:18: *Chasten thy son while there is still hope, and let not thy soul spare for his crying.*

He loves Maria. He paid for her to go to parochial school when they could barely afford it. He paid for her to have a private tutor to help her with homework. He taught her the ways of the Lord and explained to her what could keep her from going to Hell. Her soul was his responsibility.

On his way upstairs, he counted the commandments the child had broken.

One: "Thou shalt honor thy mother and father." Her behavior was out of control and there was no honor.

Two: "Thou shalt not steal." By forging their signatures, she had stolen "the integrity of our names."

Three: "Thou shalt not bear false witness." She had lied to her teachers and told untruths to her parents.

Four: "Thou shalt not kill." She had kicked another girl at the tutorial center. Any violence against humanity breaks this commandment.

"My daughter knows the commandments," Henry Banks said. "We have taught her and she still disobeyed."

He was not angry. The Lord says not to hit in anger. He was hurt. When he climbed the walnut staircase and turned to his left, Maria was waiting. The father told Maria to take her clothes off and prepare for her "strikes."

There would be seven, two for each commandment she broke. The final strike would be spared because God says have mercy.

"Get on your knees," he said, without raising his voice, "in a praying position."

The little girl, who still wears pigtails, knelt beside her white canopy bed.

"She had on her panties and training bra," her mother recalls.

Her father lifted his belt and it came down on her seven times. She yelled and she covered her bottom to break the strikes, but her hands did no good to ease the pain. The belt whipped her arms. She cried. The welts began to swell.

Proverbs 20:30: *The blueness of a wound cleanses away evil.*

* * *

The old people in the neighborhood used to say: "The police department finishes raising other people's kids." Another way of saying: If you don't raise your kids right, you'll lose them to the street corner.

As the debate rages across the country over whether to spank—as some Christian groups advocate the Bible-sanctioned striking of children, as the American Psychological Association releases its limited blessings on spankings, and more books and chapters are published—conversations in beauty shops, churches, living rooms and around kitchen tables start to sound like this:

"Kids these days just don't know how good they got it....I remember my daddy's belt....Look at them acting up....They could use a good whuppin'."

"It is a cultural thing," says Russell Adams, chairman of the Department of Afro-American Studies at Howard University. "There is almost a masochistic celebration that it happened, that it was good for me. They say it like an ordeal righteously survived. You get this kind of amen to the old days."

You know this is gonna hurt me more than it hurts you...

The whuppin' ritual has certain theatrical elements.

First, the anticipation: "Oooooh, you gonna git it! Wait until your father gets home."

Then, the interrogation: "Did you do that? No? Well, you are lying because so and so said they saw you."

Then there is the recital of the law of the house, the neighborhood, the universe: "Now you know better. How many times did I tell you not to...?"

The next stage is the laying on of hands: In some families, the child is held, often producing a hopping dance around the pole that is the parent. In other families, the command is to freeze.

"You were supposed to stand there with your hands raised up in the air," Adams recalls. "We called that the crucifixion position."

The next thing is the art of the preemptive wail, often followed by: "I haven't hit you yet!" Or: "Quit all that crying." Or: "I'm going to give you something to really cry about."

Cunning children always learn fast how much noise to make to receive mercy.

Adams: "There is always the outcry, 'Mama, you are killing me!' The crying is supposed to be a sign you got to me. You almost try to make the whipper feel wrong."

* * *

Proverbs 13:24: *He that spareth his rod hateth his son: but he that loveth him chasteneth him betimes.*

Henry Banks is sitting at his dining room table in his Victorian house in Peekskill, a small riverfront town. White ruffled curtains cover the window. A white lace tablecloth protects the table. A worn King James Bible in big print sits before him.

His is not a dusty Bible. The Scriptures are highlighted in blue, orange, yellow. Some are underlined in blue ink and red ink, indicating he has read them over and over again, consuming the Holy Writ, turning the meanings of the words over in his head.

Banks, 59, has been a minister for 15 years. Ordained by the Disciples of Christ in Brooklyn, he heads the Church in the Wilderness, whose 27-member congregation meets every Sunday right here in his living room.

Spanking is a commandment, he says, not a choice.

He's reading from the Good Book now.

"In the Old Testament, if a child is disobedient, he could be taken by his elders and stoned." He is pointing to Deuteronomy 21, verses 18 through 23.

"It is not that easy to spank, believe me. But God tells you how, where and how many strikes. This is not something you play with."

He is flipping through Proverbs, stops at 13:24 and reads slowly. *He that spareth the rod...*

This is a sermon he has preached many times.

The day after the seven lashes, Maria went to school. She wanted her teacher to know what had happened after that phone call—the impact of her words.

Maria asked her teacher for an ice pack.

The teacher sent the child to the nurse's office. The nurse called Westchester County Child Protective Services, and an hour later, social workers came to the school and drove Maria away.

"If we didn't believe there was a God, I would be in my grave," her mother says now, recounting that awful time in February.

"For seven days," says Henry Banks, "we didn't know where she was. It was pure torture. They incarcerated my daughter."

The Bankses found a lawyer through the 700 Club, a Christian television ministry. And they took the agency to court. Reveal Maria's whereabouts, the parents demanded.

Armender Banks begins to cry, remembering how she could barely hold on during the separation from her daughter. "They are nothing but the Devil," she says. "It's a horrible thing."

"It's very evil," her husband concurs. "Once they get a child into that system, you can't do anything."

The authorities made it clear: Maria could not go home until her parents promised never again to spank her. They refused. They were answering to a higher authority.

* * *

Ultimately, spanking is about control. Not just controlling your child, but running your household as you see fit—no matter what the nanny-state social planners and the supposed child-rearing experts have to say. But increasingly, parents who favor spanking are clashing with the law.

In Minneapolis, police are investigating the case of a 12-year-old girl who was whipped in church, in the presence of her congregation after she was suspended from school. In Florida, a pastor was arrested on child abuse charges after he spanked a 5-year-old child for refusing to eat a strawberry.

Any number of psychiatrists and pediatricians and social workers can be mustered to support either side.

"There is absolutely never any reason to hit a child or adolescent," writes Irwin A. Hyman in his 1997 book, *The Case Against Spanking: How to Discipline Your Child Without Hitting.* Hyman is leading a national campaign to make spanking not only illegal in all public schools but at home as well.

"Every state I know of doesn't allow foster parents to hit children," notes Hyman, a psychology professor at Temple University and director of the National Center for the Study of Corporal Punishment and Alternatives. "The only place you can legally hit kids is in schools and in the home."

The debate on spanking escalated in the late 1970s as a number of states outlawed corporal punishment in public schools. Some states still allow, and even encourage, corporal punishment in schools, including Mississippi, Texas, Arkansas, Alabama and Kentucky. A number of private and parochial schools also continue to spank.

In the past decade, advocates for spanking seem to have gained ground among parents—although earlier this year the American Academy of Pediatrics declared that spanking was "no more effective" than other forms of discipline and that corporal punishment has "negative consequences." Conversely, the American Psychological Association, which has opposed corporal punishment in schools since 1974, recently decided not to condemn spanking in every circumstance.

Some academics believe that the history of spanking among blacks can be directly tied to slavery. Adams, the Howard professor, argues that whippings—as an act of brutal control by white owners—spread into the black culture on these shores.

"There is not a record in African culture of the kind of body attack that whipping represents," he says. "The maintenance of order by physical coercion is rare in Africa."

The custom may be connected to a desire by some blacks to be like the majority culture: "We have imitations, just as we have imitations with hot combs, from those who wanted to look Caucasian. I grew up at a time when people wore clothespins on their noses to make them smaller. We would go to the movies to see Hopalong Cassidy and come back and compress our lips to make them smaller."

Blacks and others who endorse spankings might be suppressing or rationalizing their pain, some psychologists suggest.

"Most of us must admit that the most indelible and most unpleasant childhood memories are those of being hurt by our parents. Some people find the memory of such events so unpleasant they pretend that they were trivial, even funny. You'll notice that they smile when they describe what was done to them. It is shame, not pleasure, that makes them smile," writes Jordan Riak, who heads Project NoSpank, a California advocacy group.

Gary Ezzo teaches that a swat here and there on a child's backside to prevent a dangerous situation is not child abuse. He's the co-author of *On Becoming Babywise,* one of the top-selling books on child-rearing, and a franchiser of sorts when it comes to discipline. During the last 10 years, more than 1.5 million parents—most of them white—have used the Ezzo program in churches and Sunday school classes across the country.

"Spanking is not a cure-all," says Ezzo, who has been portrayed in the media—unfairly, he believes—as a pro-spanking spokesman. "While 85 to 90 percent of parents may be spanking, we in no way are saying they are all doing it correctly.

"We teach never to use a wooden spoon, never to use a father's belt.... We teach never to slap a child in the face, never to spank them on bare skin.... The dignity of the child must always be preserved during any type of punishment. You should never ridicule a child, never attack their dignity as a human being."

* * *

Ordinarily, juvenile cases are sealed by state law, but because Henry and Armender Banks made their case public, Westchester County prosecutor Alan D. Scheinkman will give the official side of the story:

"The school nurse observed the child and found reason to think there are reasonable grounds for child abuse....It was unrefuted testimony that the child was hit with a plastic belt that caused bruising and swelling."

According to Scheinkman, the Bankses initially agreed to allow Maria to stay with a "third party" while an investigation was conducted, but the "parents did not honor that agreement. And because the parents violated the agreement, that effected a removal of the child from the home, which is allowed under state law."

Removing a child from her home is not something county officials do lightly. Ted Salem, an associate commissioner in the county's department of social services, says officials may investigate 5,000 reports of child abuse and maltreatment any given year. "We will probably remove fewer than 250 children."

Was Maria's whipping excessive enough to qualify as child abuse?

"The department has never brought a case against somebody based on a slap on the wrist," answers Salem.

Scheinkman says the law respects the rights of parents to raise their children. "The law becomes involved whenever a parent crosses the line."

* * *

In a red brick building in Seat Pleasant, Md., several women in their twenties and thirties are gathered to receive lessons in what social service bureaucrats call "life skills." This particular program will help them find jobs. They are doing double duty: raising children on their own and trying to pay the bills. Keeping their kids in line is important.

Seated at a table at the side of the classroom, their teacher, Carol McCreary-Maddox, invites a discussion on how they intend to control their children while they juggle.

TuSheena Watson is remembering her parents' house in New Jersey:

"They beat us for what we did—wrong things, for wrongdoing. And I appreciate it. I appreciated it then and I appreciate it now more than ever. And I know my other brothers and sisters do as well...

"When they took us anywhere, we were like soldiers, we were in line, respectful—and because of that I know right now to this day that's why all the 10 of us had never been in trouble and incarcerated or any of the bad things."

A woman named Beverly begs to differ. "My mother beat us and three are incarcerated and one is dead," she says of her siblings. "When they got out of the house, they broke all the rules."

Beverly is 34 now. She has three boys—12, 8 and 3 months. She hated getting spanked by her mother. She believes discipline must be unwavering, but she is resolved not to spank her own kids.

"I don't see how it helped me—not that it hurt me, but it didn't help me," she says. "Her spanking me... well, we called it beating when I was growing up because that's what they were, a beating. All it did was make me scared to come to her with things.

"I don't beat my boys because I don't want them to feel like they have to beat a person in order to communicate with them, or to get them to do what they feel they should be doing."

So how does she punish her older sons? For misbehaving in school last year, 8-year-old Jocque was confined to the house all summer. Totally grounded. He couldn't go outside to play. No matter what, he had to stay inside.

McCreary-Maddox tells Beverly that some people might say confining a child to the house all summer is a more severe form of child abuse. She believes that a spanking provides an immediate lesson about what is right and what is wrong. "Kids need to know what the limits are. You don't want a child growing up to think they can get anything they want and all that will happen is a good stern talking to."

McCreary-Maddox has three children, ages 20, 17 and 12. She loves them all, and she has spanked them all—just as she was spanked as a child. She favored a wooden spoon. "Belts leave marks. I think there may have been a time when I used a belt, but suppose the buckle hits and they are scratched. That is not what you were intending to do."

Her 12-year-old, Allyssa, sits still in the campaign office where her mother volunteers after class. The ponytailed girl freely offers this opinion: "I find it unfair when parents are allowed to hit when they get mad, but we aren't able to do anything. Getting a spanking only makes me madder."

She is remembering the last one.

"I kicked this boy and I got suspended. She said go up to the room and I got a spanking. It didn't really hurt, but I cried before she hit me.

"My cousin told me to say 'Kunta Kinte,'" a reference to the scene in *Roots* in which a white slave owner tries to beat Kunta Kinte's name out of him. "He did it when he was getting a whipping and his mother started laughing."

That tactic didn't work for Allyssa. Her mother still gave her the spoon.

* * *

Proverbs 23:13-14: *Thou shalt beat him with the rod, and shalt deliver his soul from hell.*

Henry Banks presses those words on the thin pages of his Bible. The rod, he says, "that is like a belt, or a switch."

After a series of court hearings and 28 days in which Maria was kept from them, the Bankses finally agreed they would not spank the girl. A judge agreed to return Maria to her home and scheduled the whole case for dismissal in December—if the parents abide by that promise until the hearing.

Banks says he had no problem agreeing because the judge understood the Bible, and further understood that spankings are not done spontaneously.

"Spanking is not the first thing," the pastor says. "It is the last thing you do."

Besides, Banks says, Maria is now 11 and soon she will reach her age of reason—13—at which point, he says, the Bible commands him not to spank.

Since Maria came home, there have been no major problems. She hasn't had a need to be spanked, her parents say.

"She is scared she could be taken," Armender Banks says.

Maria takes a seat in the corner of the living room. Her parents tell her it's okay to talk about what happened to her. She is reluctant at first. She doesn't want to discuss the time she spent in foster care.

"That's in the past," she says. "It was bad. I didn't like it. There was a lot of cursing, drinking and piercing."

"Piercing?" her mother asks.

"Yeah, piercing body parts," Maria says. "They tried to pierce me."

"You see what can happen when a child is out of her household."

Maria says she doesn't even think much about the spanking that started this whole story. She fidgets and recites the Bible: "'Spare the rod, spoil the child.' That means give your children spankings....They spank me because they love me."

Maria asks to be excused. She is tall for her age, but inside she is still a child. It's a Saturday; she wants to play. She chases a friend into the kitchen and they beg for sodas, then run upstairs to watch television.

A few minutes pass and they run back downstairs, now wanting to walk to the riverfront for a festival. After a series of nos, then maybes, Armender and Henry Banks relent.

"But be back before the sun goes down."

The parents keep talking, the daylight fades and Armender checks her watch: 8:45 p.m.

"The sun been done gone down," she says. "Where is Maria?"

The mother climbs in her van, drives to the riverfront and scans the crowd. Neither the girl nor her friend is there.

"Maybe they already walked home," Armender says.

She drives home and opens the screen door. The house is dark. Her husband comes in. He has not seen

Maria either. It is pitch black in the foothills of the mountain-ringed town. Worry creases their faces.

This would be the perfect scenario for a spanking. But they are under court order.

They get back in the van. "Maria is going to be grounded for this," says Armender, now riding in the passenger seat.

A block from the house, Henry Banks lowers his window. Two figures are walking slowly up the street.

"There she is." He stops the van.

"You were supposed to be back before dark," Armender says. "Get in the van."

"But we were walking back," Maria pleads.

The father will hear no excuses.

"The next time you ask to go somewhere the answer is an automatic no," he says.

He wheels the van slowly up a hill, his wife at his side, his daughter sitting in the seat behind him. He is still the father. He is still the man in charge of his household. But not totally. The child has disobeyed in a blatant, dangerous way. He thinks of the time she left the yard when she was 3 and her mother burned her legs up with a switch. After that, she never left the yard without permission again.

You can see the frustration in his face. He knows that girl could have used a good spanking.

Writers' Workshop

Talking Points

1) The opening of this story mentions rhythm and is itself very rhythmic. Read the first few paragraphs aloud and analyze the different cadence of each.

2) When writing about a characteristic of a particular culture, you run the risk of trivializing or overgeneralizing. Does this story have that effect?

3) Note how this story alternates between the Banks family and general discussion about spanking. How would this story read if it were solely one focus or the other? What does the story gain by focusing on one family rather than several?

Assignment Desk

1) Find a local family that has struggled with the issue of spanking. Use them as the focus of your own story. Before you interview them, write about your own experience with spanking, either as a child or parent, or both. Use the information to develop your interview questions.

2) This story uses different voices in the narrative. Look for ways to incorporate different voices in your stories.

Deborah's choice

SEPTEMBER 27, 1998

ONSET, Mass.—Deborah Gaines sees him still, his face framed by black curly hair, his dark eyebrows arched. He is a contradiction. He is evil and benevolent. He is a murderer and a savior. He is the abortion clinic gunman, and his face haunts her.

She remembers running out of the clinic that cold December morning. He, the shooter, is chasing her, the patient. He is firing his semiautomatic rifle. The bullets are spraying all around her, banging into the metal gate through which she is trying to escape. He is staring at her as she desperately pulls at the gate, trying to get it open, trying to run. He is standing only three feet away, yet the bullets seem to bend around her and ricochet, *ding-ding-ding,* off the black steel gate.

She hears him saying something like "Darn, I'm sorry I missed you."

She keeps clawing and yanking at the gate. It finally opens and she runs for her life—but not for the life that is now about seven weeks old within her womb.

She runs and runs, pulling herself over another fence and falling flat on her back. She gets up. She doesn't know how, but she finds her feet beneath her. She is not looking back. She believes he, the man in black, is after her. She does not stop running until she crosses the street, pulls open an apartment building door and frantically pushes all the buzzers, crying for anybody to help.

Behind her, in the Preterm Health Services Clinic in the Boston suburb of Brookline, blood is pooling on the first floor. An antiabortion zealot named John Salvi III has pumped bullets into three staffers. One of them, receptionist Lee Ann Nichols, is dead.

On that day in that place, fates got up and exchanged places. One life ended and another life received a reprieve: a baby who was not yet wanted, but who would come to be named Vivian Gaines.

Deborah Gaines remembers Dec. 30, 1994, as if it happened an hour ago. She remembers it every time she looks into the small honey-colored face of her daughter, the child she now loves dearly but the same child she went to the abortion clinic that morning to get rid of because she could not afford to raise her.

Gaines, 31, is sitting at her kitchen table in the white clapboard house she rents next to a busy highway in this town on the edge of Cape Cod. The child she never wanted to have is sitting in her high chair refusing to eat her morning bowl of Cheerios. Vivian is 3; her soft brown hair is carefully pulled into a ponytail high on her head.

The pretty little girl squeals. She communicates, but with few words. She can barely say her sisters' names. She has developmental problems—emotional, physical and intellectual deficits. Doctors say that at 22 months, Vivian had the cognitive ability of a 6-month-old. She is hyperactive. She likes to grab a face and sink her nails in and not let go. "Vivian, be nice," her mother says. "Nice, nice, Vivian." The girl is a trial for her mother, who never married and has three other children.

All this helps explain why Deborah Gaines has become something of a local celebrity. People here are talking about the suit she filed against the abortion clinic, seeking damages for the trauma she says she suffered that day. It also seeks to recoup the cost of raising her child. Her suit relies on the concept of "wrongful life," making the rather novel and controversial argument that Vivian should never have been born, and therefore the clinic should defray the cost of raising an unwanted child. The suit says the clinic failed to protect clients against madmen like John Salvi and foreclosed Gaines's option to have an abortion—an argument the clinic's lawyers call patent nonsense.

The mother folds her hands on the white table that has been scrubbed clean in the white kitchen with white stucco walls. She is wearing a black pantsuit. Her soft face is troubled. She is thinking. It is all so complicated; the issues raised here are shaded in gray. But on one level, to her, it is quite simple.

"It shouldn't have happened to me," Gaines says. And somebody's got to pay for what she went through.

She looks at her daughter. She cherishes the little girl, but she knows that Vivian would not be here had Salvi not chosen that clinic in Brookline to air his rage against abortion. Salvi, 23, a devout Roman Catholic, justified killing as part of a militant mission to protect the unborn. Gaines once viewed her daughter's survival as a "sign from God," but now she's convinced what Salvi did was the work of the Devil.

"God don't kill anyone," she says. "God don't put a blessing on a murderer coming into the clinic and shooting people up."

But the troubling questions don't end there. There are these: Who is responsible for Vivian's life? Is she solely Gaines's burden? What about the father? How much responsibility does the clinic have, if any? Or the state?

Gaines doesn't fully understand all the legal issues, but says she doesn't feel she's shifting responsibility with this suit. She quotes something her mother told her when she was pregnant with her first child: "You decided to lay down and have them. You take care of them."

A WOMAN SCORNED

People who don't know Gaines are judging her life and her decisions. She picks up a local newspaper. A columnist who never called her to find out her story has labeled Gaines a welfare mother who deserves no money—and deserves to be in the sorry situation she is in. A man on the street yells that she should have just gone back the next day to the clinic and gotten the abortion.

It's true that she was receiving federal Aid to Families With Dependent Children when she became pregnant with Vivian. She knew that she could not afford to have another child. She didn't want to make her life any more difficult.

"No one knows how hard it is raising four kids by yourself," she says. No one knows how hard it is to find a job without a high school diploma. They don't know how difficult it is to find a babysitter for Vivian. How difficult it is to keep a job when she can't keep a babysitter. How difficult it is to make ends meet when the rope is too short to begin with. In her world, there are no safety nets for bad choices. In her world, when you fall there is nothing to catch you—except what's left of the welfare system.

People are talking, but they have not lived for one moment underneath her skin. Those people don't know her pain, the intense fears. They are not with her when she wakes up in the middle of the night with the nightmare visions of John Salvi shooting at her, and the medicated child she did not want to have is screaming at the top of her lungs.

Yes, she loves Vivian. Yes, she wants Vivian. The conflict is that Vivian exists.

Gaines's lawyer, Chris A. Milne, puts it this way: "The resentment is there. The love is there. It's inconsistent but she feels them both."

At the kitchen table, he flips through a report from Gaines's counselor. It shows that one month after the shooting, she was terribly confused: worried about the impact of having the baby but fearful of going back to another abortion clinic.

Milne is a well-known Boston area child advocacy lawyer who specializes in setting up trusts for children hurt in accidents and shootings. He says he is seeking between $100,000 and $500,000 for Vivian's care.

His suit, filed last year in Superior Court, argues that the owners of Preterm, aware of shootings at other clinics and the fierce and continual protests outside the clinic's own doors, should have seen Salvi, if not someone else, coming—and they should have been prepared with "full-time armed security guards, police presence, metal detectors and locked doors to protect patients such as Deborah Gaines, who were entering the clinic to exercise their lawful right to an abortion."

The lawsuit also says that Gaines suffered "posttraumatic stress disorder" after the attack, with symptoms including "frequent crying episodes, headaches, cold sweats, flashbacks, sleep irregularity, psychic numbness."

The filing anticipates the public response that she could have gone elsewhere, and argues that "she could not go back to an abortion clinic because she fears for her life."

Earlier this month, Judge Patrick F. Brady rejected a request by Preterm to dismiss the suit, allowing the case to go forward even while pronouncing himself "very, very, very, very skeptical" of the arguments.

In the past 25 years, various courts have granted damages to parents who have claimed "wrongful life." Many of those cases involved failed sterilization procedures or amniocentesis tests that failed to determine that a child would be born with genetic defects. Other cases have been won by women who felt they "lost the opportunity to terminate a pregnancy," Milne says.

In 1990, the Supreme Court of Massachusetts ruled in a landmark medical negligence case in favor of a couple who sued a doctor who had failed to sterilize the woman properly. The woman gave birth to a "normal and healthy, but unwanted, child after the physician had performed a sterilization procedure that the mother had sought for reasons founded on economic or financial considerations," the judges wrote in the case.

After the baby was born, the court ruled that the parents could receive damages to cover the cost of rearing the child to adulthood, "offset by the benefit, if any, that the parents receive or will receive from having the child."

Preterm, which has settled two cases brought by shooting victims and their families against the clinic, argues it has no responsibility to Gaines or her daughter. Says Adrian Sevier, an attorney for the clinic: "Preterm had no notice a madman like John Salvi would enter the premises and open fire. Their security was adequate and there is nothing they could have done to have prevented John Salvi's actions, and there is nothing Preterm did or did not do that caused any harm to Deborah Gaines."

At the heart of the case, to hear the lawyers tell it, is a word that has defined the abortion issue for decades: choice.

"The argument is essentially that Deborah Gaines chose not to have an abortion after December 30, 1994," Sevier says. "She was free to go to any clinic of her choice and have an abortion. She chose not to do so and she is therefore responsible for her decision."

Says Milne: "The responsibility starts with Deborah at Preterm exercising her right to have an abortion.... It's legal and she had the full right to expect that she would be given one. She was exercising her right to choose."

ONE WOMAN'S STORY

Deborah Gaines's black eyebrows are drawn on perfectly. Her hair is just so. Today she is wearing tight curls. There is still a trace of the girlish vivacity that probably impressed the judges when she won the Duncan Projects Beauty Pageant back in New Jersey, when she was 14 and she still had hope.

That was before she had her first baby at 17, before she had her second baby and her mother put her out of the house. Before she moved to a trailer park, before she fell in love and out of love and couldn't find a job and lived in a house with no heat and lived in a shelter and received a Section 8 housing certificate and then tried to live on meager checks from AFDC.

"Life just got rougher and rougher," she says. Whenever she talks to her own mother she finds strength. "My mother always says, 'Hold it to the road.' Take care of things. Be strong."

Deborah Gaines was born in the Jersey City projects, the youngest of five children. Her father was a boxmaker. Her mother was a homemaker.

Deborah learned to fight early and to defend herself. She says she was in a "little" gang. She dropped out of high school. She lived with a sister in Cherry Point, N.C., before her boyfriend found a job at a nuclear power plant in Plymouth, Mass. She packed up her son and daughter and moved north to be with the man.

"But things didn't work out and I went into a shelter for the homeless." She and her children were living in assisted housing when she met a house painter named Michael Richardson at a nice restaurant in Plymouth.

"We started talking. I was having dinner with my girlfriends. After dinner, he asked me to dance." That was May 7, 1989. "We've been together since then," Gaines says. Richardson is the father of her third child, Debbie, and of Vivian.

Over the years, Richardson has helped out almost daily with the kids, but he didn't marry Gaines or move in—that would have cut off the AFDC checks. He says he felt he couldn't make as much to support the family to offset the loss of the welfare benefits.

Gaines did hair in her kitchen, pressing and curling and braiding. And she tried to make a home for the family: Once she moved into a cottage with a nice little yard on the waterfront. They found a picket fence and painted it white. They got a dog named Rex and brought him home. They called him "Rex, Malcolm X."

But she had to move from that house on the shore because it was very cold, and she couldn't afford the oil heat. Once to keep warm she and the kids huddled together under blankets with a blow dryer.

In the early '90s, she found an apartment with wood floors, a patio, a small deck. There was just enough room for her and her three children. She had no intention of moving again. Then she woke up one morning with a familiar queasy feeling.

"I just didn't want to know what I knew—but you know I knew. So I went to a clinic in North Plymouth and they did a pregnancy test for me." It came back positive. (Gaines won't discuss whether she was using birth control at the time.)

"I just shook my head...I was feeling like, 'Debbie, you done messed up.' I mean I had so many. I was living this fantasy, you know. I always dreamed about having my own and doing for my own...and when I felt that I was pregnant I was totally devastated."

It happened just when she was trying to get herself together. She had already started to study for her GED and was planning to get a job—a result, she says, of a personal epiphany, not the pressure of welfare-to-work reform. She already had filled out the paperwork at the unemployment office.

Richardson, now 36, didn't seem eager to have another child, either. And it was coming at a bad time. He recalls thinking, "Deb's pregnant. She's trying to get ahead in life. She was going to school."

"He didn't want to say go ahead and have it or don't have it," Gaines says. "It was more like 'Make your own decision from here on.'"

"I said something has to go. I mean I can't go through this and have another child, and there's so much that I want to do."

She made her choice. She found a telephone book and made an appointment at Preterm Health Services, where an abortion would take about an hour. She was scheduled for 9 a.m.

KILLING TIME

That morning John Salvi drove his black Toyota pickup, the one with pictures of dead fetuses taped to the back window, into Brookline from New Hampshire. Dressed in black, he walked into a Planned Parenthood clinic around 10.

A woman asked Salvi whether he needed help.

"Is this Planned Parenthood?" he asked.

When the woman told him it was, he pulled out a .22-caliber semiautomatic and opened fire, killing receptionist Shannon Elizabeth Lowney. A female counselor and two male volunteer escorts in the waiting room were wounded in the spray of bullets.

Salvi calmly walked out of the clinic, got back in his truck and drove a mile west to Preterm.

Gaines and two friends, Debbi Davis and James Magazine, had arrived late at the clinic around 9:10. They parked across the street from the squat red brick building, they fed the meter quarters, and Gaines hurried to the first floor. The receptionist told her the doctors were running behind and asked if she wanted to reschedule.

"I want to go on with it today," Gaines told her.

The receptionist gave her a form that explained the procedure. After filling it out, Gaines took an elevator to the fourth-floor waiting room. It was crowded, she remembers, maybe a dozen people sitting there, holding on to their own secrets. In the uncomfortable silence, she grabbed something to read.

Around 10 a.m., Gaines impatiently put down her magazine, got up and asked, "Do you know how long it will be?"

"You're going to be next," the receptionist told her.

"I was wondering, can I step downstairs to smoke a cigarette?"

"Okay, Miss Gaines," the woman answered, "but don't be long."

Gaines raced downstairs and found her friend Magazine and asked him for a cigarette. He reached in his pocket but didn't have any.

Together they went looking for Davis, who they thought was in the car parked across the street.

About that time—10:10—John Salvi walked into

Preterm's first-floor reception area and was stopped at the front desk.

"Is this Preterm?" he asked a woman answering phones.

She told him yes.

He reached into his duffel bag, pulled out the rifle and shouted in a voice like a preacher: "This is what you get! You pray the rosary!"

He shot Lee Ann Nichols.

"Then he took a step to his left, lifted his gun and shot me," Jane Sauer, a patient administrator, remembered. Sauer rolled behind a column and heard Salvi yelling as he pumped 10 more bullets into Nichols.

Gaines, who was outside, hadn't heard those shots. She still couldn't find Davis, or the cigarettes, so she turned around to go back into the clinic.

Right inside, right away, she heard what she thought was a firecracker. Then she saw women running her way, trying to escape. They knocked her over.

She saw a man running down the hallway, firing a gun. Nothing made sense. Her instincts told her to run.

"I jumped down the steps and landed on my knees." She dropped her pocketbook but didn't bother to gather it. Everyone else, it seemed, ran to the left of the entrance. For some reason, she ran to her right. Salvi followed her.

He was still firing, maybe seven shots, but gave up the chase after she finally escaped through the black steel gate. She ran to the apartment building and somehow her friend James Magazine had ended up there, too.

"We fell to the floor. I told James, 'Please, don't make a noise.'"

But he insisted on going out to check out the chaos.

"He came back and said, 'It's okay.' He grabbed me and said, 'It's okay.'"

What happened next was a blur for Gaines. All of a sudden reporters were pushing microphones in front of her and the FBI wanted her to look at photographs. She picked Salvi out of a lineup and somehow ended up back home, she doesn't remember how.

For days, Gaines says, she was afraid to leave the house, afraid to turn the lights off, afraid to open the windows because she had pointed out Salvi. He or someone connected with him was certain to be coming after her, she thought.

Two weeks later, she found herself sitting in a mental health counselor's office. Now more than two months pregnant, she wanted help.

In a report dated Jan. 17, 1995, a therapist at the Mayflower Counseling Center wrote, "Ct. [client] has experienced intense fears that (pro-lifers) someone is going to kill her. She has had nightmares and is also experiencing flashbacks. [Client] states feelings of overwhelming guilt and confusion and fear.

"[Client] states that she is unsure of whether or not she should terminate the pregnancy. She feels it may be a sign from God to keep the child, but she states that this is an unplanned pregnancy and she doesn't want it to hold her back (planning to start school, seeking employment).

"[Client] states that she will not go back to a clinic to have an abortion because she fears for her life."

Later, a psychiatrist prescribed Ativan for Gaines's anxiety.

A follow-up reports states: "[Client] has made decision to give birth to child and not abort."

A NEW LIFE

Vivian Victoria Gaines was pushed into the world Aug. 7, 1995, arriving at a healthy 6 pounds 5 ounces.

"Oh, it's a girl!" Gaines cried. She held her and gave her a little kiss on the forehead. "I was very happy. I loved her immediately."

In the kitchen of her home, Gaines flips through a photo album that she says will someday be given to Vivian as proof of the family's love for her. Gaines is pointing to the pictures of Vivian and her sisters, Octavia and Deborah, and brother Davon. She comes across a newspaper article that she framed. The headline says, "'This beautiful child': Clinic shooting changed many lives profoundly."

Gaines is quoted as saying that she would never for a moment give credit to Salvi for saving Vivian: "I know ignorant people out there are going to say if it weren't for John Salvi, this baby wouldn't be here. But this does not make him a hero."

The shooter escaped from Brookline that day and went on to fire 20 rounds at a building housing an abortion clinic in Norfolk; he was later convicted of two murders and five counts of armed assault with intent to murder. Salvi was found dead Nov. 28, 1996, in his maximum-security prison cell with his hands and feet tied and cotton stuffed in his mouth. Authorities called it a suicide but Salvi's lawyer said he was beaten to death.

Little Vivian walks over to the table and points at the pictures. She sees herself in a pink dress, sitting in her mother's lap at 4 months. In the snapshot, Vivian has a juicy drool. Her mother is smiling.

"When Vivian was born, she had it all, like all of my children," Gaines says. "Vivian is very much loved." Michael Richardson nods and says, "She's here now, and I love her."

Gaines has put a baby gate between the porch railings to keep Vivian from running out into the heavy traffic. Her constant fear is that somehow the child will manage to open the door and run out there to her death.

She turns her back to the table for a second. Vivian darts through the living room to the front door. Gaines turns around.

"Did the baby run out there?" She gasps. Her stomach drops. She drops the album and runs after her. She catches her. Holds her hand gently. Walks the child back to safety.

CHOICES

Gaines looks at her watch. It is the first day of school for her older daughters. The school buses come, and Gaines and her three girls go to the park up the road. The mother sits on a wooden bench, watching the children play on a clear blue afternoon. The scent of saltwater is in the wind. Blowing with it is the question:

Has she ever thought about the irony of all this? Had the shooting never happened, Vivian would not even be here. Then how would she feel?

She thinks about the question. She decides it is impossible to answer. Of course Vivian wouldn't be here. But why ponder? It doesn't even make sense. Who can change history?

"I can't go back." She made choices. Choices were made for her. Things happened that were out of her control. She can't dwell on the what-ifs. The what-ifs won't feed this baby.

Maybe her life would be different if Vivian weren't here. Maybe she would really have completed her GED. She probably would have a full-time job by now. That would mean she could deal with these overdue bills, like the one for $189 for cable TV installation. Maybe she could find the $400 to fix her car and go to her uncle's funeral. It certainly would be easier to find a sitter. And maybe other parents would bring their children over to play because they wouldn't be afraid that Vivian would stroke their faces, then without warning sink her fingernails into their skin and not let go.

The child is running through the park now, oblivious, climbing up the slide. Vivian, in a blue jumpsuit with a yellow Big Bird on the front, comes speeding down fast. Her hands are in the air. She's wearing new black Hush Puppies. They have been buckled with care by her mother. Her clean white socks with the lace edges have been neatly turned down.

"Whee!" Vivian cries. Her mother is excited by this moment of pure happiness.

"But wait!" She runs to catch her. Before she can, the girl plants her feet, her new shoes, in a deep puddle. Then she races back up the ladder to the top of the slide.

"I think I'm a good mom," Gaines says. "I take care of them the best I can."

She already is planning her speech, preparing for the day Vivian asks.

"I know the question will come up: 'Mommy, if you love me now, why did you decide to get rid of me?' And I'll explain it to her like I explained it to other people. Hopefully she will understand. I'll tell her I was there to have an abortion. But things happened. Then I'm going to show her all the pictures we took."

Vivian comes down the slide again, this time backward. She bumps her head slightly. She cries. She runs to her mother. Gaines kisses her head. Holds her close.

So forget the questions. Gaines pauses and says what is the absolute truth in her head: "If she wasn't here, she wouldn't be here for a good reason."

First she chose not to have Vivian. But ultimately she chose to have her. It's a contradiction she'll have to live with.

Writers' Workshop

Talking Points

1) Note the use of short and long sentences in the first few paragraphs. What effect does this have?

2) The author asks a question in the story: Has Gaines thought about the fact that without the shooting, her daughter would not be here? Does it seem artificial for Brown to ask the question in the story? How satisfying is the answer?

3) Which section of the story do you find most powerful? How do your feelings about Gaines change in these sections?

4) Does Brown have an opinion about Gaines? What evidence in the tone and language leads you to your conclusion?

Assignment Desk

1) Abortion is one issue on which few people are neutral. Interview those who represent both views of the issue about this lawsuit and write a story.

2) Experiment with the length of sentences in your own stories. When are short sentences effective? When do you use long sentences?

Baby, don't get hooked on her

OCTOBER 11, 1998

They didn't hear me when I came home early that day. The other woman was in my kitchen. He was in her arms. He was dreamy-eyed and drooling. I could see, from where I stood, her lipstick smudged on his face. She giggled. They both laughed. They were singing some silly song, all wrapped up in each other. I had caught them in the act and they didn't know.

I spied them from the garage door. They did not hear me still, so I slammed it again. Then they both looked up at me.

She was wide-eyed, fumbling, uncertain about what to do. I hurried to wrest him from her arms. He began to cry.

Betrayal, I thought, in my own house, and in the light of day.

Insane jealousy whirled through my mind. And all he could say about the matter was "Mommy!"

I tried composing myself, yet I felt overcome. This woman was doing everything I wanted to do, except I had to work. She was in my kitchen. I wanted to be in my kitchen. She was singing to my baby in the middle of the day. I wanted to sing to him in the middle of the day. She had all the fun times. I had the middle of the night when he wouldn't go to sleep.

"Mommy," he says, looking so innocent. That word could not fully squelch my jealousy. I kissed him and calculated my revenge. My goal: Get that woman out of my house; get my baby out of her arms. That was Plan A. I had no Plan B, meaning what I would do with this baby in the middle of the day when both my husband and I had to work. At that moment, Plan B didn't seem to matter.

Babysitter jealousy was a term I could not comprehend until six months after I delivered a child, nursed him, pampered him, read to him, cradled him—then handed him off to another woman. The nanny, the babysitter, the woman who lives under the stairs, whatever you may call her, is the woman who is there to keep your baby when you cannot, who has full power over the home when both parents are out.

In some households, for more than 10 hours a day, she is there when you are not. And who knows what kind of bond they develop in those long hours when Mommy and Daddy are gone? She is possibly one of the most important people in your life. That was something I would not come to realize until much later.

* * *

I had watched *The Hand That Rocks the Cradle,* and I remembered the line from the movie. The hand on the cradle rules the house. I was having none of that: Nobody's hand was going to be rocking my baby's cradle or ruling my house. I had heard the stories from other women: "Just wait until he calls her Mommy." I had read the stories in the parenting magazines of women whining about what to do when their babies cry for the sitter over the real mommy.

As I prepared to go back to work, I prepared to mark my territory.

My mother-in-law, who has two doctorates, called the week before I was to end my maternity leave. "It's going to be hard," she said in a soothing voice, "but your baby will be able to pick you out of a crowded room of women. Don't worry, no other woman will be able to take your place."

Right, I thought, and burst into tears. He doesn't know that if I leave I'm really coming back. He's too little to understand the complicated world of economics, commutes, career maintenance.

A friend advised me to explain everything to my baby in adult words: "Listen, I am your mother. I'm going to be gone for a few hours. But I will be back. Don't even think about calling this woman Mommy. I am your mommy. I will always be your mommy. Okay? Now give Mommy—your real mommy—a hug."

With the baby prepared by this lecture, I moved to other areas. I had to walk a fine line of contradictions. I had to let this woman know I trusted her but I didn't trust her. I wanted to let her know I was leaving the house but I would always be there. I wanted her to know she had some control but I ruled.

I asked her to write down the baby's daily schedule: when he slept, when he ate, what they did. It was okay for her to hold him, but only after I left. It was okay for her to feed him, but I would decide what he ate. I picked his favorite red cup.

I combed his hair and dressed him. I read to him every morning: *Guess How Much I Love You.* I could have had five minutes to put my lipstick on and run out the door, but I would sit there calmly in the big over-stuffed chair, acting as if I had not another care or thought in the world until I finished that book and he knew that I loved him to the "moon and back."

Then I would drive to work listening to the oh-so-caring Dr. Laura, who would tell any parent working to quit her job, move to a more affordable area and make sure there was always one parent home with the kid. I would slump in my seat, bite my lip and think of ways to be there. At the end of the working day, I would race home. Anybody in my way became an intolerable hurdle between me and my baby.

There was no advice in the "What to Expect" books about this kind of motherhood-induced insanity. My husband had absolutely no idea why I was so obsessed with getting rid of the sitter. "When I came home from work today," I argued, "she was in the basement cleaning and he was all the way upstairs taking a nap."

"What's wrong with that?" my spouse asked, clearly puzzled.

I couldn't explain, so I clearly had to make a better case.

She microwaved his milk. Crumbs were on his face when I got home. She let him sleep in his shoes

My husband could find nothing wrong in those infractions.

I did nutty things like call home in the middle of the day to see whether I could catch him screaming in the background.

He never was. He was always happy. And she was always pleasant, patiently answering all my questions. I tried like a government prosecutor to find something egregious that she'd done, so I would have cause to get rid of her. But nothing she said or did could convince my husband that she was evil or incompetent.

Then one night when we were trying to teach the baby to fall asleep by himself, I heard him down the hall yelling, "Mommy! Daddy!" No response. (The book says to wait a few minutes before you answer—otherwise babies think they can control you.)

"Mommy? Where are you? Daddy, where are you?" our son asked.

Then we heard: "Raquel?"

And then it hit me: This child trusted her. And needed her. If he called out for her at a moment of need, then that meant he liked her. And if he liked her, that meant she liked him. And if they liked each other, it meant somehow he was telling me he had a good babysitter.

Slowly I began to see beyond the green that clouded my vision, and I grew to praise this woman. I could see that she was really good with him. She taught him the alphabet before he was 11 months old. She prepared a whole curriculum for him. One day I came home early and they were taking bowls from the cupboard, getting ready to work on a lesson in gravity. In moments of joy away from her, he would recount the little silly songs that she taught him.

I came to realize that my life—the one that holds down the three jobs of household, baby and work—would be much more difficult without her.

Finally, I knew it: I don't want her out of my kitchen. I don't want her out of my house. Now, when I hear the sound of the car outside at 9:18 a.m.—when I am trying to feed him one last spoonful of oatmeal and he is squirming and I have six minutes to get dressed and get out the door—the expectant voice I hear is my own.

"Raquel?"

Writers' Workshop

Talking Points

1) Does the headline of this story give away the secret meaning of the lead? Since reporters don't usually see headlines before publication, how can a writer anticipate potential problems?

2) Brown uses humor in this story. Which parts seem funny to you? Does the humor strengthen or weaken the essay?

3) Why does Brown choose to not identify or personalize the nanny?

Assignment Desk

1) Rewrite this personal essay as a news story about women returning to jobs outside the home and leaving their children in the care of nannies.

2) Write a personal essay about a difficult transition in your life. Can you use a lead with a secret meaning?

The accused

NOVEMBER 1, 1998

CHICAGO—The persistent sound of someone trying to saw through thick plastic woke her from a deep sleep. She slid heavily out of bed and followed the sound that was coming from down the hall, from the bathroom. The rasping of metal on plastic reminded her that nothing had changed. Her 7-year-old, her baby boy, was still facing charges of first-degree murder.

She found him in the bathroom with a butter knife, futilely trying to free his leg of an electronic shackle. He sat cross-legged on the floor, naked, yanking at the hard black plastic strip that a judge had ordered clamped around his ankle. He slid his chunky fingers under the shackle and tried frantically to pry it off—not having sense enough to know he could not free himself, and his mother could not free him either. He was caught, trapped.

This chubby-cheeked boy, barely four feet tall, had spent much of the week in court. Reporters from across the country studied his caramel face, his fat braids, his missing two front teeth, and wrote down every detail.

A prosecutor, a blond woman with short hair and a crisp green suit, had sliced the air with her finger, then pointed at him and his 8-year-old friend, and proclaimed them callous killers. She argued that an 11-year-old girl had been fatally "brutalized at their hands."

For eight hours in court that day, attorneys argued back and forth about whether the 7- and 8-year-old boys were a danger to society. When the boys stood up, deputies raced behind them. When they went to the potty, deputies stood guard. But the judge knew that the children, under state law, couldn't be placed in a locked facility. So he sent them home, to be monitored by their parents and the custom-made electronic shackles.

The 7-year-old, believed to be the youngest murder defendant in the city's history, didn't fully understand what was happening. Because of his speech disorder, he couldn't or wouldn't talk about it. All he knew was that because of the uncomfortable shackle he couldn't nap that Saturday afternoon, and he wanted to take a bath.

"It don't come off," his mother sleepily reminded him.

"Man, why they got to put this stuff on me?" he grumbled, the words barely distinct because of his speech impediment.

"If you don't leave it alone, the sheriff is going to be here," she scolded.

The phone rang. The sheriff's office was on the other end. Deputies wanted to speak to the boy to make sure he was not trying to escape from the house.

The mother put him on, and he recited his ABCs and numbers until they were satisfied they had their prisoner.

* * *

"Police Say Suspects Not Too Small to Kill," declared the lead headline in the *Chicago Tribune* on Aug. 11, two days after the two boys supposedly confessed to the murder of their neighborhood playmate, Ryan LaShaun Harris. "We are certain we have the right individuals," a Chicago homicide sergeant said.

Within a month, the charges were dropped and the shackles unbuckled. Investigators found semen on the panties of the victim. Boys that age cannot produce semen. Now, suddenly, the evidence pointed to someone else—someone much older, someone powerful, someone the boys' parents and their neighbors had always suspected was the real killer, the one who battered that pretty little girl, crushed her skull, beat her face, rammed foliage up her nose, pushed her panties so far down her throat that she swallowed her tongue, making sure that if she did not die of the beating, she would most certainly die from lack of breath.

Ryan Harris was slain in a poor South Side neighborhood that had seen many other heinous murders. When the news of the boys' arrest was flashed nationally, many gasped and thought, *Why not?*

Why not—when kids were shooting kids in alleys, parks, school halls and playgrounds? Why not—when not far from this neighborhood two boys, 12 and 13, had dropped a 5-year-old out of a 14th-story window because he wouldn't steal candy? People, especially those who don't live on the South Side, seemed more than willing to believe the worst about kids—black kids in particular.

The police version of events—that the 7-year-old had knocked Ryan off her bicycle with a rock, then dragged her body into the weeds with the help of his friend—was based on an interrogation of a shy child with speech problems who could easily be coaxed into saying anything an adult wanted to hear. Yet to this day, the police and the city refuse to apologize to the boys or to their parents. Saying the case is still under investigation, officials will not comment further.

There is one central question they really can't answer. Perhaps nobody can.

How does a little boy who still sucks his thumb put his life back together after he has been accused of murder?

How does he wash away the dry taste of a police interrogation room, the stain of the fingerprint ink, and the thick, lingering suspicion? How can he go on playing tag, walk to the store to get candy, go to school, when the grown-ups who caused all of this—"the mean police," as he calls them—won't just say they're sorry, and clear his name?

You don't remove the stigma by simply dismissing the charge.

* * *

The mother says it happened after church the other Sunday. Some kids called him a name: "I don't want to play with you anymore, you little murderer," one boy shouted. "My mama told me you murdered that girl."

"He will always be suspect. He will always be known as the youngest murder suspect in Chicago's history," says his mother. She is 28, round-faced, a hard-working woman who keeps her four children well behaved.

It's 7 a.m., and she is pressing his hair. It sizzles. His sisters, 6 and 8, and brother, 10, sit at the kitchen table in the small apartment above her mother-in-law's house. The mother takes the pressing comb and puts it in the stove's blue flames. He's having his second-grade pictures taken this morning at his new school, where the children don't know he was "the 7-year-old accused killer." Only the principal, his teacher and the counselor know.

The boy's long hair hangs nearly shoulder-length. He is proud of it, and of his perfect-attendance trophies from last year. An industrious child, he liked to help out at the corner store and the Laundromat, offering to sweep the floor for quarters.

All that has changed since the charges were filed. The family had to move. He doesn't like to talk about his arrest. He does not like to talk much at all—for when he speaks, he is often misunderstood. His voice is deep and gruff, and his tongue gets tied. The words bump together: "Amgoingtoschool. Don'tbe laughing atme. Yourhair isalmostlongas mine."

His mother knows what he's saying and interprets.

A court-appointed psychiatrist diagnosed him as having something called a receptive/expressive language disorder. "If you ask him where is his right hand, he will point to his left," his mother explains. But it goes deeper than that.

"I'll say, 'Where did you go last night?' And he'll say, 'To the store.' And I'll say, 'No, we went to McDonald's.'"

The family may have actually gone to the store. But once he's told it was McDonald's, the boy would believe it to be true, she says.

So: If you told this boy that he killed somebody, he'd believe that, too.

* * *

The mystery begins on July 27, in a neighborhood known as Englewood. That afternoon, Ryan Harris, a straight-A student who wanted to be a basketball player, didn't come home after riding a borrowed bicycle. Ryan had been spending the summer with her godmother.

In Englewood when a little girl is missing, residents tend to fear the worst. Her family called police, mobilized a search party and passed out hand-printed fliers, with a photo of a smiling Ryan Harris standing in front of a chalkboard, her braids pulled up in a ponytail.

Ryan's body was found the next day behind an isolated row house in an overgrown lot near the railroad tracks. The medical examiner determined she died of trauma to the head and asphyxiation. A collective, almost primal scream came from the community. Somebody was hunting their little girls and had made a kill. The residents, poor and powerless as they were, demanded that the killer be found.

Police began investigating older men, but then got an anonymous call saying the murder was connected to some boys throwing rocks. Detectives went to talk to Ryan's relatives, who told them that a few days before Ryan died, she and her little sister were going to the corner store to buy candy when two boys started throwing rocks at them.

"You better get back home and don't come around here," one of the boys yelled at the girls, according to police reports.

"I want that bike right there," a boy yelled, pointing to the blue bike Ryan was riding.

Ryan got scared and pedaled away.

* * *

The 7-year-old's parents were high school sweethearts who married four years after graduation. She got an associate's degree in liberal arts from a local college. They both found work in fast food. She is a manager at a KFC franchise and he is a fry cook. On Sunday, Aug. 9, both were at work.

The boy was at his grandmother's when police knocked on her door. They needed to ask the 7-year-old just a few questions. It seemed he had some information and might be able to help them out. The grandmother told the detectives she was taking him to church, but would be sure to stop by the police station after services that afternoon.

A slender woman who wears her hair primly pulled back, the grandmother drove the boy there about 5 p.m. She says that when they arrived, a detective greeted him: "Hey, big guy, come with me."

The detective took the boy to the lieutenant's office, a small room with a desk, a telephone, a typewriter, a computer, four file cabinets and three chairs. According to a police report on the interrogation, the door was left open so that the boy's grandmother could see him.

The detectives, James Cassidy, who is white, and Allen Nathaniel, who is black, introduced themselves. But before they asked him any questions about the dead girl, they made small talk. They asked him about his favorite sport (basketball), what kinds of things he liked to do (play with trucks), how old he was and whether he was looking forward to going to school.

Then they began the real questions.

"Do you know the difference between the truth and a lie?" a detective leaned over and asked.

"You should never lie," the boy told police, according to the report. To tell the truth is to tell "what really happened" and a lie is "when someone makes up something."

"To tell the truth is good," a detective said. "To tell a lie is bad.... Good boys only tell the truth."

"Are you a good boy?" a detective asked him.

Yes, he told them.

The officers then asked him to hold their hands "because we were all friends."

The boy gave Cassidy his left hand and Nathaniel his right.

The detectives showed him a poster with Ryan Harris's picture and asked the boy, "Do you know the girl who was killed?"

"Without further questioning," the detectives' report says, the boy told them this story: He and the 8-year-old were playing and throwing rocks. When they saw Ryan riding her bicycle, the 7-year-old threw a rock and hit the girl in the head, knocking her off her bike.

"After she fell off the bicycle she wasn't moving so he and [the 8-year-old] each took one of the girl's arms and moved her into the weeds where they began 'to play with her soft,'" the report said. "He said they took her panties off and put them in the girl's mouth and rubbed leaves on her."

According to the report, the boy told police, "They put leaves in the girl's nose and also a stem." And police said the two took the bicycle and moved it into the weeds by the railroad tracks, where someone must have taken it because they never saw it again.

Police won't comment on the interrogation, which was not taped, but a source close to the investigation, who did not want to be identified, put it this way: "At some point in the conversation, police were being told things that were very disturbing by the 7-year-old. He said things that implicated himself. The cops were stunned.

"They said, 'We dragged her.' There were drag marks on her body. They said they put things in her nose. There was dirt and leaves in her nose."

At that point, Cassidy left the room and Nathaniel continued talking to the boy about basketball and school.

In another room, officers approached the 8-year-old and his mother, and told them they wanted to get a witness statement from him. Police said she allowed them to talk to the boy alone, saying, "I want you to get to the bottom of this."

The 8-year-old was given a soda and put through the same routine. He and Detective Cassidy talked about lying, and how good boys don't lie. The report says that each suspect was given a simplified version of the Miranda warning: The boys were told that they didn't have to talk if they didn't want to, and if they asked for a lawyer, then the detectives "wouldn't talk to them anymore."

Neither boy knew what a lawyer was.

According to the report, the children were told that a lawyer "protects people who are said to have done something bad." Court was a place "where if you were accused of doing something bad you would have to go there and a person called a judge would decide if you really did something bad or not."

The 8-year-old told police that he met the 7-year-old behind a house and the younger boy threw a rock, hitting the girl in the head, and she fell off her bike. He told police the 7-year-old did "something to the girl who wasn't moving," the report says.

The older boy said he didn't want to watch, so he turned his head away. Then he got on his bicycle and rode home to watch cartoons.

The boys were given McDonald's Happy Meals, then were arrested and charged with first-degree murder.

The homicide case of Ryan LaShaun Harris was classified as "Cleared/Closed by Arrest."

* * *

By 6 p.m., the 7-year-old's mother was ending her shift at KFC. She arrived at her mother's house, but the boy and his grandmother were still not back and her older son told her they had gone to the police station. She panicked, thinking, "What is going on?"

Still in her uniform, she jumped in her car and sped down the expressway. She ran into the station and saw someone she knew: the mother of the 8-year-old. "You are not going to believe what's going on," the woman said.

She tried to find her son, but an officer told her the boy couldn't leave just yet because he had admitted hitting Ryan with a rock.

Later, in a green spiral notebook, the mother recorded her version of a conversation with the unidentified officer. "Now he's not being charged with anything," she quotes him as saying. "The way I see it, it was an accident, so don't be mad at him. He's going home and if you don't tell, we won't either."

She looked at him in disbelief and asked, "What about the rape allegations?"

He said, "Oh, that was just the media's imagination. You go back in the room with him while we complete our paperwork."

She went numb. An accident, she thought. She sat in a room across the hall. She didn't think anything was wrong until her son had to go to the washroom.

Police stopped him.

"Where are you going?" boomed an officer. "He needs to be escorted."

Now she knew something serious was going on.

"They won't let him out of sight," she said. "I saw a detective go back with him. I kept hearing 'DCFS'"—the Department of Children and Family Services.

Thirty minutes passed. She panicked again. "Where is he?"

A youth officer came into the room, asked her to step next door, and told her without stopping for breath or giving her a wall to lean on that her 7-year-old baby was charged with murder.

"Are you out of your mind?" she screamed. "This is a child. Are you crazy?"

She had to pull herself together. She had to listen closely to what they said. She needed to know what was going to happen next. She recorded the conversation in her mind and later put it down in her notebook, her diary.

The officers told her that her son had confessed to hitting the girl with a rock, dragging her body into weeds, stuffing "foliage" in her nose and playing with her "very softly."

It was a setup, she thought. "My son can't talk," she argued. "If he speaks a whole sentence, you might be able to pick two words out of the sentence. You must be crazy."

She told them not to talk to the boy again unless he had a lawyer. That much she knew from watching TV.

They told her she had a choice: Sign the boy over to Hargrove Hospital, a psychiatric center on Chicago's West Side, or DCFS would take custody of him until he went to trial. Her mind went blank. She wrung her hands and did what any decent mother would have done.

She signed the papers that allowed him to go to the hospital.

"DCFS you don't want to play with," she says. "They get your child and you will never see him again."

On the way to the hospital, he fell asleep sucking his thumb.

* * *

The next day, the court assigned two public defenders to the 7-year-old: Catherine Ferguson, a tough-talking lawyer who grew up on the South Side, and Elizabeth Tarzia, who was about to have her own baby.

They hadn't even met the boys before a hearing that would decide if there was probable cause for holding them.

"We were waiting for the kids to come when we saw these two little figures walking down the hall with five or six deputies," Ferguson remembers.

The boys were hysterical, crying, slobbering, calling for their mothers.

"It was the kind of cry when someone loses a mom," Ferguson says. "My partner starts to cry. I said, 'You gotta pull it together.'"

When the 7-year-old met his attorney, he wiped his face and asked whether he could go home.

"I tried to change the subject," Ferguson recalls. "I said, 'Well, you got a whole lot of boogers running down your face. I'm going to get some candy. What kind do you like?'"

"Honey buns," the boy told her. She had never seen or heard of that pastry. She went to the vending machine and bought Skittles.

Under the fluorescent lights of the courtroom, the boys climbed onto chairs between their attorneys. Their feet dangled above the floor. A courtroom artist

gave them crayons so they could draw pictures on legal
pads. When they stood before the judge, they were crying so much that he stopped the hearing and asked the
boys' mothers to stand behind them.

"But a sheriff told me, 'You can't touch him,'" the 7-
year-old's mother says. "We couldn't hug them or
touch them."

* * *

On the night of Aug. 9, lawyer Andre Grant got a
call from a woman who called herself Miss Rosetta. It
was a name he fondly remembered from his days growing up in the Washington Park housing project. "The
woman practically raised me," Grant recalls. Now her
children had had children, and she was the grandmother of an 8-year-old boy—a boy who had been
charged with murder and needed help.

Tall and slim, Grant is a former prosecutor who likes
to take on the system. He headed to the police station.

The boy was sitting in a dirty interrogation room,
crying. Cops were looming over him, the lawyer says.
Grant asked all the officers to leave the room.

"I told him his grandma had hired me to represent
him and I knew his mom. And I told him I was a
lawyer. And I asked him if he knew what a lawyer was.

"He said no. I asked him if he knew who I was. He
said yes. I said, 'Who am I?' He said, 'You are another
police.' I said, 'No, I'm not the police. I'm here to help
you. I'm going to fight for you.'"

The boy's face showed he didn't know whether to
trust him. He wouldn't stop crying.

Grant had to figure out a way to get to him.

He leaned over and asked: "Do you like the Power
Rangers?" The boy, looking bewildered, said yes.
"Who's your favorite Power Ranger?" Grant asked.

"The blue Power Ranger," the boy said, his eyes a
little wider.

"I'm the blue Power Ranger," Grant said. "I'm going to fight for you."

The boy stopped crying.

* * *

While editors around the country front-paged the
story on the boys, their neighbors, playmates, attorneys
and ministers on the South Side said it didn't make
sense. Didn't make sense that the kids were riding their

bike in a field choked with weeds. Didn't make sense that two little boys could produce the kind of blows to bring a taller girl to death. Didn't make sense that they could be a part of something so terrible and then participate in the search to find the girl.

Community leaders urged police to keep looking for Ryan's killer. Citing the historical racism in the Chicago police department, they raised that issue even though the superintendent of police and the commander of the district are both black. The police countered by saying race had nothing to do with the arrests, that the boys knew too much about the crime. But neighbors said other kids had seen the body before police made it to the scene and word of what they saw raced through the neighborhood grapevine. Anybody could have known those things.

State's Attorney Richard Devine said: "The police would not have filed the charges and we would not be pursuing them unless there was evidence to support the charges. Police officers are not out there to find some people to throw a charge at, particularly a 7- and 8-year-old."

But three weeks later, investigators got a call from the state crime lab that blew their case apart. The call came a day before the boys were scheduled to go back to court for another hearing. A DNA report had found semen on the girl's panties.

When the fax came in, prosecutors were waiting. "We were surprised," says a source in the case. "There was an immediate recognition we would drop the charges."

On Sept. 4, they took the new evidence to the hearing. Defense attorneys were waiting. The prosecutor stood up and read a statement dismissing the charges.

"Everybody was looking at them with jaws dropped," public defender Ferguson recalls. "Then it was like, 'How dare you? Why didn't you find that out before you charged them?'"

After four weeks, the boys were set free. The police still refuse to rule out that they were somehow involved.

"At this stage, all you can say is that the charges went away," says the law enforcement source. "Nobody has been charged in the Ryan Harris case."

Checking the DNA against a database, the lab found a close match with a man called Eddie Durr. But the match was not perfect, leading police to believe the semen belonged to someone related to him. They found his brother, Floyd Durr, 29, who had been arrested this summer after a series of sexual assaults. Floyd Durr's DNA matched perfectly, the police say.

Durr, a convicted sex offender who lived in Englewood, is being held without bond in three other cases. He recently pleaded innocent to sexually attacking three neighborhood girls earlier this year, ages 15, 10 and 11.

Durr, who has not been charged in the Harris case, has denied killing the girl. He allegedly told police he saw two little boys playing near a house. According to police reports, he said he happened upon the girl after she was dead and performed a sexual act that stained her underwear.

"I think that's a lie," says Grant, the 8-year-old's attorney. "They know this guy's the guy. They know doggone well these children aren't involved."

* * *

The day is gone in Englewood. The 8-year-old's father is in a fit of anger. When Andre Grant arrives, the father stops him on the sidewalk.

"You know what I heard last night? A bump. It's 4 o'clock in the morning and my baby runs in the room: 'Daddy, it's a man!'"

The father is a mechanic who plies his trade on the street in front of his aging brown house. He paces in front of the chain-link gate. His face is pulsing with rage.

"I got to get out of here. I'm going to take my baby and go. Kids are running up to him at school saying, 'Why did you kill that girl?'" the father says. "I got to go. Money, no money, we've got to get out of here."

Up the creaky steps, past a mixed-breed chow, the little boy sits curled in a green chair, too close to the television. He's 4 feet 2, with a round brown face and big brown eyes. He smiles, gives his lawyer a handshake and then a high five.

He is watching a show about volcanoes. A gray and white kitten jumps in the boy's lap. He strokes the kitten's fur.

"Look at that smile," Grant says. "The first time I saw him, I knew he could not have done that. Look at his smile."

The boy says nothing.

"You know he's been asking about you," the boy's mother says to the lawyer.

Grant tells the boy he can call him any time, and reaches into his jacket pocket and hands him a business card.

Call me, he says. Do you remember my name?

"You're the blue Power Ranger," the boy says.

* * *

Thanks to the conventions of the juvenile justice system and journalism, the names of the boys have not been released. But that doesn't mean people don't know.

"I have this empty feeling," the 7-year-old's mother says. "Because you know he got a label. He's like the youngest child in the United States to ever be accused of murder. People won't say it, but I know they'll always think it."

She is sitting in the dimly lit but spotless kitchen. Her daughters are playing at the table, copying letters and counting.

It was hard for the boy to start school. His old school didn't want to enroll a murder suspect, so his mother placed him in one 15 minutes away.

The first day back, his mother held his hand, but when he saw the big building he screamed, "Those people are mean in there. Don't leave me!"

She couldn't calm him, so she took him home.

The next day, he was better. But the day after that, when the teacher was not looking, he slipped out of the classroom and they found him balled up sucking his thumb in a corner.

It's over, but it's not over.

Immeasurable damage has been done. You can see it in the boys' eyes. They feel that at any time, the police could come knocking at their doors.

The 7-year-old told his mother: "They think I killed that little girl. She was my friend."

His mother told him: "Anybody say you hurt that girl, that you killed that girl, is ignorant. We ignore ignorant people."

She is angry: "We still don't know who killed that girl," she says. "I want to prove my son's innocence. He won't stay outside and play. He won't eat honey buns no more. When we go to the store, he gets a big fat juicy pickle."

"We may never get to the truth of what happened now," public defender Ferguson says. "We always thought he saw something. I don't know if he dreamed it up or they [the detectives] said it. Every time you ask him, it comes out different."

He doesn't talk about it now. And his parents are not going to ask him. The police want to interview him again, but the lawyers have refused.

Grant also has refused to submit the 8-year-old to more questions.

"I said, 'You've got to be joking.' There is not a parent in America that would take their children back to the police station...when they were framed the first time."

After the judge ordered the boys unleashed, they still walked and thought as they did when they had the monitors on. Like the prisoner so used to the chain that when he is freed he forgets how to run.

The 7-year-old's mother told him the news: "You are free. You can go outside and play."

She pushed him to the front door, but he wouldn't budge.

"Don't wannago," he said. "You tryingtotrick me."

He grabbed his mother's leg.

Writers' Workshop

Talking Points

1) Brown begins this story with a long anecdote. Is it more effective or less effective than a non-anecdotal lead?

2) Analyze the end of section two, beginning with "There is one central question they really can't answer." How does the writer use specific, vivid details to illustrate how difficult it will be for the 7-year-old to lead a normal life?

3) This is an anonymous story; we never learn the names of the accused or the mother. Does this hurt the story? How does the writer make them seem real to readers despite their anonymity? Where does anonymity hurt the story?

4) Do you think the boys had some involvement in the crime? What do you think Brown believes? How is this question addressed in the story?

Assignment Desk

1) Write another possible lead for this story. How does it compare with this one?

2) Note the quick characterizations of adults in this story. How can you incorporate such portrait sketches in your own stories?

A conversation with
DeNeen L. Brown

KEITH WOODS: Tell me something about your strategies for getting ready to write.

DeNEEN BROWN: I often want to start in the moment, and start with the tension up front. Like with the Clark piece, I wanted to show him at his weakest moment. My concern all the time is to bring readers in, to bring them in really fast.

This is not my own idea, but this is the idea I've gained from many years of writing. The idea for a story is to introduce a sympathetic character, have them confront some kind of tension, some kind of hurdle, and try to figure out what the resolution is.

And I want, in many of my stories, to introduce the sympathetic character in their moment of weakness.

And why that choice?

Because it's something I think most of us who are perceptive people can identify with. Because we all have our weaknesses. And to reveal somebody's weakness is almost like telling their secrets.

As humans, we always want to know what somebody else's secret is. And if you look at those stories, one of the themes is the secrets that are unfolding.

I want the reader's complete attention when I begin the story. I don't want them to leave me.

In the case of "Deborah's Choice," there's some question about who the sympathetic character is, and I guess, depending upon what you bring to that piece as a reader, she immediately becomes a pariah or a sympathetic character.

I guess the theme of that piece was almost, "Thou shalt not judge." I just want to lay out this woman's life and let people know that it's too easy to judge her, because many of us could be in that kind of situation. When you're living in that kind of poverty, there are so many kinds of human complications that I think people can't relate to, and it makes it easy to judge a person like her.

So I wanted to show, as much as I could, what was going on in her head, what was going on in her life that would bring her to the point where she is now.

Well, in some ways, I guess, you're making a judgment of her; you're deciding that she's worth suspending judgment.

Right. The thing is that I can identify with her in a way that I think a number of people may have difficulty doing. I have people in my family who are in that situation. Life is hard, and they just can't get out of this kind of circle, this kind of cesspool of poverty. And I guess my goal in that piece was to show that she is not unusual.

There are some people who are going to walk away from that story thinking, "She's still no good, and she made a bad decision," but there are others—and these are the people I was trying to reach—who could relate to her.

So you bring some of yourself to the story?

Yes. Definitely.

You have a couple of pieces that are fairly close to first person—one of them *is* first person. In the Clark story and in "The Accused" you brought something of yourself to them, didn't you?

The Clark story was supposed to be part of a larger package. So I guess when I sat down to write that, I felt like I didn't have anything to lose. Because it wasn't supposed to be this major story, and I thought, "I'm just going to try something here. I'm just going to show this man for who he is rather than one of those straight, hard-news profiles where you're bringing in all the critics—and this is what his supporters say, and this is what his critics say. And this is what he's done and this is what he hasn't done"—which is all in the story.

But I also wanted to reveal as much about this man's emotions and what was going on in his head as I could. And I was lucky enough that Clark revealed that to me in a series of interviews.

How many interviews?

I had four interviews with him. I had an initial interview, where it was almost like breaking the ice with him.

I had broken the story about his evaluation, that he had gotten a poor evaluation. So he was mad at me for putting that in the paper. And when my editors decided to assign me to write a profile of him, I had to figure out a way to go deeper with him. The first interview was the standard answers to my questions, and then at the end of the interview, I put my pen down, and put my notepad down and said, "OK. You're very good. You've given me the answers that I was looking for, but tell me who you are."

It was like a turning point for us. He started talking. And then it grew from there. I would ask to spend the day with him, and then I'd go back for follow-up interviews with follow-up questions, making sure that I had certain stuff in his life right. That was it.

What about the moment of putting the pen down? Do you think that turned the corner?

Well, oftentimes I think when we're interviewing people, we have to develop a relationship and trust them. They have to trust us. And often they don't until they're able to see the reporter as a person. Once they feel some level of trust, then they start feeding you a little bit more and a little bit more. And then checking to see what your reaction is to that information.

Oftentimes, in my interviews, I will reveal something to them, too. It's almost like a back and forth. If somebody talks about their mother, I'm like, "Oh, you know, that happened to me." Or, "My mother is like that."

Or with Clark, he was a deacon, and my father is a minister, so we could relate on that level. In a lot of my interviews, I'm letting them know where I'm coming from.

I'm struck by the presence of faith in three of the five stories. Are there influences that give you license to use that with some authority in the way that you do?

I'm a preacher's kid. So I know parts of the Bible well, and there are many parts I don't know well. But I think faith plays a huge role in the lives of many African-Americans. I guess many of my subjects are African-Americans.

It's kind of a big theme in my own life. I'm just reaching a point of clarity about the world and about the kinds of things that I was taught when I was growing up, and they're all beginning to make sense.

You make use of language with a familiar touch. I have a sense of your familiarity with the world about which you're writing by the language that you choose. The decision to use "whuppin'" for example. Tell me about some of those decisions.

I believe if we use the true language of people without defining it, then it helps the conversation.

I mean, for example, in these stories, I could have used "whipping," which is more standard English, and most of the readership of the *Post* could understand this without definition, without the "comma, meaning spanking." But I often strive in my writing here at the *Post* to speak to some African-Americans in their language, so that the language is familiar to them, and they feel as though I'm speaking to them. Of course, not all African-Americans speak this way. I feel like other writers speak to other communities without defining what they're talking about.

You didn't, in fact, define some things. Like the hot comb in the Chicago story. You didn't define that.

Right. I thought this was a scene that many black people would be able to relate to, especially black women.

What about people who are not black who are reading that story?

I assume that if there are things in the story about a certain culture that I didn't stop to explain, then it would be one of those teachable moments for people.

I mean, there are some of these things about black culture that we explain a lot. We explain our hair. We explain, "OK. I'm wearing braids now, but yes, I do wash my hair." Those kinds of questions that you're bombarded with all the time.

I'm taking some ownership of the language myself. I guess that's the best way to put it. It's an ownership that will allow me to speak to readers who I think will be able to relate, the same way that other cultures kind of write about people.

Where do you get that from?

Many of the writers that I read speak in those languages, like Toni Morrison and Zora Neale Hurston and Jamaica Kinkaid. But if you read their books, there are certain analogies in their books, and stories that are told, but you have to bring something to the book in order to get something back from it. And I guess that's what I'm trying to do in my stories. I'm trying to make people stretch. I think you'll be enriched by this when you've finished reading the story. And then if there are things that you don't understand, perhaps you can strike up a conversation with somebody or call me.

I was particularly struck in "A Good Whuppin'" by the lack of self-consciousness about using, not just the language, but using the syntax. "Burned her legs up" was one that just stopped me, because I said, "Oh, that's from the neighborhood."

In the whuppin' story, obviously the woman in the lead was telling her story, but it was the little girl in me who was getting this whuppin'. And I could relate to her so well, you know, the sting of the switch.

It's like bringing my own life experiences to these stories and just kind of folding them into the stories that other people are telling.

But the thing about writing for the Style section is it gives you the freedom to do that. There's one line in that story where I say, "Don't get it wrong." And that's me. That's my voice.

You made mention of surprises in your writing and there were a couple of surprises in several of the stories. In the whuppin' story, the surprise comes when we learn that the child is taken away and sent to foster care. Are you conscious of what you're doing in getting me that far into the story and then shaking me up with another surprise?

I was really struggling when I wrote those stories. This whole kind of narrative writing was new to me. And I knew that I just couldn't tell you everything at the top of the story.

I guess in all of these stories, there had to be somewhat of a mystery to them. And in order for you to stay with me, there needed to be a nugget of information that you, as a reader, had to seek. And little by little, it would be revealed to you.

How did you find the people for this story?

I was desperate, trying to find somebody who would talk about whuppin's. I ended up calling a source, a teacher I knew, and saying, "Do you know anybody who still whips and is willing to admit it?" And she was working on some political campaign at that time, and she just put the phone down and yelled in the political campaign office, "Anybody here want to talk to somebody about whippings?"

It's almost by chance that you come up with these people.

One of the campaign workers happened to run a welfare-to-work program, and she actually spanked her kids, and then she knew of other women who spanked, and I thought, "Perfect. Let me go out and talk to them."

And I did, and TuSheena was very vocal, and very vivid and colorful, so she became the lead. Out of necessity, almost.

Talk about your voice and the role you think it plays in your writing.

Well, this is an interesting question. I don't know whether you experienced this as a writer, but writing is sometimes like a spiritual process. Sometimes writers talk about going into a trance-like mode or they're just, like, channeling.

There are writers here who'll sit at the keyboard, and they're rocking back and forth, rocking back and forth, trying to get in touch with the muse. I don't rock back and forth, but there's definitely a muse that I need to get in touch with, and he or she, or whatever it is, comes, and I'll wake up in the middle of the night and I'll scribble on a notebook. You know. "This is it!"

Or I'll sit at a keyboard, and I'll write something out without punctuating or capitalizing the stuff, because I don't want to slow down. I'm too slow of a typist to get it all down before it goes away.

So that's kind of how the voice as a writer comes in and out when I'm writing these stories. I guess in the same way that when people write music, or write songs, the ideas are fleeting, so you've got to get them down. The writer's voice is fleeting, so I've got to get it down or I have to have a ritual to get back in touch with it.

In "Deborah's Choice" there are a couple of places where the first quote is in Gaines's voice, in quotation marks, but you continue to speak for her, without attribution: " 'No one knows how hard it is raising four kids by yourself,' she says," and then there are, I think, four sentences that follow in which you continue to make statements.

Right. The first part, basically, is from my reporting, from my interviews with her. She kind of said all of that, but not as succinctly as I did. I mean, she talked to me about babysitting and keeping a job, and stuff like that, and I felt like those points needed to be made, in just that rhythm. It was like writing to music. There's a rhythm in stories that is very strong, and you'll often see it in other stories, where people do three beats, you know: "This and this and this." This, this, AND this.

And if they put two more "thises" in, it would mess it up. But these are really her words, but in my rhythm.

What happens when you're writing stories that are well outside of those places that are so familiar to you?

Well, I can write 'em. Sometimes they're not as intrinsic to me, because I'm not as familiar with the subject matter, but I've been working as a reporter for 12 years or so, and I've written all kinds of stories.

Let me ask the question differently. In these stories, you're not writing about something that you had to go and discover. You're writing about things that you know. Would I be able to tell when you're outside of that arena?

Well, maybe, maybe not. Stories usually come in three categories. Man versus nature, man versus himself, man versus an institution. And when you think about the human complexities, it's universal. I guess that's the word I'm looking for. So yes, there are stories that are about other cultures, other people. One comes to mind, when I was covering Fairfax County courts. Fairfax is a predominantly white, affluent county outside D.C.

And there was a story about this couple whose daughter had been killed in a drunk-driving crash. And they were making the drunken driver pay a dollar a week; write a check made out to the victim for a dollar a week for 18 years.

I didn't really have that much in common with these people. At the time I was in my 20s, and they were, like, maybe 50. I didn't have kids then. But I could kind of relate to the human theme of forgiveness.

You know, there are common, universal themes that override all the cultures and people. And even back then, when I was a very young writer, I probably did this without realizing it, but I chose that theme of forgiveness, and I thought the story worked.

You push to the universal when you try to tell a story. If I've been whipped, if I've ever faced a real dilemma in my life in the way that Deborah has, or grappled with the contradictions of parenting, then I can relate to these stories. Can you be as familiar with the use of language and syntax when telling the Fairfax story?

I can try. I can try by my reporting and by interviewing. I guess, you know, it would take me almost twice as long to get to that point, where I would be as familiar with their stories to write it in such a way.

I wouldn't get it on the first beat. I'd get it after spending a day. And oftentimes I will interview somebody until I get it, because I think it's easier to write the stories after you get it.

Do you recognize it as a handicap when you're reporting at any time?

Yes. There are some people I completely don't understand. There are some cultures I really don't understand. But I try to reach that point of understanding just by asking questions over and over and over, and if I have time, living their lives.

Let me ask you about another part of your writing. How often do you use re-creation in your storytelling and what do you think about that as a technique in writing?

It's a technique I've been studying. It's getting the subject to tell you, in the most minute detail, "What were you wearing? What were you thinking at the time? What were you doing? What did your fingers look like?"

I mean, it's those kinds of tedious questions that allow me to re-create the scene. Sometimes, I'll go back to the subject again and again and again to make sure that I got it right.

Like in "The Accused." Obviously, I wasn't there in the house when the child was trying to take off his shackle, but his mother related that, and the lawyers related that, and I just kept going back to her: "OK. What did the shackle look like? Where was he sitting? What was he wearing?"

I think you can re-create scenes. I think sometimes as a journalist you have to re-create things, because you can't be there all the time. It's best when you're there, but sometimes you can't be there. And as long as it's true.

**There are places, like the lead of "The Accused,"
where you decide, "I'm going to talk as one who was
there."**

Right. When I sat at that kitchen table, and this woman
was telling me about the effect that this whole ordeal had
on her child, and when she then told me about this afternoon when she woke up, and she found her little boy
with the butter knife, I thought, "God. This is so good."

You know, you can't make it up. Fiction would not
be better than this. And I thought, "I've got to use this
in my story," so I had to get that.

Of course, I wasn't there, so I lost the moment. But,
as a writer, I'm able to re-create that. If I were a photographer, I wouldn't be able to re-create it.

And the same thing with the ending. When she told
me how afraid he was to go out of the house, I just
thought this had to be the kicker because it kind of
summed up all of the emotions. You know, he grabbed
his mother's leg; and we all want at some point in our
lives to grab our mother's leg.

**You made a different choice in "Deborah's Choice."
In the lead of that story, and then again when you
take us to the preterm clinic, I don't have any doubt
whatsoever that you are recounting something that
was told to you.**

There is the same sense of immediacy, real tension, in
the lead of "Deborah's Choice." But a different style.

I remember when I sat down to talk with her, and I
got to the point where I needed her to recount what
happened that day, she started crying, and I was like,
"OK. If you can't deal with it, then we'll just rest."

But, of course, I really wanted to use the story. I was
struck when I talked with her about how this was mem-
orized, and how there was almost a blurred line between
reality and dream. I remember when my editors read it,
they said, "Well, we can't tell whether this is a dream or
this is reality."

And so I guess I wrote that to match the state of
mind she was in when she was recounting this scene.

**There's a tremendous amount of detail in the sto-
ries. I think one of my favorite lines in "Deborah's**

Choice" is "Vivian has a juicy drool." When you say that she has bills, you put numbers to them. There are some places in the superintendent's story where the use of the observation is obviously intentional and not just, "Well, let me just put it in the story."

When I sit down to write a story, I want people to see the story, I want people to feel what I feel, hear what I hear, taste what I taste, smell what I smell. So those are kind of the basic Writing 101 things that I'm using. The colors, the smell, the marked-up pages of his Bible.

I remember when I was in Deborah's house, just being struck by this kind of constant stream of saliva that fell from Vivian's mouth. So, when you're recounting something, if you can recount it in the kind of detail that people can relate to, people can see, then I think it's more successful than if I were to say that she had a wet face, or that she kept her mouth open.

Oftentimes, when I'm in these situations interviewing people, I have a finite amount of time. As they're speaking and the tape recorder is rolling, I'm writing down these details all the time. It's like, what am I struck by? Her kitchen is perfectly clean. It's black and white. A little girl sitting in her high chair, but she's not eating her Cheerios, all the things that are happening around me as this woman was telling her story.

Two hours to get all of this stuff and get out of there before she got too tired of talking to me.

It does bring a sense of authenticity to the writing.

Yeah. I was working with an editor in Style who was just amazing. His name is Rich Leiby. He was like an editor and a writing coach.

So I'd come back to the office after reporting these stories, for example, after the whuppin' story, and he'd say, "What is the story about?" And I'd say, "Oh, it's about this man and his daughter, and his daughter has been taken away from him, and dah dah dah dah."

And he'd say, "No. This story is about control." So you boil it down to one word and you write around this word. It made so much sense. It goes back to human nature. People can identify with those kinds of one-word themes.

How did you come up with: "His is not a dusty Bible"? Talk about those turns of phrase when you go beyond reporting and just pick a really good phrase. Do you know when you've done it?

I never really know when I've done it, because I'm always second-guessing myself, and I'm always leery that the editor will come to me and say, "Come on. This is overwriting." So I always overwrite first, and then my editor pulls me back.

The "dusty Bible" thing, that was something I was struck by when I was sitting at his dining room table. It's like, "Man, look at all these highlights." He would highlight different verses in orange highlighter, the kind you used in college. Or blue, or yellow, or green, and it was throughout his entire Bible, and I was trying to figure out a way to describe that, because my Bible is very dusty.

Oh, is that where the comparison comes in?

Yeah. I think so. I was thinking, "God, my Bible is so dusty, and look, this man uses every page of his Bible." Maybe it kind of goes back to something my grandmother had told me, "You don't want a dusty Bible."

In the "Deborah's Choice" story was the phrase, "On that day in that place, fates got up and exchanged places."

That was a line I had to fight for in the editing process. My editor took that out initially because he thought I was reaching too much.

How did you win that battle?

You know, I'm very shy and sometimes don't fight like other reporters fight for every word. So usually I let it go. But this time, I thought, "No, that's the best line in the story." It made what was going on there kind of vivid. That was kind of my muse writing, I think.

I think we're all seeking this meaning of life, trying to figure out whether we're predestined, or whether we have true free will. That's a question that I'm always raising in my head, and I guess it may have been in the back of my head when I wrote this piece. I was just very struck by the fact that this child lived when her mother went there for an abortion, and that this woman who got up that morning to start her day, started her day, went to work, and she died, and I was just very struck by those comparisons.

My editor took that out because he thought that it made it sound like the story would be about the woman who died. But the story was really about Vivian and Deborah.

I just remember saying, "Can't I just fight for this one line?" I don't remember my argument. I just remembered saying, "I really like this line in the story. Can we put it back?"

And you won?

Yeah. And I was happy with that.

Now, let me transition to transitions. I find that I am conscious of when I'm moving in a story. In "Superintendent Tries Moving a Mountain" you ask a question: "How did Clark get to this mountain?" And now we're going back to 1942. In "Deborah's Choice," you begin with a description of her. "Deborah Gaines's black eyebrows are drawn on perfectly," and that takes you to the housing project's beauty pageant, and that takes you back to when she was 17.

When I wrote the transition, "To get back to Clark's childhood, you have to take such and such and such," it came from the interview. I don't know why I asked him how do you get back there, but in the interview, he knew exactly which roads to take, which highways to take, and I remember when I was sitting down to write this story, and I got to a point where I needed to tell something about his childhood, I thought it made sense to use this approach—kind of a map. I like the way that turned out. I liked the way that worked.

You do a lot of physical description of people, and you used that as a transition in Deborah's story.

Yeah, and again, I just want the readers to be as close up to these people as I am. It's almost like putting a magnifying glass on people. I was struck by the fact that she was the beauty queen of this project, and there is irony in that.

You talked at the very beginning of our conversation about your decision to make sure that I understood Deborah totally and had to suspend my judgment. And then toward the end of the piece, Vivian becomes whole. She's out in the park. And she's going up and down the slide. And now I'm saying, as the reader, "Oh. So here is where I see the relationship between mother and child."

Right. I definitely wanted the reader to know that this woman loves this baby. I mean, she could say that she loves the baby, but you could see how much she loved this baby. I could see that, and I wanted to relate that to the reader, by how much care she took with dressing her, combing her hair, and the socks turned down just so. I just wanted those details to be in the story so that readers could take away from this that this mother loves this child, despite the fact that she was suing the clinic for the cost of raising her.

All of your stories end with a distinct statement by the person who is writing the story. You got it on the front page of the newspaper just as surely as you got it in the Style section. So, what's to stop writers from using this style more liberally than we tend to at the moment?

There's a kind of revolution here at the paper. Our editors really want us to *write* stories. There are stories that are reported well, but there's a difference between reporting a story and writing it.

And so I took them up on that challenge, to just write a story in a way that a writer would write a story, as opposed to the way a reporter would write a story. If that makes sense.

Do you think, as a student of the craft, that that's a direction we ought to be trying to take?

Well, it's kind of a dangerous place to be as reporters, as journalists, because there's this really fine, fine, fine line between strict news and editorializing, and you tread that line. I'm treading that line in these stories, and obviously in many of the stories I just go over completely. I just kind of fall over.

But I think we're at a point in journalism where readers want more from papers. When they pick up the paper in the morning, they want a story that's going to move them. Of course, they want the facts and all of that; but I think other readers really want to be moved, and in order to do that, we need really, really good features—well-written features—that will bring readers in and move them and make them expect that they will get something more out of the newspaper than just news. Because if you wake up in the morning and you look at the front page, many of the stories you've already heard about either on your drive home or on the evening news or on the 11 o'clock news. So you're looking to newspapers to add something more to that. And we can do that in our writing.

The Oregonian

Erin Hoover Barnett

Finalist, Non-Deadline Writing

Erin Hoover Barnett has been a member of *The Oregonian*'s Health, Medicine & Science Team since 1996. Barnett graduated from Carleton College in 1987 and began at community weeklies in Chicago. After moving to Portland in 1990, she became a free-lance contributor to *The Oregonian,* and then took a temporary assignment covering the city's public schools. She joined the staff full time in 1994 as a night police reporter. She and reporter James Long won second prize in that year's "Best of the West" competition for their re-creation of the Storm King Mountain fire in Colorado that killed nine Oregon firefighters.

Barnett is always on the lookout for compelling stories about personal triumph and strength. She found her most challenging material covering the thorny issue of physician-assisted suicide in Oregon, where a landmark law took effect in late 1997 after a long court battle and an unsuccessful attempt at repeal. The result: a powerful four-part series about Brian Lovell's struggle to face his impending death in time to control it with a lethal dose of pills. In the last installment, reprinted here, Barnett illuminates the heartbreaking dilemmas that the changing American way of death pose for terminally ill patients, their families, and medical caregivers.

Hope slips away in final vigil

NOVEMBER 25, 1998

Brian Lovell never wanted his 3-year-old daughter to see him like this.

"Wrapped up in tubes," he called it.

But it was getting harder to hide the IV lines. They ran from his chest to the morphine bag and pump in his waist pack.

During his 21 months with colon cancer, Brian had willed himself through two major surgeries, nauseating treatments and leg pains that felt like electrical shocks. He put himself through all that because he still wanted to live. He was only 37.

Now that the end was clearly near, the best he could hope for was a peaceful death. He wanted all of his options available to achieve that.

That's why, on Sept. 13, 1998, he asked his Hillsboro oncologist to help him pursue assisted suicide. And that's why, four days later, he dragged himself to see the Tualatin doctor who would consider writing him the lethal prescription.

"Things aren't progressing the way I'd like them to. I'm losing my vocal capabilities. I'm not thinking," Brian told Dr. Nancy Crumpacker, who also is a cancer doctor.

"Trying to read the paper this morning, what normally would have taken me 20 minutes, took me 45 to 50 minutes," he said.

Brian always thought the option for assisted suicide could allow him to remain in command until the end. But he didn't comprehend how formidable it could be to look death in the eye and harness it.

Under the law, Brian still had 10 days of the 15-day waiting period to go before he could get the lethal medication.

He didn't think about what might happen if he needed the medication sooner.

* * *

Brian's wife, Martha, had repeatedly promised him she would help keep him from suffering.

That promise gave both of them strength as they faced his cancer.

But that promise was becoming harder and harder to keep.

On Monday, Sept. 21, the searing pains began radiating down Brian's legs again.

A hospice nurse bumped Brian's IV morphine to 600 milligrams an hour: half again as much as he had been getting.

Brian struggled to form sentences now. He was having strange dreams. One was about a child who turned out to be a dog.

Washington County Hospice nurses visited several times daily. But Martha had to monitor his IVs and change the bag of fluids and the batteries in the pumps. She had to inject anti-nausea medication every few hours into one of his tubes, the tubes that Brian didn't want 3-year-old Samantha to see.

Brian was vomiting so much now that Martha wasn't sure he could even take the lethal prescription for assisted suicide if—when it came—he wanted it.

"I don't know what's going to happen," Martha said, exhausted.

* * *

On Wednesday, hospice workers set up a hospital bed in the living room of Brian and Martha's Hillsboro home. Brian lay covered in a pastel quilt in the place where his recliner used to be.

By that time, cancer had completely paralyzed his small intestine.

The organ could no longer process food. But waste had to exit Brian's body somehow. Brian began to vomit fecal matter.

Crumpacker, at age 51 partial to simple dresses and sensible shoes, visited Brian at home that day to see how he was doing and whether he still thought he wanted the lethal prescription.

She wound up holding Brian's bucket for him and rubbing his back.

She had decided when he came to her office the previous week that he was an appropriate candidate for assisted suicide under the law. She had told him he had many options. They could implant a medication pump near his spine if he needed better pain relief. He could control his dying by deciding to stop eating.

Or he could use a lethal dose under the Oregon Death With Dignity Act.

The law makes patients wait 15 days from when they first formally request a prescription from their doctor. They then can have the massive overdose of barbiturate capsules, intended to shut down the brain.

The law says you have to take the drugs yourself, so someone else isn't killing you. But that also means you can't be on the brink of death. You still have to be able to swallow.

Brian told Crumpacker he still hadn't decided for sure that he would commit assisted suicide. But he knew he didn't want surgery for another medication pump. And he didn't want to die slowly of starvation like he watched his grandpa do.

Brian didn't know it, but Crumpacker had been sitting in the row in front of him a year earlier when he had appeared on the local talk show "Town Hall." There, he had articulately expressed his interest in assisted suicide. The fact that his views hadn't changed helped convince her that he wasn't requesting a prescription because he was depressed.

Brian's stomach hurt and he was agitated, tossing about and occasionally vomiting. He began getting injections of lorazepam that day to help ease his nausea and control his anxiety.

He was reaching the point that makes assisted suicide a possibility; when being dead seems better than being alive.

* * *

Brian could no longer fit all of his medications in the pack around his waist. Now fat bags of morphine, fluids and lorazepam hung from a silver IV rack next to Brian's bed, with IV lines funneling into the catheter in his chest.

Rushing into Brian's veins along with the medication was the realization that his independence was sliding away from him.

He fought his helplessness. When the hospice nurse arrived that afternoon, he refused to use the commode. Weak and groggy as he was, he was going to walk to the bathroom.

The nurse helped him up. Brian sat on the edge of the bed in his gray sweat suit looking haggard.

His daughter, Samantha, wearing a little white tunic with red hearts, wandered into the living room.

She suddenly turned away from Brian.

"Did you say 'Hi' to daddy?" Martha asked her. Samantha shook her head. She curled her lower lip. She seemed almost angry.

Then she turned around to face the hospital bed, the tubes, Daddy.

She waved a little wave.

Brian waved back slowly. Like a windshield wiper pushing snow.

* * *

That Thursday night, Brian kissed Samantha again and again before Martha sent her to stay with friends.

Martha told Brian he must have a catheter slid into his bladder. He had not urinated for hours, risking infection.

A hospice nurse arrived and inserted the tube. Brian winced. He gritted his teeth.

For Brian, that catheter tube was the final indignity. About 11:30 p.m., his wife heard his morphine pump drop to the floor.

Martha ran to discover Brian sitting up with about a foot of the urinary catheter pulled out. Her close friend Sandi Fisher was right behind her.

Try sliding the tube back in, the hospice nurse said on the phone. Martha tried. Brian grimaced. The nurse said she would come.

Martha sat next to her agonized husband, pushing the button on his pump every 10 minutes to give him an extra morphine hit.

The hospice nurse arrived. She hugged Martha. Martha held Brian's hand. The nurse tried unsuccessfully to get the catheter back in.

Brian looked first at Martha and then at the nurse.

"I'm done," he said in a hoarse voice.

"I want to go now. I want to go *now.*"

But Brian had waited too long for this moment to arrive. The medicine was still four days from his grasp.

The choice to die was no longer his.

He looked again at Martha. Tears were streaming down her face.

"You promised me," he whispered fiercely.

"You promised me."

"You promised me."

Hysterical, Martha called Dr. Gerald Gibbs. He was still Brian's primary physician.

Gibbs said there was nothing they could do until morning. She would have to ignore Brian.

But how could she?

She had promised Brian she would not let him suffer. Should she break the security code on the morphine pump, try to give Brian an overdose and worry about getting prosecuted later?

Martha called Crumpacker.

Crumpacker told her that her promise to Brian was not to play God and let him die immediately.

Her promise was to keep him comfortable.

Martha calmed down.

* * *

Crumpacker hung up the phone. It was 1:45 a.m. on Friday. She was supposed to leave on an early flight for a long weekend with her husband.

Now she knew she couldn't go. She dropped off her husband at the airport. She called Martha at 6 a.m.

Martha had not slept all night. Brian tried to pull out his chest catheter, the only remaining route to get medicine into his bloodstream. He sweated. He threw up more fecal matter.

Crumpacker said she would be there soon. She had an idea.

It was too late for assisted suicide. She could not deliver the medication to him until the waiting period ended Monday. Moreover, his blocked intestine would prevent him from absorbing the lethal mixture.

So Crumpacker ventured into the ethically touchy realm of aggressive end-of-life care.

In rare situations, doctors will use drugs to sedate a dying patient who is in agony. It's called palliative sedation, and it is legal. But palliative sedation is dicey because the drugs can also shut down the brain so much that the patient stops breathing.

Many hospice programs, in these situations, will sedate a patient by raising the levels of morphine and lorazepam, drugs that the patient usually is getting already.

These medications didn't seem to be working well for Brian, so Crumpacker thought it made sense to switch to a barbiturate.

The main job of barbiturates is sedation. They do the job well with a much smaller dose than usually is needed with morphine, which is chiefly a pain killer.

But barbiturates are so good at sedation that they can also kill you quickly. That's why people use them to commit suicide. And that's why they make doctors nervous.

The ethics of any kind of palliative sedation hinge on intent. The doctor's intent must be to ease suffering, not to kill the patient.

The barbiturate Crumpacker was considering was thiopental, commonly used for anesthesia or to control seizures. It is also used in the Netherlands for euthanasia, the intentional killing of a suffering patient.

Crumpacker knew that if she gave Brian too much and he stopped breathing immediately, it could look like euthanasia.

Euthanasia is illegal.

* * *

When Crumpacker arrived at 8:30 a.m., Brian was still miserable, stuck between life and death.

Crumpacker suggested the thiopental. Gibbs, Brian's attending physician, would call in the prescription.

Martha sat down beside her husband and stroked his hand. She told him that Crumpacker was going to make him feel more comfortable, if he would just wait a few more hours.

Brian agreed to hold on.

Martha called Brian's parents, his brother and his friend from boyhood, Roger Bennett.

This would be a good time to come and see Brian, she told them. It could be the last time Brian is lucid enough to say good-bye.

* * *

A pharmacist with Providence Health System read Gibbs' order for medication that slid out of the fax machine at their Northeast Portland office. Washington County Hospital uses Providence for its pharmacy services. The pharmacist consulted the supervisor, veteran hospice pharmacist Milo Haas.

The order surprised Haas. It seemed like a sudden shift when the patient could tolerate more lorazepam and morphine.

Haas called Gibbs.

The phone conversation was short, and it left Gibbs with a distinct impression: "In their official opinion," Gibbs recalled, "to use this medication was equivalent to euthanasia."

Gibbs had not realized the thiopental might be controversial. He did know that this was not the climate for risk taking. Just that week, a U.S. Senate committee advanced a bill that would allow the federal government to investigate doctors who prescribe drugs for assisted suicide or euthanasia.

Gibbs canceled the order for thiopental. He requested more morphine and lorazepam instead. Then he called Martha.

Martha listened as Gibbs explained what happened. He said he had no experience with thiopental and didn't want to put hospice in an uncomfortable situation since he is their medical director.

He told Martha she would have to appoint Crumpacker as Brian's attending physician if Brian wanted the thiopental.

"Fine," Martha said. "You're fired."

* * *

Crumpacker was in a grocery store parking lot when her cellular phone rang.

It was Jean Kludas, the patient care coordinator for Washington County Hospice. Kludas had gotten a similarly jolting call from the Providence pharmacist.

Kludas told Crumpacker that hospice could not get involved with this drug. They could continue to care for Brian. But if Crumpacker was going to get the thiopental, she was on her own to administer it.

Crumpacker was frustrated. She thought the drug could make Brian comfortable.

She drove home and called Martha. She told her it would take her a while longer to get the drug.

Crumpacker called William "Frosty" Comer, another pharmacist who specializes in administering intravenous drugs at home.

Comer had come to terms with his support for assisted suicide by vowing to help keep patients from needing it. He viewed the use of the thiopental to calm Brian's agitation as one of those situations. This was not euthanasia. It was not assisted suicide. It was good end-of-life care.

* * *

Martha was at Brian's bedside when Crumpacker and a nurse arrived about 6 p.m. Crumpacker with her sleeping bag in case she needed to spend the night.

Martha had spent the afternoon trying to keep Brian from reaching for his IVs and getting out of bed. Gibbs noticed his agitation when he dropped by to visit.

A hospice nurse had stopped Brian's intravenous fluids and bumped him to 1,000 milligrams of morphine and 10 milligrams of lorazepam an hour, extreme amounts even for dying patients.

When Crumpacker got there, she said Brian was sleeping. But the pained expression on his pale face remained.

"The drug is here, Brian," Crumpacker told him. "I'm going to make you comfortable."

Brian nodded groggily.

Crumpacker and the nurse, who is specially trained in administering IV medications at home, stopped the morphine infusion.

Martha watched her husband's furrowed brow.

Crumpacker picked up the syringe. She didn't know how much would be needed to calm him. She didn't want to give him too much.

She injected 50 milligrams of thiopental into Brian's intravenous line over five minutes, far less than he would have needed for anesthesia before surgery.

Suddenly, Brian's face relaxed.

The arm he had crooked over his head slid down to his chest.

Martha exhaled.

She had kept her promise.

"It was like gold. It was like air," she said. "The relief of that bag coming in the house and finally, he was better."

* * *

Crumpacker stayed until midnight when Martha's sister, an intensive care nurse from another state, arrived.

After giving Brian the initial dose of thiopental, Crumpacker had started an infusion pump that delivered 50 milligrams an hour. Crumpacker told Martha's sister how to work the infusion. She left her phone number by every telephone.

Martha and her sister pulled out the sofa bed. Her sister checked on Brian, moving his infusion up by 10 milligrams at one point when he became agitated.

Martha slept for the first time in three nights.

* * *

The next day, Brian's parents and Roger sat with Brian in the living room. He was sleeping peacefully. Martha's friend Sandi offered Brian's dad some coffee. She asked if anyone wanted anything.

Brian opened his eyes a little.

"Yeah, I'll have a couple beers," he said.

Sandi even thought she saw him smile.

Brian was still in control.

Crumpacker came by late that morning, as did a hospice nurse. Gibbs stopped by a half hour later. Gibbs was impressed by how peaceful Brian looked. The two doctors and the hospice nurse left momentarily.

Martha was about to leave the house for the first time all week. They needed groceries.

But she heard Brian's mother shriek from his bedside.

Brian had opened his eyes and was no longer breathing.

"My boy. He's gone!" his mom cried.

Martha ran in from the kitchen, sat on her husband's bed and took his hand. She moved close to look in his eyes.

She told him it was OK.

He could go now.

She said she saw his soul leave his eyes.

She lay on his bed for a long time.

Martha's 17-year-old son, Matthew, stood behind his mother. He braided her hair and massaged her back.

Martha stroked Brian's arm where so many of his IVs had been.

"No more," she said. "No more."

* * *

The hospice nurse returned to the house. She had a special blanket called a passage quilt. She laid it over Brian's still-warm body.

When the man from the mortuary took Brian away, the nurse removed the quilt.

She walked over to Martha, standing on the stoop outside her home, watching her husband go.

The nurse wrapped Martha in the quilt.

"A hug," the nurse said, "from Brian."

Lessons Learned

BY ERIN HOOVER BARNETT

Lesson #1: Be flexible. The Oregon Death With Dignity Act, the nation's only law allowing physician-assisted suicide, finally took effect in late 1997. My ultimate mission, it seemed, was to write about a person who used the lethal drugs.

But it turned out that the real story was in making the choice to die. My team leader, Sally Cheriel, and the editor on "Brian's Journey," Amanda Bennett, helped me to see that. The challenge of that choice became the theme to the four-day series on Brian, as captured in my lead on the first day: "Brian Lovell had a lot to live for. And that made choosing to die especially hard."

Lesson #2: Maintain integrity. This was *his* life—and death—not *my* story. I realized when I met Brian Lovell in August 1998 that to get this story I needed to be willing to lose it.

Brian was dying of colon cancer and had publicly supported assisted suicide but had not started the two-week process to get the lethal prescription himself. For me to have story, Brian needed to pursue that prescription. But at 37, Brian was focused on living. I needed to sign on for the ride, knowing he could get better or die without getting the lethal dose.

Photographer Ross William Hamilton and I pored over the ethical minefields with our editors. We consulted Bob Steele at Poynter. Were we encouraging Brian to kill himself just by being there? We decided to emphasize that we were interested in Brian's journey, not his destination.

Initially our worries were overblown. Brian was not about to swallow 90 barbiturate pills for the sake of our story. The will to live is the most powerful force imaginable, which I later realized was central to the story.

But as Brian got sicker, ethical limit-setting became important. I went with Brian and his wife, Martha, to see Brian's last CT scan. His doctor told me in private that Brian's cancer was paralyzing his intestines, and that he could die a horrible death from vomiting and starvation. But his doctor soft-pedaled the news to Brian. He told him he would die of "malnutrition."

I felt sick knowing what he was really facing. I knew that if I told him and Martha what the doctor told me, it could encourage Brian to get his lethal prescription. If I kept quiet, I would feel some responsibility if Brian did die a horrible death and couldn't get the lethal dose in time to escape.

I decided to back away from that ledge. I asked Brian if his doctor was giving him all the information he wanted. Brian said yes. He said he was happy to take things one day at a time. I realized something essential that I would have missed: The real challenge behind physician-assisted suicide is facing death. Brian was not facing death yet and he wouldn't until being dead seemed better than being alive.

Lesson #3. Be diplomatic. Ross and I wanted to be there if and when Brian took a lethal dose. We broached the topic gently with Brian and Martha. We were careful not to imply that he *should* take the drugs, but just that if he did, we wanted to be there. They said no. Martha said she would never forgive herself if we distracted her from attending to Brian. We backed off, hoping we could keep the option open.

But as Brian drew closer to death, the Lovells naturally pulled away from us. We tried to get them to think about what they would want from this story and how we needed to be with them to do a good job. We walked a difficult line between getting the material we needed and respecting their privacy.

Lesson #4. Get the support you need. Sally let me call her at home when I needed to process an experience with Brian. Amanda always knew when I needed a pep talk and always delivered. My husband lived "Brian's Journey" with me, helping me work through dilemmas, critiquing my drafts, and making me laugh. Ross and I worked as partners and served as each other's sounding boards. And for the hard stuff—like how it might feel to watch Brian swallow a lethal dose—I visited a professional counselor.

Lesson #5. It can be OK to be human. In the evening after Brian died, Ross and I asked if we could join Martha and her friends. Ross left his camera in the car. I stuffed my notebook in my purse. We stood with Martha in the kitchen of her home, locked in a three-way hug, and cried.

Bartholomew Sullivan

Deadline News Reporting

Bartholomew Sullivan is a reporter for *The Commercial Appeal* in Memphis, Tenn. A native of St. Louis, Mo., he graduated with a bachelor's degree in political science from the University of Santa Clara, where he was editor of the campus newspaper. After briefly attending law school, he began his newspaper career in 1982 as a rural beat reporter for *The Gettysburg* (Pa.) *Times*. From there, he worked as a county reporter for *The Carlisle* (Pa.) *Times* before moving to *The Palm Beach* (Fla.) *Times,* switching over to *The Palm Beach Post* after the two papers merged. At the *Post* he covered a series of municipal beats and general assignment duties, including the annual Everglades alligator hunt.

He joined *The Commercial Appeal* in October 1992 and for the past six years has been the tri-state regional reporter, covering breaking news events and trials in

Tennessee, Mississippi, and Arkansas. He is co-author of *The Blood of Innocents,* about an Arkansas triple-murder case.

Sullivan's beat represents just the kind of deadline reporting that the Jesse Laventhol Prize recognizes: journalism as a timed sport. Whether he's covering the trial of a Ku Klux Klan wizard for a three-decades-old murder, the funeral of music legend Carl Perkins, or one of the tornadoes that regularly bring destruction and tragedy to the countryside of his region, Sullivan's hallmarks are attention to detail, empathetic reporting, and informed and evocative prose to communicate the human connections behind the news of the day.

—Christopher Scanlan

Perkins's fans pay homage to the man

JACKSON, Tenn.—Giants of five decades of country and rock music paid a songful tribute Friday to Carl Perkins, with Wynonna Judd at one point noting, "Y'know, the Beatles were in his fan club."

Former Beatle George Harrison, rockabilly's Jerry Lee Lewis and country stars Garth Brooks, Ricky Skaggs and Billy Ray Cyrus led a list of luminaries at the overflow funeral at the R.E. Womack Chapel on the campus of Lambuth University.

In an impromptu tribute toward the end of the 1½-hour service, Judd asked Harrison to join musicians onstage. Retuning an accoustic guitar borrowed from Skaggs, Harrison said, "I think somebody out there must know this. It's from Carl's first album." The congregation was electrified as the aging rocker sang the old rockabilly lyrics: "True love, baby, that's what you give to me."

Except for an organ flourish, Harrison's contribution ended the church service. It was the benediction.

Everyone who spoke at Friday's service recalled Perkins's humility and charity, his sincerity and abiding faith. The son of sharecroppers, Perkins rose to fame singing of blue suede shoes. He died Monday after a series of strokes. His death at 65 prompted an outpouring of respect from legends of the music world as well as lifelong local friends from Jackson, his hometown.

His old friend and Methodist minister Dr. John A. Jones recalled Perkins's kindness to a girl whose father had died, his work for abused children, his humor and his travails.

Using the 23rd Psalm for a text, Jones said he had seen Perkins "waller in green pastures" but said Perkins "knew the Lord had taken him to still waters."

"Today all of Carl's longings are satisfied," he added. Later, Jones exhorted the crowd to join him in a chorus of "Old Time Religion."

Judd—who joined Cyrus and Skaggs in a rousing version of Perkins's "Daddy Sang Bass" as the crowd got to its feet—also sang the hymn "How Great Thou Art" with a mixed chorus. At another point, she reminisced about talking to Perkins and seeing a document she said belonged "in a vault": proof of the Beatles' fan club status.

"Carl was the coolest cat I've ever known," she said. "I never heard Carl sound resentful for the fact that he wrote a song somebody else pretty much got most of the credit for," an apparent reference to Elvis Presley's success with "Blue Suede Shoes."

Former Beatle Paul McCartney, in a video clip played to the crowd, described his former band members' admiration for Perkins's sound as kids growing up in Liverpool, although he said they had to slow it down to get the lyrics. "We became really serious, big fans of Carl Perkins," he said.

The congregation also heard recorded musical tributes from Elton John, Eric Clapton and George Martin.

Judd also read from a note pinned to a flower arrangement sent by Bob Dylan: "He really stood for freedom. That whole sound stood for all the degrees of freedom. It would just jump right off the turntable.... We wanted to go where that was happening," Dylan wrote.

Gov. Don Sundquist recalled college days dancing to "Blue Suede Shoes" in blue suede shoes.

"Our state of Tennessee is known the world over for our music," Sundquist said in tribute. "Our friend Carl Perkins is one of the reasons....His music and style changed music itself, influencing generations of performers."

"Tennessee has lost a dear friend, a great ambassador, a big part of our musical soul."

Billy Ray Cyrus was on the program to sing "Amazing Grace" but instead strummed a song he said he wrote after a walk in the woods this week. "Angels will sing when they call out your name," he sang as he strummed his left-handed guitar. "Goodbye."

Singer Johnny Rivers said "being around Carl and his guitar was like going to school....He had a gentle, soft-spoken manner."

"Carl, the world is a better place because you were here," he added. "No one can ever step on your blue suede shoes, but we can be glad we were able to touch them. They're way too deep to fill."

Many in the crowd of 650 that filled the red brick chapel stood in the damp, 40-degree chill for three hours before getting into the 2 p.m. service. An overflow of several hundred more watched proceedings from the Lambuth student union, where Jackson's ABC television affiliate WBBJ ran the event live and without interruption.

After the service, Harrison, 54, gave 62-year-old Jerry Lee Lewis a bear hug and introduced him to his wife, Olivia, as a crowd of students and fans trampled the muddy perimeter of a rope line. Harrison left for the cemetery in a Lincoln bearing the vanity licence plate "Suede." Someone shouted, "Thanks for coming, George."

Jeannie Sims, 55, drove down from Paris, Tenn., to stand in the long line and pay her respects. "I was the right age to be very wound up by all that," she said of Perkins's music. "And he was truly a very good person."

Leroy and Sadie Gipson of Jonesboro, Ark., drove 175 miles to give their idol a sendoff. For both, the music and Perkins's evident faith made it more than a funeral, they said.

"It was more rejoicing," said Leroy, 65. "It's hard to explain, but this was a celebration."

Writers' Workshop

Talking Points

1) Celebrities and fans gathered together at the funeral of Carl Perkins. Note the structure of the story. How are voices of the two groups balanced in the article?

2) Few celebrities have additional identification; the writer assumes they are well-known. Do readers need more identification for Wynonna Judd, George Martin, or others?

3) How much biographical information about Perkins is included in the article? Is more background necessary?

Assignment Desk

1) Write an obituary about another famous musician. In your research, note what colleagues and fans have said about the musician.

2) Listen to the music of Carl Perkins. Write a review about his music.

Tornado sneaks into Manila, killing 2 kids just as sirens wail

APRIL 17, 1998

MANILA, Ark.—It killed first, then it came into town.

With almost no warning, a tornado dropped from the skies over northeast Arkansas just before 3 a.m. Thursday, smashing the mobile home of 5-year-old Brittany and 2½-year-old Kasey Lomax just as warning sirens began to wail.

Then it crossed a plowed but unplanted field, smashed a brake-parts factory and a Dollar General Store, and spun down Olympia Street, snapping 100-year-old trees like pencils.

"It was one excellent, big, humming roar," said Larry Carpenter, 38, who saw what was coming and climbed into a Laundromat dryer to wait out the storm.

The Lomax children died before rescue workers and their parents, Wayne and Candy Lomax, could lift the floorboards from their shattered bodies, a shaken and muddy Manila Police Chief Jackie Hill said later.

"When you pick up two small kids and hold them in your arms—I've got kids—it breaks your heart," he said.

The twister also injured 21 people—several seriously —and damaged or destroyed 163 homes and 25 other buildings in this usually quiet Mississippi County town of 6,410 about 70 miles northwest of Memphis.

Gov. Mike Huckabee toured the town in the early afternoon and later declared Mississippi County—as well as Craighead, Lonoke and Pulaski counties, which suffered minor damage from tornadoes—a disaster area.

After he met with the grandparents of the Lomax children, he said, he "walked away with the most helpless feeling," but vowed to commit the resources at his disposal to help those in need.

Manila Mayor Jimmy White declared a dusk-to-dawn curfew to prevent looting as 30 National Guardsmen from the 875th Engineer Battalion, based in Jonesboro, began arriving in the late afternoon.

"We had virtually no warning," White said. "But when you've got one that comes out of nowhere, you never have enough time."

Mississippi County Sheriff Leroy Meadows said sirens went off just 30 seconds before it hit. Several residents said they were already seeing serious damage by the time they began to hear the sirens.

"When the siren went off, there was already a tree lying on my porch," said Mabel Healey, 67. "If I'd have gone out, it would've killed me."

But as the whine of chain saws rent the air all around, Healey said she'd gotten off comparatively easy. "On down the street—it makes you cry."

National Weather Service meteorologist James W. Duke said the region was placed under a severe thunderstorm warning at 2:36 a.m. At 2:42 a.m., it was upgraded to a tornado warning, and the Memphis weather service office called the Manila Volunteer Fire Department phone number, automatically alerting all 25 of its members through a system in place for such emergencies.

Someone set off the town wide alarm seconds later.

Manila Patrolman Joni Isebell, 32, was on duty and driving down Main Street when her car was lifted off the ground.

"It was just floating. I was scared," she said. But she was most worried for her children, Mikki and Dennis, staying with their grandmother west of town, where reports of trapped children—the Lomaxes—were coming over her police radio.

By the time she got there, the wall of her mother's house had been torn away, but her children had escaped injury wedged between a bed and a couch. If they had been at home in her trailer home, they might not have made it, she speculated later. The trailer was blown to smithereens—a pile of debris mixed with evergreen boughs.

"I'll never live in another trailer," Isebell said. As Isebell described the evening, another siren began wailing in the distance, and some relatives monitoring a police scanner reported funnel clouds sighted in Lake City and Black Oak. Thursday's noon tornado warning was lifted at 4 p.m.

The destructive power of the predawn storm knocked Brian Pate's house off its foundation and dropped a huge black walnut tree onto his Taurus station wagon.

"My 6-year-old woke us up around 3 o'clock and said the siren was going off," said Pate, 29. "We got in the hallway and that's when it picked the house up and moved it about three foot."

By his neighbors' assessments, Melvin Browning, 53, had the nicest backyard in Manila, with an old English walnut, ferns and a row of pine trees—a 27-year labor of love. Now, it's demolished, the trees bent and snapped off at odd angles; a shed upended.

Browning said he was asleep when the wall of his bedroom began to cave in. He made a race for the storm cellar, but got only as far as the utility room.

The afternoon before the storm, Browning video-taped his granddaughter in the backyard, collecting hidden Easter eggs. As he ate a bologna sandwich supplied by the American Red Cross, he said he was most grateful his granddaughter's life had been spared.

"It was a sad sight when daylight came," he said as he crunched through hallways strewn with glass. "But all this can be replaced. Life can't."

As he spoke, neighbor Therese McDonald, 44, dropped by with her daughter, Dreama, 4. The child had "sensed something" moments before the storm hit, McDonald said. "She was just jerking from head to toe."

"I grabbed her and said 'Dreama, let's go,'" McDonald said. "We got in the bathtub and went to praying."

All down Olympia, Boston, Baltimore and Ark. 18, aluminum siding hung from utility wires, fiberglass insulation clung to tree limbs and trash was scattered everywhere. So many evergreen trees were knocked down or stripped that some areas smelled like a Christmas tree lot; other areas smelled of natural gas. At one house, open to the sky after a roof had been torn off, dolls still sat on a bookshelf, undisturbed.

Charles Galloway, 42, said his family huddled in the hallway as his house "kind of jumped up and down." The back of the house blew away and a tree landed on his car.

Cherokee Sammons, 25, said she tried to make it to a shelter with her 4-month-old son, but was lifted off the ground and thrown under a car. She received nine stiches to her scalp. She was trying to get a ride to Memphis, where her son, Tyler, and daughter, Danielle, 4, had been airlifted to Le Bonheur Children's Medical Center.

William Martin, 36, went outside to cut off the natural gas when he saw the storm throwing debris into the air from his bedroom window. When he got outside, he was looking up into the eye of the storm. "It's not over. We're in the middle of it," he recalled thinking. He and his wife hid in a closet as a utility pole crashed down on their roof.

Grace Halpain had lived 82 years without seeing a tornado. Her cats woke her up as the wind picked up and the power went out Thursday morning.

"It come up all at once," she said, as she tuned one ear to a battery-powered radio.

Writers' Workshop

Talking Points

1) Analyze the lead. What makes those eight words so powerful? How would the impact of the lead change if "it" was changed to "the tornado"?

2) Note the powerful verbs in the story, e.g. "dropped," "smashing." How do these affect the tone of the story?

3) "...some areas smelled like a Christmas tree lot; other areas smelled of natural gas." Many stories include details of what reporters see and hear; fewer include the sense of smell. Note how this adds a powerful layer of description to the story.

4) The seventh paragraph includes many numbers. Does it bog down the story?

Assignment Desk

1) Note how this story blends the reactions of people in town with those of public officials. Does your own writing start with officials and then move to residents? Look for ways to include more voices in your stories.

2) On your next story, include what you smell, as well as what you see and hear.

Ex-Klan leader convicted of killing Dahmer

AUGUST 22, 1998

HATTIESBURG, Miss.—It has taken 32 years, but it looks like justice has finally come to Ellie Dahmer and her children.

In slightly more than three hours of deliberations Friday, a Forrest County jury found Sam Bowers, the former Imperial Wizard of the White Knights of the Ku Klux Klan, guilty of the 1966 murder of civil rights activist Vernon Dahmer.

The historic verdict and life sentence followed four mistrials in the 1960s in which jurors deadlocked on charges that Bowers orchestrated the firebombing that killed Dahmer, injured his 10-year-old daughter and destroyed his home and grocery. Witnesses said Bowers, now 73, ordered the killing because Dahmer (pronounced DAY-mer) was allowing black voters to pay their poll taxes in his store.

Immediately after reading the verdict, Circuit Judge Richard W. McKenzie polled the jury, then ordered Bowers into custody. He will be sent to the Mississippi State Penitentiary at Parchman sometime next week. Before sentencing, McKenzie asked Bowers if he had anything to say. "No, sir," he said. He had taken off the Mickey Mouse lapel pin he'd worn all week.

The conviction of Bowers, combined with a guilty verdict four years ago in the retrial of the man accused of killing Medgar Evers, was seen by some as proof of a changing racial climate in Mississippi.

When McKenzie banged his gavel at the close of the four-day trial, the courtroom erupted in cheers. Forrest County Asst. Dist. Atty. Robert B. Helfrich choked back tears. Retired FBI agents who'd spent the prime of their lives battling Klan violence and had returned to testify this week embraced each other, misty eyed. Mrs. Dahmer, in a balcony overlooking the defense table where she had spent all week, hugged her children.

Outside the courthouse, dabbing her eyes with a balled-up tissue, she spoke for her family and her husband.

"I'm filled with joy," she said. "The tears I'm shedding, I'm shedding for Vernon. I know he's looking at us today....It's a happy moment for us—one we've waited for for about 30 years."

Said Helfrich: "This is the Dahmers' day. They have waited too long for it."

Everyone in the Forrest County Courthouse this week knew that history was being made. Named in 1909 for Confederate Gen. Nathan Bedford Forrest, who founded the original Ku Klux Klan, the county and its county seat have been a focal point in the civil rights struggle since the late 1950s.

Dist. Atty. E. Lindsay Carter noted Friday that he had been asked by many people not to reopen the case, and was widely praised for the courage to take it on.

Others, like Bob Stringer, the surprise witness who came forward last year to say he'd overheard Bowers and Deavours Nix plan the attack, said it was the right thing to do. Nix, 72, faces trial on arson charges in the same incident.

"I'm just proud. This is about people helping people. I'm just glad I could help," Stringer said.

But what some saw as courage and righting a wrong, the defense team saw as pandering to a political constituency, the theme of defense lawyer Travis Buckley's often wandering closing argument.

"I started out by telling you that this was a case that was wound up by political expediency and driven by members of the press," Buckley told jurors. "I say to you now that this is a case where Mr. Bowers's life is being offered upon that altar to be sacrificed...to promote political ambition." Later, he vowed to appeal the conviction.

Most will remember the Bowers defense for the testimony of Nix, who said he joined the Klan when he heard of its "benevolent" mission and its delivery of fruit baskets at Christmastime.

Atty. Gen. Mike Moore, who attended the trial Thursday and was here for the verdict Friday, poked fun at the strategy of putting Nix on the stand.

"Fruit baskets at Christmas: that about sums up the defense in this case," he said. "The jury laughed at the defense the entire trial."

For most in the courtroom, the fifth Bowers trial and the verdict Friday was a victory as sweet as the 1994 conviction of Byron De La Beckwith for the 1963 murder of NAACP field secretary Evers in Jackson.

Dahmer's killing occurred just as Klansmen were being called before the U.S. House of Representatives Un-American Activities Committee. The firebombing was aimed at sending a message to Washington, according to testimony.

Dahmer, his wife and three children were asleep in the predawn hours of Jan. 10, 1966, when two carloads of Klansmen, bearing shotguns and 12 gallons of gasoline, attacked the Dahmers' rural home and grocery about five miles north of Hattiesburg. Dahmer fired back at the attackers but was severely burned. He died that afternoon, his lungs seared by burning gasoline fumes. He was 58.

In their closing arguments Friday, Special Asst. Atty. Gen. Lee Martin and Helfrich urged jurors to look at the consistent evidence of guilt, not the moral character of the former Klansmen who testified against the former Imperial Wizard.

Billy Roy Pitts, the chief witness in the earlier trials and again this week, admitted on the stand to having an extramarital affair while in protective custody. Another witness left her Klansman husband shortly after the Dahmer killing and lived with a man without marrying him, a point the defense hammered home.

Martin asked jurors to consider the testimony of Cathy Lucy, the former wife of Klansman Burris Dunn of Jackson, who recalled Bowers arriving at her house with headlines of Dahmer's death from the daily newspaper and "jubilant" at what his "boys" had done to the Dahmer family.

Helfrich banged an index finger on the rail of the jury box as he recalled Thursday's testimony in which a string of Bowers's Jones County friends testified that he was a solid businessman, a Christian—"a gentleman." One of the witnesses was Nix, who called Bowers a "real, real nice man."

"They talk of gentlemen," Helfrich whispered. Then, shouting, he said: "These people don't have a gentle bone in their bodies. They were nightriders and henchmen. They attacked a sleeping family and destroyed all they owned."

Then recalling Pitts's testimony that as he fled from the burning house he heard a man's voice—"in distress"—Helfrich reached his conclusion. "A man's voice is still in distress...because Sam Bowers is still walking the street."

Since he was tried on an indictment that had been "passed to the file" at the end of his last trial in the '60s, Bowers was found guilty under the law as it stood at the time. Although a current-day life sentence in Mississippi means life in prison, Bowers will be eligible to apply for parole in 10 years, said Martin of the Attorney General's office.

Awaiting the verdict in the courtroom Friday morning were three of the four FBI agents who testified for the state in the case. Lindsay, the district attorney, called them "my right stuff."

Retired agents James W. Awe, Loren Brooks, Charles Killion and Jim Ingram, now Mississippi's Commissioner of Public Safety, are walking Civil Rights Era textbooks on the Klan and its secret ways. Said Ingram: "We are about the only ones still alive or who still have their mental faculties who could be here, who could testify to the significant elements." Awe said they'd probably set a record for returning to testify after so many years.

But for all the agents who tried to bring peace through law enforcement, there were more who tried to use what Jeanette M. Smith called "the movement." She'd attended Bowers's first trial in 1967.

Her late husband, Dr. C.E. Smith of Memphis, took over as president of the NAACP in Forrest County when Dahmer was killed, and she served in the same capacity later herself. Smith recalled the constant harassment her family received after her husband was invited to be one of the few black people in Forrest County permitted to vote, but refused if everyone couldn't.

"The emphasis was on voter registration, but after Mr. Dahmer's death, things began to escalate," she remembered. "They'd call and say, 'Do you know where your children are?' They'd come by and throw skunks in the yard. They did all kinds of things to instill terror.

"It means so much to me to see justice done," she said.

But she doesn't want revenge. "You have to forgive because some of the worst people I know have the finest children."

Rev. Will Campbell, 74, of Mt. Juliet, Tenn., who was the only white man present at the founding of the Southern Christian Leadership Conference and walked the first black children into Little Rock Central High, was greeted in the courtroom as an old friend by both Ellie Dahmer and Sam Bowers.

Asked about the ease with which he walked the divide, he said, "You don't take sides in a tragedy. It is a tragedy and we're all caught up in this drama."

The former Baptist chaplain at Ole Miss said he'd known Vernon Dahmer for years before he was killed, attending voting rights meetings. But he realized that he needed to talk to enemies of the movement while writing a book about an Episcopal priest caught in the integration struggles at the University of Mississippi and, through an intermediary, spent time with Bowers.

At one point, Bowers stopped at a cemetery to pray over a tombstone, Campbell recalled, and when he returned to the car, he had tears in his eyes.

"Animals don't cry," said Campbell. "Human beings cry at the foot of a friend's grave."

Plater Hamilton, who teaches "tolerance education" at Tulane University's Southern Institute, said the lesson of the trial is that "the system works but it requires people to push it." There are other Klansmen still awaiting their day in court, he said.

"The message from Forrest County is that those people should be afraid—that justice will catch up with them."

Writers' Workshop

Talking Points

1) "...it looks like justice has finally come to Ellie Dahmer and her children." Is this objective reporting or commentary? How does the writer support this statement? How does the thesis frame the rest of the story?

2) The fourth paragraph says Bowers "had taken off the Mickey Mouse lapel pin he'd worn all week." Note the specific detail. What does the detail signal to the reader? Look for other examples of such details in the story.

3) The trial occurred more than 30 years after the killing. How does the writer weave the background into the story? How does it affect the flow of the story?

4) Does the reporter have a point of view? On what do you base your opinion?

Assignment Desk

1) Murder trials inherently are full of drama. Cover a murder trial and write about the personalities involved.

2) Look for ways to include specific details in more of your stories.

A conversation with
Bartholomew Sullivan

CHRISTOPHER SCANLAN: How would you describe your beat?

BARTHOLOMEW SULLIVAN: I'm the regional reporter based in Memphis, and I travel to all the stories in the territory of 50 or 60 counties between our state capital bureaus in Little Rock, Ark., and Nashville, Tenn., and Jackson, Miss. All that territory in between those state capitals is mine to explore, so I get to do whatever's the best story in the region pretty much every day.

How often do you write?

I probably write something four days a week. I cover a lot of trials, and so when some crisis isn't breaking out, I've probably got a murder trial or jury selection getting under way somewhere in one of these counties.

There's something happening, obviously, in a territory that big every day, and so if I can get to it in time, we try to be there. This paper used to have a lot more bureaus in these rural territories than we do now, and so I sort of make up for that by putting on my track shoes and getting to the scenes.

Do you spend a lot of time in hotels?

Well, yeah. I get to work on a little Toshiba portable computer and sort of making the hotel room be the office for a while.

Kind of "Have laptop, will travel." What's in your traveling kit?

I always have a suitcase in the trunk with some basic stuff: shirts and ties and an extra pair of socks, and that kind of thing, but that's about it. I'm just sort of pretty much ready to go when I need to.

What do you carry for your reporting tools?

If it's a very short-term thing, like that tornado, I have a stack of reporters' notebooks and a lot of pens and two tape recorders, because I find that one of them'll go on the fritz at some point, and extra batteries and things like that.

When and why do you use a tape recorder?

In a courtroom situation, I often can't, and in emergency crisis kinds of situations, I usually don't. But you want to be absolutely accurate, especially in paper-of-record type stuff, especially talking to politicians or public officials whose decisions about things are potentially being called into question. You want to make sure you get 'em right, so I like to get 'em on tape, if I can.

So where'd you learn to write?

I got a pretty good education. The Jesuits do a pretty nice job where I went to school, at Santa Clara, and I've always read widely and I think that's the whole answer—you read a lot, you learn how to write. I learned how to write fast because two of my early newspaper jobs, the *Evening Sentinel* in Carlisle, Pa., and *The Palm Beach Times,* made me come in at 6 in the morning and meet a 10 or 11 o'clock deadline. And so I was always really racing, and you learn how to write fast that way.

I grew up in St. Louis, so I grew up reading the *The Post-Dispatch,* and I've always read *The New York Times.* I always liked John Darnton and Christopher Wren. I've always thought they were particularly beautiful stylists. Everybody reads Hemingway and his bylines as well as the fiction—all kinds of things. I read all the time, and I like to read journalists. I'm reading Max Frankel's book right now.

How old were you when you decided you wanted to be a reporter?

I started off expecting to be a lawyer and I started law school, then got out real fast and fell into this line of work because I'd been editing my college newspaper and I liked doing it. I studied politics in college. I have yet to take a journalism class.

Tell me a bit about *The Commercial Appeal.* How would you describe the paper?

It's by far the dominant daily newspaper for a whole region. It's bigger than any of the other papers—*The Tennessean* or the the *Democrat Gazette* in Little Rock or the *Clarion-Ledger* in Jackson. So everyone who lives in this region and has to read a newspaper because of what they do for a living, or wants to read it because they want to be informed, reads *this* newspaper. And so it's got a lot of influence. It's an important newspaper and it takes its responsibilities seriously.

Have you always had the same job there?

I came in as a county reporter covering the Shelby County government, but I did that only briefly and then this came available. I've already described it as sort of a dream job, to cover the best story every day in this wide region and get to know the region at the same time, by doing a lot of traveling.

Are a lot of your stories self-assigned?

There are very few times when I'll be told to do something. When the Manila tornado struck or we had some tremendous tornadoes that killed a lot more people in Jackson, Tenn., about a month and a half ago, they're just automatically in my territory. So sometimes the event assigns me. But otherwise, when I decide which trials to cover—sometimes there are two or three trials going on in this region and I can do only one—it'll usually be my decision.

If you're writing, say, four times a week, is the assumption that you're writing daily, you're writing for the next day's paper? Do you like that kind of deadline?

It's very satisfying work. Deadline reporting is this adrenaline rush, and you get to use everything you've learned in the process of meeting a daily deadline for 16 years. It's satisfying. You get to see your work the next day.

Are there times you wished that you had another couple of days?

Sometimes. When I'm writing profile stories, I get more time to do them and sometimes by Tuesday or Wednesday, something that was a daily story is also turning out to be something of a trend or something like that. I'll write a Sunday kind of feature story, and I'll get a couple of days to write that. But most everything is on a pretty short time span.

How do you select the best story of the day? What are the distinguishing characteristics?

If we're talking about news, it'll be the thing that has the biggest impact in the region or the most significant trend or the kind of thing that's getting people's attention. Obviously, we're in the newspaper business here, and television to some extent is going to drive what we know about in these territories. When a fertilizer plant explodes in Helena, Ark., television is going to be there before we are. If we're there at the same time, they're going to be broadcasting sooner than we are. We are, to some extent, dictated to by that medium.

But sometimes we're way out in front of everybody and breaking stories that nobody knew anything about and getting followed by television, which is sort of the way it should be, it seems to me.

Those stories are sometimes stories of heroic people doing things that are superhuman, or trials that people forgot about or didn't keep up with.

You just kind of keep your attention on what's going on in the region and get a sense of what the best of several options will be.

What sources for story ideas and assignments do you rely on?

I talk to an awful lot of prosecutors, police chiefs, sheriffs on a regular basis, especially the ones who are closer to Memphis. I check in with circuit court clerks all the time. If it's an explosion or a fire or a train wreck, I'm going to hear about it because the photo desk knows about it.

Tell me about Carl Perkins's funeral.

We knew that Carl Perkins had been ill for a long period of time. Then he died on a Monday. The music critic wrote the A-1 obituary and quoted Sam Phillips, the guy who discovered Elvis Presley and all the people who would have known Carl Perkins, and I assumed that our music guy would go to the funeral. It was announced that there would be a very public funeral at this college campus and a lot of people would be allowed to get in. I found out Thursday night, without having made any preparations, that our music guy *wasn't* going, and I thought that the newspaper probably needed to be there, so I volunteered. I went off pretty much cold—no background. I couldn't get any information from the funeral home, so I drove to Jackson, about 80 miles east of here, with the assumption that I would get no access and cover a crowd kind of story.

I went to the funeral home and got pushed around by the folks who were interested in getting the luminaries in and out of this place, and I couldn't get any access there. Some little Napoleon from the funeral home would shunt us off into a corridor, and I'd wander out and look at the flower arrangements.

I remember looking at a flower arrangement sent by Bob Dylan. He wrote a nice message to Perkins's family. I jotted that down, and they threatened to throw me out.

So finally I got tired of that and I went over to where the funeral was actually going to occur, and I stood in this long line with all these people who were real fans of Carl Perkins, but just regular people.

And I went into the church and just listened to what was going on. I didn't know that George Harrison was even in the church until Wynonna Judd noted that he was in the crowd. But at the very end of the funeral, he was asked to come up on stage and he sang "Your True Love," which brought the house down. It wasn't exactly like a funeral. There were all kinds of music stars there and they said a lot of nice things about Carl Perkins, but they also put together some very fine music, and it was an important kind of cultural event.

I didn't have much of a long conversation with anybody. But it was just a nice thing to be able to sort of eavesdrop on.

Then what did you do?

Then I got in my car and drove back to Memphis and wrote the story. It's a good long way back, so you get to collect your thoughts on Interstate 40.

So when you're driving home from the funeral, has the writing process begun?

I've usually got a pretty good working lead by the time I get into the newsroom, and most of the time when I know that I really want something to sing, I've usually heard the kicker already, and I've already marked it in my notebook, and I know generally what the highlights of the story are going to be and what ground I need to cover.

But finding the sort of elements of what will end up being a pretty good story, yeah, I've usually worked it out in the car or on the way home.

I like the pacing of that paragraph—"Except for an organ flourish, Harrison's contribution ended the church service." And then you do a full stop—"It was the benediction." Was that a conscious decision?

I think so. I was raised a Roman Catholic but I do go to a lot of Protestant services in this region. A lot of important things happen inside churches around here, so you sort of pick up on the language of the dominant tradition. That would be something that people around here are familiar with, more familiar than I think some Roman Catholics would be—the term "benediction," and its meaning.

Do you have a reader in mind when you're writing?

Just somebody who's thinking clearly and cares about reading newspapers, I think.

Let's talk about the tornado in Manila.

When I woke up that morning, the middle of April of last year, I knew I was going to go to a tornado because the television and the radio were already screaming that people had been killed in Arkansas and people had been killed in west Tennessee across the river. So it was more or less a decision of which hot spot I was going to go to. And so I called my metro editor. We decided that I was going to Manila, and they had just sent a couple of photographers on their way to Manila. I went to Manila and I spent all day there.

I'd been there once before when the mayor had been charged with animal cruelty because he had authorized the police to shoot stray dogs, and the Humane Society got all up in arms about that. So I knew a little bit about the lay of the land. But everything was torn to shreds, and you could drive in just so far and then everything else was walking. Talking about the story today, I remembered that I parked right next to a puddle of muddy water and I walked around in soaking wet shoes all day that day. I walked all the streets of Manila and talked to as many people as I could, and everybody was out. I mentioned the smell of the evergreen trees, because all those trees had been just snapped off—and I said it smelled like a Christmas tree lot.

I've covered a lot of tornadoes in the past, and so I knew that generally what I wanted to look for was people who had really gone through this thing and could really make the experience of it come alive in what they said. One of the nice things about my territory, this part of the country, is that people speak very naturally. It's a Southern area and Manila is a very rural Southern area, and so people will actually talk to a reporter with a notebook in his hand. They're not too sophisticated to talk to him and they're not cynical and they're not saying, "No comment" and this kind of thing—they'll actually talk to you.

And so I found some very, very nice folks who were willing to describe what they'd gone through, and I ran into that guy who told me that he'd climbed inside of a Laundromat dryer.

The photographer, Lee Daughteridge, and I were standing in the doorway of this Laundromat when the rain was still coming down and this guy made that comment about the "excellent, big, humming roar." If somebody speaks like that, he's got to be quoted, so I quoted him.

"It killed first, then it came into town." You remember when you wrote that lead?

I know I wrote it in my head on the way back. I just sort of liked the sound of it, and it was accurate, and it was sort of dramatic—maybe overly dramatic—but I thought it was interesting that this thing had crossed this little community that wasn't really part of the town, but then had come in. It'd gone across that field, and then hit the town very solidly, but where it had killed was outside of town. Everybody who was in the town of Manila was beat up pretty badly, but nobody was killed there.

That sort of sounded right to my ear.

What's your goal on a story like this?

I'm trying to find the kinds of people who can commu nicate a real experience of this kind of shocking thing they've just lived through. I don't think they're about trying to teach anybody any lessons about going to the fall-out shelter when the tornado siren goes off or anything like that; it's just communicating what these people have been through. Obviously you've got to get all the facts right. You've got to find out how many people were killed from the police chief or the sheriff or something like that. You've got to make sure of details —how does she spell "Nancy" and all that kind of thing. But I think what I'm really looking for is the person who says something or does something, some mannerism or something, that shows that we're paying attention and there's some sort of deeper sense that we're communicating part of this person's life, maybe what the academic journalists call "authenticity" or something like that.

Why do you want to do that?

I think you really need a lot of detail in order to communicate to people you really have seen what you're reporting and let them take from that whatever meaning they find in it.

Are there particular ways you approach people that you have found to be exceptionally useful in getting them to be themselves and to tell you exactly what happened?

You learn a lot of things about what *not* to do, I guess, when you watch television, television reporters. And so one thing I think I've learned—and everybody who does this for any length of time learns this—is just to be real respectful of the people you want to talk with because, if you're haughty or arrogant or insistent or fawning or anything like that, it's not going to work, most likely, and you won't get what you're looking for.

I want to put 'em at ease, let 'em know that this is a newspaper; we're trying to get a whole sense of what they've gone through, and we're not just going to make it into some sort of sideshow and then move on to the next thing. These individuals we're trying to talk with are important and we care about what they have to say.

If a young reporter were to ask you for advice on going into a small rural community where a tragedy has occurred, what advice would you give?

Be absolutely respectful of the situation you're in. Talk to the people who look like they might be in a position to want to say something, and avoid like the plague those who are obviously too distraught to communicate with you. You're a stranger and they've had a tremendous experience that has in some cases ruined their lives or ruined it at least temporarily, and they don't want to talk to newspaper reporters or anybody else except their families or their doctors or somebody like that, and leave 'em alone. You can describe, of course, that there are people who are distraught all around and that they are not in a position to talk and leave it at that. But obviously you'll find people who will be willing to talk, and sometimes you get lucky

enough and they're real articulate and they say something that's amazing, and so you listen for that.

**If we could see your notebook for this story, what
kind of things would we see?**

I'd have made note very carefully of what all was there
and what all had been smashed. And I might have put
an asterisk in the margin because I'd want to make sure
that I mark off things that I know I need to get in the
story. With things that I know I'm quoting directly, I
just put quotation marks around.

**I noticed you have the age for pretty much every-
body in Manila. Why do you ask everybody their
age?**

This is sort of police beat journalism here. We went
into a crisis and we need to get the details, and that's a
detail that people are going to want to know—if this
guy's 90 years old or 16. It characterizes this guy and,
in the case of Mr. Melvin Browning, he's a middle-
aged guy and his gardening is his labor of love.

**There's a journalism teacher named Melvin Men-
cher who says that all stories have what he calls
"non-negotiable necessities." And it sounds like for
this kind of story, the ages of the people involved is
a non-negotiable necessity.**

I think so, yeah. My very first editor on a daily newspaper, a guy named James Kalbaugh at *The Gettysburg
Times,* one time threatened to make me drive all the
way back out to a borough council meeting to get a
guy's middle initial because it was the style of that paper that everybody whose name appeared in the paper
had a middle initial, because this guy had the attitude
that anybody who appears in the newspaper is in their
Sunday best—they want to look their best—so that requires a middle initial. I always get middle initials
now—I still do.

**Speaking of Sunday best, when you go to a town like
Manila on an assignment like this, what are you
wearing?**

A shirt and tie.

Why?

Except for in a very unusual circumstance, I'm representing this newspaper. Because it's this old-fashioned, old institutional force in this region, I think people expect *The Commercial Appeal* to come to them in a shirt and tie.

Can we talk a bit about the smells? Do you often put olfactory images in your stories?

I sometimes do. Sometimes when it seems like it will characterize a place—like the smell of those trees that had been knocked down—you would take note of it, if you were walking down that street.

So when it's obvious, yeah. I take note of it. When I go to an explosion, I tell you what it smells like.

When you're writing a story like this, are you writing it with your notebook at your side? How do you actually go about writing a story like the Manila tornado story?

I've got to have a working lead. And so I sit down and I sort of boil everything down to the thing that I think is the essential, most important first impression that I want to make. I make that into a working lead. It will change sometimes, but often it doesn't.

And once I write a lead, it flows. I go back to the asterisks in my notebook, and put those things in the proper order, and find the quotations that are particularly telling, and get the best ones high, and the ones that just convey information, the quotation from a police chief who says that the sirens went off at the same time that the tornado hit, that's an important and relevant detail. It may end up figuring in lawsuits down the line, so you need to get it in the story, but you don't necessarily need to get it in real high.

I'm looking at your word choice. "But as the whine of chain saws rent the air all around..." Tell me a bit about the thinking that goes into the use of the word "rent."

I think it's the right word. I'm trying to convey that there's an air of confusion and noise and repair and emergency and all that kind of thing, all in a short space, so I used it. I could have said "sounded loudly," or "screamed," or something like, that, but I thought "rent" sounded better.

Do you write with a dictionary by your side, or a thesaurus, or are you just drawing on your reading and your life as a reporter and writer and reader when you write?

It's writing and reading and liking the sound of this language, and wanting to use the right word. I'm not trying to find some obscure word to confuse people.

I was advised one time that I wrote like a lawyer, and that it would be better if I'd write like a truck driver.

And I took that advice seriously. I got enough of an education to use the right word, but sometimes the right word is just a little beyond the regular readership, and you take that into consideration and make it simpler.

Talk about "Ex-Klan Leader Convicted of Killing Dahmer."

I really wanted to go to the Bowers trial, and let me make note that right at the end of the year, *Life* magazine came out with the best pictures, the most evocative pictures of 1998, and there was a picture of Ellie Dahmer walking out of the courthouse with the prosecutor and the attorney general of the state of Mississippi, and all of her family all around her. This was just one of the most important things that happened in 1998.

You could tell that the people were really yearning for justice, that there were really obvious truths, and really serious lies, being told in that courtroom, and you could feel it.

And that made a reporter like me very aware of a solemn responsibility. I was saying that I cover a lot of trials, but this one was really a special thing.

It struck me that the victim in this case had been denied justice, his family had been denied justice, in several mistrials over a long period of time. But he was just one guy. Vernon Dahmer wasn't representing the state of Mississippi as the field secretary of the NAACP, like Medger Evers. He was standing up to these thugs on his own, defending his own family, and he was burned alive. This kind of crime was just inconceivable.

The hallmark of this story, for me, is the sense of history that suffuses it. I want to know more about the history. What kind of background did you do on the story, or did you learn all this history there?

No, there are certain cases, the civil rights cases, around this area that you just know because you *have* to know them. This is where Martin Luther King was killed, and so everybody knows all the intricate details of that history, and the integration of Ole Miss in the early '60s, and the people involved in that. All these sorts of important historical events occurred right around this area, and for people who take the time to study up on it, this was an important case, and we knew that this guy was the head of the Ku Klux Klan for that part of Mississippi— I think for all of Mississippi at the time. And he was still around, and he was still walking the streets of his home town, sort of a hero to the bigots. And this is a story that people needed to get to the end of.

How do you learn the history? Have you gone back and read the paper's coverage from that period?

I did do some of that, yes. And I interviewed the prosecuting attorney, who said that he'd been urged not to reopen this case, because he would bring out all kinds of things people didn't want to be reminded of. So he told me a good bit of the history. And the guy who's now the head of the public safety department for the state of Mississippi was one of the lead detectives for the FBI on the case years earlier. So these guys were history textbooks just available to chat with.

Why did you end with Plater Hamilton?

We're all about the business of public policy here. There are a lot of unsolved cases out there. There are a lot of Klansmen who should be looking over their shoulders. I thought, "What an interesting thing to say." This is one down. There are still some more to go.

When you first started working, would you have written these stories just like this?

I don't think so. I think I've learned a good bit. I learned a lot in Florida, because there's so much competition there, and I had some fine editors there. The speed, I think I got pretty early on.

What are some of the things you've learned that would be useful to someone trying to get better?

I think just recognizing the important responsibility we have in intruding in people's lives. We want to give a true and accurate account of what we're seeing, and try to get to some sort of deeper sense of the things we're observing. We just have to be real careful about dealing honestly with people, and being respectful.

You learn certain tricks of the trade. I want to have that tape recorder available when I'm talking to politicians. I want to make sure that my bag is packed and in my trunk. I want to have telephone credit cards and that kind of stuff available, and a cell phone, if I can get one. It's the practical type of things that you learn.

How about important lessons about reporting or writing that you learned that make the difference between these stories and what you might have been writing, or how you may have written them back in Gettysburg or Carlisle?

Taking a lot of notes on just what's going on around you is an important thing I've learned to do, to jot down the color of the walls, or the color of the carpeting, or the color of somebody's eyes, or some smell, or some irritating noise in the background. You can just take all that down, or put it in a corner somewhere of the notebook, and put a box around it, and you may want to make note of some or all of this in the story later on. But at least you've got it.

And the same thing with ages and middle initials, and that kind of thing. Just have it in case you want to use it, or in case some editor says you have to have it, and then you've got it.

How long do you want to keep doing this kind of work?

I think I want to do it as long as I can, as long as I'm healthy. It's very satisfying stuff to do, I think. And it's a very daily kind of assessment of abilities and sometimes you get something good done.

What advice would you give somebody wanting to do better deadline writing?

Well, I guess one thing I'd say is that you should try to spend as much time on the ground as you can. And observe as much and listen to as much as you possibly can. Realize that the deadline is going to be there, and squeeze as much time into the interviews and things like that as you can. And just leave the writing to the last hour before the deadline. That way you can get more in that notebook and you can get more inside your head, and you're going to write a better story. Don't worry about the deadline. You've got to meet the deadline, so it's not really an option.

You don't want to try to be too chummy with people; that's something I see a lot, I guess. People trying to almost befriend people they just want to talk to briefly. This is a serious line of work. We're not trying to befriend these people. We're trying to tell the story, so just treat it that way, and if people aren't receptive to you being straight with them, move on to somebody else.

The New York Times

Seth Mydans

Finalist, Deadline News Reporting

Seth Mydans is *The New York Times* bureau chief in Bangkok, Thailand. He joined the *Times* in 1983 as a metropolitan reporter after working as a *Newsweek* correspondent in Moscow, London, and Bangkok from 1981 to 1983. He was a correspondent for the Associated Press from 1973 to 1981 in Moscow, Bangkok, London, New York, and Boston. At the *Times,* he has been a national correspondent stationed in Los Angeles and a foreign correspondent in Moscow and Manila before being appointed Bangkok bureau chief in 1996. Mydans is a graduate of Harvard College and worked for an American construction consortium in Vietnam from 1968 to 1971. He is currently on assignment in Cambodia.

In "The Demons of a Despot," Mydans displays his familiarity with the region and its tragic history and his command of the telling phrase. In 23 paragraphs, Mydans communicates the significance of Pol Pot's death and the lingering impact of his reign of mass murder on the lives of Thai people whom Mydans describes, unforgettably, as "eight million victims of post-traumatic stress disorder."

The demons of a despot

APRIL 17, 1998

SIEM REAP, Cambodia, April 16—This was a nation bereaved today, but not a nation in mourning. It was a nation liberated in some small measure from the shadow of its past traumas, but it was left empty-handed, without answers to some of its most painful questions.

"I wish Pol Pot were still alive," said Oum Bun Thoeun, a legal assistant, after hearing news of the death of the creator of Cambodia's killing fields. "I still want to know what happened, why Pol Pot killed so many people, why he killed my brothers. Yes, I would like to hear him say why he killed them."

Pol Pot, the man responsible for the deaths of more than one million people during four years of terror in the late 1970s, died late Wednesday night at 73 in a small thatched hut in the mountains of northern Cambodia. Foreign journalists viewed his body today.

His death came as Government soldiers and renegade guerrillas from his Khmer Rouge movement were closing in on him and as the international community was preparing for his capture and trial for crimes against humanity.

Now he is another of history's mass killers who escaped retribution.

"Usually you are sad when you have lost a loved one," said Youk Chhang, who heads a research center that has been collecting evidence in preparation for a trial of Pol Pot and other Khmer Rouge leaders.

"This time we are sad because we have lost a criminal we cannot punish," he said. "I wish to see him in court. I wish to see him in handcuffs. I wish to see him suffer the way he made me suffer."

For nearly 19 years, since the Khmer Rouge were driven from power by a Vietnamese invasion, the author of the nation's suffering remained in command of a guerrilla insurgency in the jungles of western and northern Cambodia.

Though he was never a real threat to the country's successive governments, his very presence cast a shadow over the nation he all but destroyed. The continuing violence, political feuds, corruption and social fragility of Cambodia are his legacy.

From 1975 to 1979 he and his black-clad followers killed off the educated classes of the country, its monks, its minority groups, its technicians and its artists. Many others died of starvation, disease and overwork. Virtually every Cambodian alive today lost a relative.

This is a nation of eight million victims of post-traumatic stress disorder.

It is a nation that has still not come to terms with its past, where torturers live side by side with their victims, and the bones and skulls of the dead lie unburied in heaps on the sites of Pol Pot's killing fields.

Many Cambodians seemed to shrink from the idea of a trial, preferring not to look too closely at the horrors of their past or to disturb the demons of their present, in what many people here insisted was a spirit of Buddhist forgiveness.

But reactions today seemed to belie that seeming passivity. At least from the man at the top, whose name is still spoken in lowered voices, people said today that they had hoped for an accounting.

"He was an old man and he didn't have any power, so he was not frightening to me anymore," said Ahmad Yahya, a member of Parliament who lost several brothers and cousins to the Khmer Rouge. "But I lament that he passed away, like I lost something, lost some answers."

Today is the final day of Cambodia's three-day New Year festival and the streets of this provincial capital were filled with merrymaking. In the park outside the Summer Palace of King Sihanouk, and on the walkways surrounding the ancient ruins of Angkor Wat, people splashed each other with water and white powder.

It was a festival that had just been completed 23 years ago, on April 17, 1975, when the Khmer Rouge marched into the capital of Phnom Penh and emptied it of its three million residents, starting their murderous regime.

Many people among the crowds today had not yet heard the news of Pol Pot's death. Some were skeptical, after years of rumors and disinformation from the Khmer Rouge.

"Died? I don't think so," said Crouch Chanda, a secretary from Phnom Penh who was visiting the temples with her small daughter. "This is political, you know. We have heard this many times but it has never been true."

If the news was true, she said, she would be disappointed. "When I heard on the Voice of America that he would be put on trial I was very happy," she said. "He made many people suffer."

But Youk Chhang, who heads the Documentation Center of Cambodia, a private research office partly financed by the United States, said there were still accountings to be made.

After the defection of most of the Khmer Rouge guerrillas, a small core of Pol Pot's close lieutenants remain at large in the Dangrek Mountains in northern Cambodia, close to the border of Thailand.

"A lot of people think the death of Pol Pot is the end of the Khmer Rouge," Youk Chhang said. "That's not true. Ta Mok is still at large. Nuon Chea. Khieu Samphan. We should not let them escape justice. I have 150,000 pages of high-level documents and I can get them to any lawyer in the world by e-mail within 15 minutes."

The Huntsville Times

Peter St. Onge

Finalist, Deadline News Reporting

Peter St. Onge is a columnist for *The Huntsville* (Ala.) *Times,* where he also writes news and features. Before joining the *Times* in 1995, he worked as a sports columnist at the *Waterbury* (Conn.) *Republican-American* and *The Anniston* (Ala.) *Star.* He has won multiple awards in the Associated Press Sports Editors competition, including first-place honors in column writing and features in 1995, and has twice been a finalist for a Livingston Award. He graduated from the University of Missouri in 1991.

In "Law Upheld in Jonesboro, But the Anguish Remains," St. Onge offers readers his attempt at understanding the inexplicable in a report of the sentencing of the two boys convicted of killing four girls and a teacher, and wounding 10 others, at Westside Middle School outside Jonesboro, Ark. He reflects the sorrow and frustration of a community, and a nation, with a column that demonstrates how even when explanations are offered, they don't answer the question, "Why?"

Law upheld in Jonesboro, but the anguish remains

AUGUST 12, 1998

JONESBORO, Ark.—They rose slowly, one by one, shuffling through the silence to the front of the courtroom, wearing white ribbons, carrying statements written on looseleaf that shook as they spoke. Mostly, the families of the Westside school shootings brought questions, soon to be unanswered, because, as most parents understand, children have difficulty explaining the most benign of wrongdoings, never mind the most horrific.

On Tuesday, at the Craighead County Courthouse, 12-year-old Andrew Golden and 14-year-old Mitchell Johnson answered legally, at least, for their crimes of March 24th.

In a courtroom protected by metal detectors and bomb-sniffing dogs, Mitchell admitted Tuesday—his 14th birthday—to taking part in the killings. He stood before Judge Ralph Wilson Jr. for just 10 minutes, not much longer than the bloody ambush that left four schoolmates and a teacher dead.

Then Andrew was found guilty by Wilson after the judge rejected his claim of temporary insanity.

And so, in an unusual public juvenile hearing, each was adjudicated delinquent for the acts of murdering four girls and a teacher and wounding 10 others at Westside Middle School, just outside Jonesboro.

The boys were sentenced to a youth detention center near Little Rock, where they will begin a confinement that should last at least until their 18th birthdays, their 21st if the state builds an adequate facility as promised by Gov. Mike Huckabee.

"Here the punishment will not fit the crime," lamented Wilson, who added 90 days in jail should the boys be released before they turn 21.

It all could have been decided months ago, in a closed courtroom, as is the case with most every juvenile proceeding. But Wilson, not usually considered a big-picture guy around the courthouse, decided his community needed more than a whispered conclusion to the killings.

Shooing precedent aside, he moved the juvenile hearing to the large courtroom in the building and reserved 130 seats for victims' families, shooters' families, and Westside students and staff.

He allowed the boys to wear civilian clothes instead of the mandatory blue-and-white striped uniforms for accused male delinquents. Andrew wore a green polo shirt, jeans and the new $120 Doc Martens boots he had put in the getaway van before the shootings. Mitchell got to wear a collarless cotton shirt with jeans and hiking shoes.

The boys entered the courtroom just after 10 a.m., their eyes swiveling to look at the people looking at them. This was part of Wilson's purpose, for the victims and families to see the boys, for the boys to see the victims and families, for the chance that some thread of understanding could pass one way or another.

Or if not, for the chance at least to vent.

That came after lunch, after Mitchell had pleaded guilty and Andrew was declared the same in the face of quick and overwhelming evidence.

Mitchell Wright, husband of slain teacher Shannon Wright, was first to speak for the families. Each had been mailed a victim's impact statement form that contained such questions as "How has this affected you?" to help keep grief focused. But when Wright sat at the witness stand, he absently set his statement aside.

"I not only lost a wife, I lost a best friend, thanks to you two," he said, looking at the boys. "My son looks for his mother to come back. I have to explain to him that his mother's in heaven. I have to explain what you two did."

He continued: "Shannon and I had dreams of having another child this year. We had plans for a new house. You have robbed a 3-year-old of innocence."

He said there was no way the killings were unintentional.

"You can't tell me it was random, son, not with the scope on that gun," Wright said, his face red, his eyes beginning to tear.

Mitchell's Remington Woodsmaster .30-06 rifle had a telescopic sight, and the evidence at Tuesday's hearing was that at least two bullets from that rifle hit Shannon Wright.

Mitchell Johnson rocked back and forth at the words, nodding his head and wiping his eyes. Andrew stared blankly, expressionless as he had been throughout the hearing. When Andrew's attorney, Val Price, objected and the judge cautioned Wright not to speak directly to the boys, Wright smiled wryly and continued.

He talked about how his wife had helped Andrew work through a difficult class puppet project this year. He talked about how his wife had nothing but praise for Mitchell when he was in her class a year ago.

He said, finally, that he wished he could sit and talk with the boys someday and find out why.

"That's what everyone wants to know," he said.

When the victims were done, young Mitchell stood with his own sheet of paper. "As I have sat during the last four months, I have had the opportunity to think about what happened on March 24, 1998."

He read haltingly, rocking back and forth, crying through the words, just a few hours after celebrating his birthday with his family.

"I am sorry," he said. "I understand that it may be impossible for some of you to forgive me."

And: "I never really felt anyone would be hurt. I thought we would shoot over everyone's heads."

And: "I hope that anyone who will listen to these words will know how sorry I am."

Minutes later, he and Andrew were escorted out of the courtroom, the hearing over, the audience stunned at the statement, angry at his explanation.

Said Wright later: "When I looked at that boy in the eyes, he didn't look very sorry to me."

So the pain continues, as it will through birthdays, anniversaries and the inevitable appeals.

In Mitchell's short time before the judge, he held his mother's hand while his father put his hand on his shoulder. His mother, Gretchen Woodard, told Wilson that her son understood what he was doing, but his father, Scott Johnson, objected.

"I do not concur with this plea, but he's making it on advice of his counsel and mother," said Johnson, of Grand Meadow, Minn., south of the Twin Cities. He complained later he wasn't allowed to hire a lawyer of his choosing for the boy.

Val Price quickly promised to fight Wilson's refusal to consider insanity or incompetence arguments that he raised Tuesday. Price argued that the boy was too young to understand the crime or the hearing. Wilson ruled that insanity or incompetence pleas do not apply to juvenile cases.

But Tuesday wasn't only about that kind of justice. It was a day made public for the Westside families, a chance to see the too-young killers, to talk to them, to empty out the last of the emptiness.

"I'm relieved it's over," Mitchell Wright said. "But there's no satisfaction. For any of these families, there's no justice."

Lessons Learned

BY PETER ST. ONGE

I felt a bit of guilt when I first got the assignment to cover the Jonesboro school shootings hearing. I had not been to Jonesboro when the shootings had occurred almost five months before. I had not done any follow stories, or columns, or perspective pieces, unlike the fine reporters I had read in the months since.

My qualifications: My editor had graciously entered my name in a drawing to select one national print pool reporter.

In other words: I won the lottery.

So yes, guilt. Perhaps a little fear, too, but no more than the usual jelly legs most of us get with big assignments. But the quickest route past any deadline anxiety is to go back to the fundamentals—fill your notebook, then empty it smartly.

For this assignment, I drove to Jonesboro early, read clips at the *Jonesboro Sun,* talked to the patient and generous writers there, called school officials, teachers, ministers, parents of the boys on trial, and parents of the girls they killed. Not everyone wanted to talk, of course, but those who did provided details big and small, from how parents were prepared by prosecutors for the hearing, to what kind of boots one of the boys would be wearing. At the hearing, I looked for similar details, anything that would help the reader stop and look around, not just race through the plotline.

Also, I wanted to offer some perspective. The news writers I most enjoy reading are those who expand news events, tell me both what's happening and what's really happening. In Jonesboro, the news was easy—one young boy, 14-year-old Mitchell Johnson, pled guilty to the delinquent acts of murdering four girls and a teacher and wounding nine others at Westside Middle School. The other boy, 12-year-old Andrew Golden, was quickly found guilty of the same.

But the story was really that the hearing had been opened to the public and the press. The decision had been made by Circuit Chancery Judge Ralph Wilson Jr., who wanted the parents of the victims to have an opportunity to see the two boys, to speak to them, to reach for some sort of closure. The story of this hearing wasn't about the crimes, which the community had endured again and again. The story was about healing—or at least trying to.

Once that showed itself, I was able to focus on the imagery in the courtroom. The young boys alternating between blankness and tears. The victims' parents and relatives shaking as they read their statements from the stand. The inevitable questions about why—and the unsatisfactory answers that followed.

Those parents and those questions became my lead, followed by the legal news of the hearing, followed by the rest of the story. By then, my job was to stay out of the way, keep the story simple, chronological, logical. Good stories have their own kind of rhythm. The best we can do sometimes is give them texture. Observe. Report. It won't make the jelly legs go away. But it's an easy lesson for most any kind of story.

The Star-Ledger

Mike Vaccaro

Finalist, Deadline News Reporting

Mike Vaccaro is a general sports columnist for *The Star-Ledger* in Newark. He joined the paper in 1998 after covering sports for *The Kansas City Star,* the Middletown (N.Y.) *Times Herald,* the *Northwest Arkansas Times,* and the *Olean* (N.Y.) *Times Herald.* He has also been a contributing columnist for MSNBC. Vaccaro was named one of the 10 best sports columnists in America in 1998 by the Associated Press Sports Editors. The group has recognized him six times for distinguished sports writing. He is a graduate of St. Bonaventure University.

Vaccaro has covered hundreds of sporting events, including three Final Fours and two World Series, but counts as a highlight the 10-month period when he witnessed the final games of Michael Jordan and Wayne Gretzky and the record-breaking hits of Mark McGwire. In "As McGwire Hits Homer 62, Time Stands Still," Vaccaro shows the staying power of words on a page to re-create a magical moment even after you've seen it with your own eyes.

As McGwire hits homer 62, time stands still

SEPTEMBER 9, 1998

For an odd, uneasy moment, nobody knew what to do. Nobody knew what to say. It happened that quickly. Fifty thousand people, all of them having spent the summer waiting for this moment, praying for it, gasped for an instant, tracing with their eyes the path of a baseball as it streaked like a laser beam off the bat of Mark McGwire.

It was 8:18 p.m., Central time, on the 13,492nd day in which the major league record for home runs in a season stood at 61, held by Roger Maris and shared only for the previous 30 hours and 56 minutes by McGwire.

McGwire had leapt at the first offering from Chicago Cubs pitcher Steve Tracheel, a fastball that was rapidly dropping toward the dirt. McGwire made solid contact with the ball anyway, muscling it on a low line toward the 330-foot sign in left field. It was a most un-McGwire-like blast; so many of his drives seem to scrape the sky on their way toward the outermost regions of a ballpark. And that was the reason for the sudden silence with two outs in the fourth inning. Had he gotten enough of it? Would it stay in the air long enough to clear the fence?

He had. It would. The first clue came from Cubs left fielder Glenallen Hill, who started to chase the ball, then slowed to a trot, then stopped altogether, knowing he would have the best view of anybody for what was about to happen.

It was then that the ball disappeared behind the fence, just beneath the Konica Copiers sign and the electrically lit "K" indicating the one batter that Cardinals starter Kent Mercker had struck out. And it was then that the crowd at last emitted an ear-splitting roar that cut through the night, spilled out across the Mississippi River, and reached every corner of a nation that has been transfixed by McGwire's pursuit since the earliest hours of the season.

"I was so shocked," McGwire said moments after the Cardinals defeated the Cubs, 6-3. "I didn't think it had enough to get out. After I stepped on first, I don't remember anything after that. It's an incredible feeling. But I thought, 'Oh, my God, we still have to play the game.'

"I can honestly say I did it," McGwire said. "I'm very proud of what I've accomplished."

There was a dual irony to where the ball landed, 341 feet away from where it was launched. For one thing, it marked the shortest distance—by six feet—of all of McGwire's homers this year. It also ended months of speculation about how much the ball might fetch from collectors and memorabilia hounds, because it wound up out of reach of any of the spectators. It was retrieved instead by a Busch Stadium groundskeeper named Tim Forneris, who immediately returned the ball to McGwire.

McGwire punched the air with his fists and began one of the most triumphant tours of the basepaths ever witnessed, one that will stand alongside Henry Aaron's 715th home run on April 8, 1974. In fact, just as two unexpected visitors accompanied Aaron on his historic trot around the bases, an interloper tried to join the proceedings last night, sprinting across the outfield before he was reigned in by security.

McGwire hugged first base coach Dave McKay— who last month estimated that he has served up some 8,000 batting practice homers to McGwire since 1987— and did so with such glee that McGwire nearly forgot to touch first base. McKay made sure that wouldn't happen. Then McGwire accepted congratulations from Cubs infielders Mark Grace, Mickey Morandini and Jose Hernandez before saluting third baseman Gary Gaetti, a former teammate, and hugging Gaetti on the way past.

By the time he arrived at home plate, McGwire was in the midst of a mob of teammates. He spotted his 10-year-old son, Matthew, and lifted him into the air with both hands.

Sammy Sosa, the Cubs right fielder who has been so much a part of this mano-a-mano struggle with McGwire—and who, through six innings last night, hadn't added to his total of 58—jogged in from right field to embrace McGwire and instead found himself lifted to the sky by McGwire as well.

All around him, flashbulbs crackled and people waved towels, flags, home-made banners and hastily scribbled signs. The uppermost floors of a hotel bordering the stadium unveiled a congratulatory message that took up two stories. In dead center field, just above the scoreboard, a giant image of McGwire was unveiled against the number 62.

McGwire then walked over to the field boxes where Maris' children were sitting. On Monday, after McGwire had tied their father with No. 61, the Marises had clapped politely, almost sadly. But last night, they seemed as filled with joy as the rest of Busch Stadium was.

Before the game, McGwire had met privately with the family in a room off the Cardinals clubhouse. They asked him to take a few practice swings with the bat their father had used to hit No. 61 off Tracy Stallard on Oct. 1, 1961, two years to the day before McGwire was born.

He did. And then he clutched the bat close to his chest, as if letting it touch his heart.

"Roger," he had said then, "you're with me."

A few hours later, the whole baseball continent would join him. The ovation would last 11 minutes, the memory for a lifetime.

Lessons Learned

BY MIKE VACCARO

One of the first truths of the sports writing trade, the one old-timers always pass along to the newest generations, is this: If you are a fan, and you wish to remain a fan, do something else for a living. Because sports writing, over time, will beat the sports fan out of you. Nobody ever believes this at first, of course. Don't we become sportswriters in the first place because we are allowed to combine two loves—sports and writing—and earn a paycheck in the bargain?

Isn't that what the gig is all about?

It takes about five minutes to learn the truth and the wisdom of that advice, however. Up close, athletes can be happy, angry, guttersnipes, generous, ill-tempered, patient—in other words, painfully human. Getting to know professional athletes, you quickly understand that the invisible line separating stars from their fans is easily blurred.

And the sad truth is you stop caring as much as you once did.

Or even as much as you would still like.

Mark McGwire and Sammy Sosa changed all of that in the summer of 1998, and as a result they provided a curious challenge to the horde of journalists who followed them from city to city. It was difficult not to root—quietly, of course—for either one of them as they tried to break Roger Maris's sacred record of 61 home runs in a season, set 37 years before. It was impossible—or almost impossible—not to get caught up in the swirl.

Since all of us wanted to be there when the record fell, and because we all wanted every one of our words, insights, and observations to be perfect, it was important to detach ourselves almost completely from what was around us. And that was difficult, especially since wherever we went, in shopping malls, on airplanes, in ballparks, this was the only thing people wanted to talk about. Mark and Sammy. Sammy and Mark. It was always around us.

Part of this—a small part—can be attributed to America's continuing fascination with baseball, and the numbers inherent to the game. But much more, I believe, was the context of the times. Every day, news of McGwire and Sosa's latest exploits was juxtaposed with the newest dispatches from the Bill-and-Monica circus in Washington. People turned to baseball to forget the messiness of everyday life.

But to get caught up in the emotions of all of this would have been to perform a disservice to readers. And that was the biggest challenge, providing readers with readable, informative stories: Tell the news, don't get caught up in your own "brilliant" writing; in short, do the job you're supposed to.

Obviously, there are other journalists who must do this every day. It is clearly difficult to not get overly emotionally involved when covering an assassination, a school shooting, a war. In its own way, the home run chase was different. For a few weeks, we were tempted to forget the old advice, forget our own experiences, and just be sports fans again. Judging from the pile of fine work written and reported from this summer, I think it's obvious that most of us succeeded in letting the sports fan inside us out for a few moments, before returning to our jobs as professionals. Hard, yes. But worthwhile. Definitely worthwhile.

Part of the Tacoma Team. Front row: Lisa Kremer, Sandi Doughton, and Bruce Rushton. Back row: Aimee Green, Skip Card, and Stacey Burns. Not pictured: reporter Kris Sherman, editor Randy McCarthy, senior editor Suki Dardarian, and the visual journalists.

The News Tribune
Team Deadline News Reporting

Mount Rainier looms large in the lives of the people who produce *The News Tribune* in Tacoma, Wash. They report on its role as a major recreational and environmental resource. Some climb it; most consider it "our mountain." So when word of a serious summertime avalanche reached the newsroom in June 1998, the news staff mobilized to bring readers the story. The next day's edition featured an expanded section of first-day coverage about the accident that killed one climber and left others clinging to ropes and rocks on the side of Mount Rainier.

But the work that won them this year's Jesse Laventhol Prize for Team Deadline News Reporting was a second-day story that told the story of the avalanche from the perspectives of the climbers and their rescuers. With one reporter on the mountain, two in the foothills interviewing survivors and rescuers, and others standing watch at local hospitals, they fed reports to writer Sandi Doughton who assembled a riveting narrative about disaster and a dramatic rescue. The story was a team effort that drew on the efforts of photographers and graphic artists to produce a compelling package.

Editors and reporters recall the steps and decisions they made, and following their accounts is a companion story detailing the involvement of the paper's visual journalists. The reporting team included Doughton, reporters Lisa Kremer, Aimee Green, Bruce Rushton, Skip Card, Kris Sherman, editor Randy McCarthy, senior editor Suki Dardarian, and intern Stacey Burns. The visual journalists were Casey Madison, director of photography; photographer Peter Haley; and graphic artists Derrik Quenzer and Roy Gallop.

—Christopher Scanlan

'We were really hanging by a thread'

JUNE 13, 1998

Swept from her feet by a churning wave of snow, Ruth Mahre fought to stop her slide. She jabbed repeatedly at the snow with her ice ax, but the tool wouldn't bite into the deep, mushy mass.

As Thursday's avalanche propelled her toward a rocky cliff high on Mount Rainier, images of death flooded her mind.

"When you're flying down rocks, and snow is pushing you down, and the people roped to you are pulling you down, you can't stop, you don't think you're going to live," recalled the 25-year-old climbing guide.

When she finally came to a stop, the situation was hardly less perilous.

Mahre and her rope team of four climbers were tangled with another five-person team, and several were dangling across the face of Disappointment Cleaver—a jagged fin of rock and ice at 11,400 feet.

The nylon rope that tethered Mahre's team to a fixed line on the slope above was nearly severed by sharp, volcanic rocks. Only a few strands remained intact.

"We were really hanging by a thread," she said, "If anybody moved, we were going down the cliff."

It would be nearly 24 hours before Mahre and some of her fellow climbers were back on the pavement at Paradise Ranger Station at Mount Rainier National Park, after one of the mountain's most dramatic rescues.

One of their number—29-year-old Patrick Nestler of Connecticut—perished from exposure. Eight were treated for injuries and released from area hospitals.

But in the sunshine that bathed the mountain Friday, shadows from the tragedy didn't deter scores of other climbers determined to pit themselves against the mountain.

"If you live by your fears, you stay at home," said Karen Peterson of Denver, who hoped to reach the top.

Several of those who nearly lost their personal battles with Rainier showed less bravado.

"I don't think so," whispered a red-eyed Scott Pressman, one of the rescued climbers, when asked whether he would tackle the mountain again.

* * *

Until the avalanche struck, the day had been a glorious one.

Most of the nearly 30 people who had paid $745 each to participate in Rainier Mountaineering Inc.'s five-day mountain-climbing school had reached the 14,411-foot summit early in the morning. It was the fourth day of the class, and the students, from all across the country, had forged friendships from hours spent in camp and on the slopes.

Curt Hewitt, 47, was one of the lead guides. Hewitt left Minnesota 15 years ago to become a guide with RMI.

"This was one of the most spectacular days I've ever seen," he said. "It was like that right up to the accident. It was euphoria, and then chaos."

About 2 p.m., two teams of five had reached the 45-degree, downslope edge of the cleaver, one of the most treacherous points on the climb.

An 800-foot safety line stretched across the snow, anchored in place by 3-foot aluminum spikes driven into snow and rock. Climbing team members were roped to each other, and at least one member of each group also hooked onto the safety line for the brief dash across the sheer stretch.

Clipped to the fixed rope, Hewitt was leading the first team across the traverse. The second was waiting its turn.

Pressman, a 48-year-old ophthalmologist from Boise in the second team, watched a cantaloupe-sized snowball tumble down the slope above and mushroom with appalling speed and ferocity.

"It was just a snowball," he said. "By the time it got down to the safety line, it was a full-fledged avalanche."

Kent Swanson, a 53-year-old Maryland businessman, was in the first group, midway across the traverse.

"I heard someone yell, 'Slide!' and then 'Run!'" he said.

The first group ran—but not fast enough.

"We had made it two-thirds of the way across, and then the wave hit us," said Hewitt. "I just kind of submarined under the snow."

The weight of five people and the force of the snow overwhelmed the fixed safety line. One of the aluminum anchors ripped out, then another. A single anchor held.

Hewitt gripped his ice ax with his right hand and in the left gripped two ropes—the fixed line and the one that connected him to his team. He came to a stop almost completely buried, his arm wrenched behind his back—the weight of four people hanging from the ropes wrapped around his left hand. He thought his fingers were being pulled off.

As soon as they spotted the avalanche, the second group of climbers hit the ground and dug in their ice axes and crampons. They thought the snowfall might pass them by.

But when the fixed safety line whipped loose, it pulled them down with the others.

"All I know is, I opened my mouth and said, 'God save us,' and my mouth filled with snow and I was over the edge," said Allen Fedor, a 30-year-old vinyl decking salesman from Minnesota.

Fedor estimates he slid 350 feet down the mountain, then fell 40 feet through the air before landing on a ledge and beginning to slide further.

"The rope came taut 5 feet before the second edge," he said. "It would've been eternity after that."

When the toppling mass of snow, rock, ice and humanity came to a rest, Hewitt managed to pull his radio from his backpack and call for help.

"Mayday, mayday!" he shouted. "The Cleaver has slid!"

* * *

On the other side of the rock wedge, 400 feet above the avalanche, Wreatha Carner was camped with her paralyzed husband, Peter Rieke, who is attempting to climb the mountain in a hand-cranked "snow pod."

She saw the snow slide and falling climbers, and used her cell phone to call in the first alert. And she listened to the victims' screams for nearly four hours, Carner said in a note carried down the mountain by another climber.

Her first instinct was to try to reach Nestler, who was suspended in space nearly 100 feet down the face of the cliff. But a crevasse blocked her path, and all she could do was watch.

* * *

Near the summit, climbing ranger Mike Gauthier was savoring his day off. He had climbed to the top with a snowboard on his back, and was preparing to shred the mountain.

His radio crackled and spat out the bad news: An avalanche had swept away several climbers. Their condition was unknown.

A man who numbers his summit conquests in the hundreds, Gauthier knew the area and knew it could be bad.

He jumped on his board and sped down. It took him 20 minutes to reach the accident site, where at least five RMI guides already had started the rescue efforts.

As he approached the area, Gauthier had to leave his board and pick his way on foot through a field of "hang-fire," the unstable debris from an avalanche.

What he saw was frightening.

The fixed safety line was taut and straining, and one of the ropes that held the climbers appeared on the verge of snapping.

"It was just down to the inner strands," Gauthier said.

Hewitt's team was strung out above the lip of the cliff. Deborah Lynn from Manhattan Beach, Calif., was clinging to rocks 30 feet below the edge of the cliff. She also was being doused by a frigid river of snow melt.

In the second group, Mahre's rope was wrapped around a large rock at the edge of the cliff, holding her snug against the boulder. The weight of other climbers tugged at her body.

"The rock felt solid," she said. "The people below me didn't feel so solid."

At the other end of the rope, Pressman also clung to the edge of the cliff. In between, three climbers were strung like a necklace along the rock face.

Nestler was in the worst position: hanging in the middle, with nothing to support him.

The wet snow had soaked all of the climbers, and they shivered as they clung immobile to their perches.

"If any one of these people moved, we were all gone," said climber Gregg Swanson, brother of Kent Swanson.

Heidi Eichner, who has been an RMI guide for five years, was the first to reach Mahre.

"When I got there, I could not believe it," Eichner said. "It was incredibly dangerous."

For the climbers, the rescuers' arrival helped allay the terror.

"They walked around like angel's wings," said Gregg Swanson.

* * *

For the rescuers, the scary work had just begun.

"It wasn't frantic. No one was screaming or yelling or going crazy," Gauthier said. "But we hustled."

The first priority was to replace the frayed rope and anchor the climbers snugly to the mountainside. To do that, they needed line and other equipment, which they scavenged from other climbing parties.

"We started stripping gear from whoever we could," Gauthier said.

It took about 90 minutes to completely replace and reposition the loose and frayed rope. Even before they finished, the rescuers also freed Hewitt's hand from the ropes that threatened to crush his bones.

Some of the rescuers rappelled down the cliff, to check on each of the climbers.

They couldn't reach Nestler, who was hanging out of sight.

"All you could see was a rope going over the edge," said Eichner.

But they heard him scream and groan.

Next, the rescuers, who included Gauthier and several RMI guides, fashioned pulley systems to hoist the climbers to safety. Rescuers then rappelled down to each victim, and hooked them up.

Lynn, the woman stuck in the freezing waterfall, was first. She was blue, incoherent and slipping in and out of consciousness when they reached her, three hours after the rescue began.

Nestler, however, was impossible to reach. Instead, rescuers decided to lower him to the base of the cliff.

Lou Whittaker, owner of RMI and a world-renowned mountain climber, took an Army helicopter to the site

with other RMI guides. Arriving about three hours after the avalanche, they began climbing to the base of
the cliff to get to Nestler.

The terrain was hazardous, riddled with crevasses.
They had to break a fresh trail.

Nestler was dead by the time the rescuers lowered
him to the ground. According to an autopsy, he died of
hypothermia about two hours after the avalanche.

Whittaker said the skillful rescue operation prevented other fatalities.

"Without the incredible coordination, we would
have had more deaths," he said.

The avalanche itself wasn't that big, Gauthier said.
He estimated it was 40 yards wide and between 6 and
10 inches deep. It was, however, extremely dangerous
because of the location—above a sheer cliff.

More than 80 people worked on the rescue, from volunteer groups to climbing guides and military personnel.

Most of the victims remained calm, as did the rescuers, Gauthier said.

Whittaker brought warm Gatorade for the chilled
climbers and rescue team. And his mere presence was
comforting, some of the climbers said.

The most severely injured of the victims were lowered down the mountain on litters, to Ingraham Flat, a
broad, open area where climbers often spend the night
before their final ascent.

Others walked.

The avalanche occurred shortly after 2 p.m., and the
last of the victims was safe by 7:45 p.m.

The U.S. Army Chinook helicopter from Fort Lewis
picked up the injured people and Nestler's body, and
flew them to Madigan Army Medical Center.

"They treated us like we were little babies," Fedor
said of the tender care administered by the chopper
crew.

Everyone was quiet as the helicopter lifted off about
9:15 p.m.

"The sun was setting," Gauthier said. "It was just
beautiful. The truth of it was, it was fabulously beautiful."

Several of the injured climbers choked up as they
neared Madigan.

"The tears are coming from the guys and gals who were wondering if they'd make it," Whittaker said. "When you land, you feel good."

From Madigan, the climbers were taken by ambulance to several hospitals, where they were treated for injuries ranging from sore wrists to torn ligaments and neck strain.

Mahre and others who were unharmed spent the night on the mountain and hiked down Friday.

When she reached Paradise, Mahre—sister of Phil and Steve Mahre, Olympic medalists in skiing—kissed and hugged her colleagues, and her brown, mixed-breed dog, Fraulein.

"I thought about you on the way down," she told the wriggling dog.

Other climbers returned to Ashford on Friday to wait for their belongings to be brought down the mountain.

Sharing experiences and reliving the details, four of the climbers fought tears and laughed over the good parts of their week together.

"The more I talk about it, the more I can't believe it," said Gregg Swanson.

All praised their guides and rescuers.

"These guys put their lives at risk," Pressman said.

At Paradise, Whittaker—who, perhaps, knows Mount Rainier as well as anyone—mused about the mountain and its power and appeal.

"Rainier has lot of secrets that we're always learning," he said. "We have to remember it's an indifferent mountain. We love it, but it doesn't necessarily love us."

Staff writers Sandi Doughton, Lisa Kremer, Bruce Rushton, Stacey Burns, Aimee Green, and Skip Card contributed to this report.

Writers' Workshop

Talking Points

1) In the opening section, the writers must paint a picture of an unfamiliar landscape while establishing a quick-paced narrative. Examine the descriptions and how they create images in the reader's mind with economy.

2) In the second section, the writers face another challenge—getting the reader to visualize the ropes and mountaineering gear that climbers use. Can you effectively visualize what is being discussed? Does this section change the pace of the story?

3) Each section of the story ends with a quote. How do you think these were chosen? What function do they serve?

Assignment Desk

1) Details are critical to this story, from the technical aspects of mountain climbing to the name of Ruth Mahre's dog, Fraulein. Look for ways you can incorporate telling details into your stories.

2) There have been several recent mountain-climbing tragedies. Read Jon Krakauer's book, *Into Thin Air,* for an account of a deadly climb up Mount Everest.

Recalling deadline with
The News Tribune

Suki Dardarian, senior editor

About 3 o'clock we have a big news meeting in the middle of the newsroom. And we had heard that there was some sort of an accident on Mount Rainier. Within a few minutes, we realized that it was something that had the potential to go out on A-1 rather than just a brief "Climbers Get Lost."

This city and this South Puget Sound region's kinship with that mountain is very close. It's our mountain, and anything that happens on that mountain, we should be chronicling.

Everybody heard about the avalanche on TV. But a newspaper can bring so much more context—telling people how it happened and how it affects them. I don't necessarily just mean what happened, but how did it happen, why did it happen, who was involved, what's going to happen now?

Breaking news helps bring out the best in us sometimes. It shakes you out of "this is just a job." It really gives you that sense of mission.

Often editors can fall into some of the logistical things. "Do you have all the film you need? Do you have a pen? Is so-and-so coming in to do this?"

But what enabled us, I think, to do something better was our ability to focus on the bigger picture. What is it that we really want to give our readers, and how can we deploy our resources in a way to most effectively get there?

Deadline tip:

It's not just getting to the scene. It's getting the *right* people to the *right* scenes, getting the right people writing and editing the content, thinking ahead about how you want it to look and sound, and what your end point is. That was our mission for the day. And I think that made everybody's job clearer. You set an overall tone and a mission for the day, rather than just "cover it." We were able to say, "We want to tell the story of what happened on the side of that mountain."

Aimee Green, suburban reporter

At 5 o'clock, we got a call in the bureau where I work that there was an avalanche. I called down and asked our crime team editor if they needed any help.

He said no. But I decided to go down to the main newsroom anyway. I found out that they needed me. They started snatching any reporters they could get.

I was out there on the curb outside Tacoma General Hospital for eight hours—into the early morning hours of the first day after the avalanche.

Around 10:30 I started thinking, "I've never turned in a story past 10:30. I can't imagine why they would want me to stay here." I guess I sort of had a hunch. I didn't eat dinner or anything. I just was expecting the ambulance to come around the corner any moment.

Then the ambulance came in. The photographer got some quick shots of Kent Swanson, the 53-year-old climber, coming in on a stretcher. And I think we yelled out some questions, and he just said, "Glad to be back."

Then we waited. He finally came out with a broken leg at 1:30 or 2 in the morning. By that time, there were 23 reporters in the lobby of Tacoma General, a lot with TV cameras. Swanson was in pretty good spirits but really sunburned and unshaven.

He recounted how the avalanche happened. He heard someone from above him yell, "Slide," and then a second later, "Run," but he couldn't. There was this gush of violent wet snow that swept him and the other climbers off their feet. They just sort of floated on top of it.

He said he slid 30 or 40 feet and thought he was dead. All they could do was wait for the rescue helicopter. They waited four hours in their icy spot.

Deadline tip:

Wait. Stick it out. There's always that possibility that you can be in the right place.

It was a really good interview. I was surprised, with someone who was injured and had been through all that trauma. I hadn't really been in that scene, where there are so many national media there. I just decided to ask every question I had on my mind. And he was able to answer them. I didn't shy away in the crowd, where you're yelling out your questions and stuff.

I had so many questions to ask him about every little thing, like, "What were you wearing?" "What time did you get up this morning?" "Did you hear the snow coming?" "How long did you wait?" "What did you talk about while you were waiting?" "Did you think you were going to die?"

Kris Sherman, reporter

I volunteered initially to go to one of the hospitals. The climbers were going to be flown to Gray Army Air Field at Fort Lewis.

The Fort Lewis people were very reluctant to let the media on base, and after much negotiation, we got the public relations people to let us on the base when the helicopter landed.

We couldn't talk to any of the survivors, so I filed a story based on what I got from the helicopter pilots. And then I was directed to a local hospital called Allenmore, where we knew one of the victims was being treated.

A photographer, Janet Jensen, and I went to Allenmore. We were the only reporters there, and we tried desperately to get permission to talk to the person who was being treated. And although he had only relatively minor injuries, he was not interested at all in talking to us.

In the midst of doing that, however, Janet got a page asking her to go to Tacoma General Hospital, where one of the climbers was having an impromptu midnight news conference.

We covered the news conference with that particular climber, and then, as the media were still swarming around trying to get more information, Janet and I kept talking about how we had to find out where these people were staying.

Todd Kelley, the spokesman for the hospital, was overseeing the conference. I snared him and took him aside, and said, "Look Todd. We need to know where these people are going. Do you have any idea, or can you find out?"

And so he found out and gave us the tip that they were being taken to Lou Whittaker's bunkhouse at Ashford, Wash., which is on the way to Mount Rainier, and that they were spending the night there.

So it was based on that that we got a team together and went knocking on the door the next morning, and were able to get to the climbers before anyone else did.

I was pretty frustrated when we were just sitting at Allenmore. We couldn't get to this injured guy, and we were very frustrated, but then it became almost like it was a challenge. Janet and I looked at each other and said, "By golly, we're going to figure this out."

Because that is, of course, one of the big challenges in journalism—to try to get information that people are trying to hide from you, whether it's where they're taking a group of climbers who have been injured in an avalanche, or whether it's sensitive documents of a government that's trying to hide the reckless way it spends the public's money.

Deadline tip:

Approach it like you would any other story. We all approach deadline stories all the time, and I think that the best thing I've learned over time is, it doesn't matter how important the story is. If you start thinking, "Wow, this is a big story," and allow yourself to be overwhelmed by it before you've even started, you can handicap yourself.

Say to yourself, "I'm going to work harder on this one. I'm going to try to do it better because it's a good story, but I'm not going to let the story intimidate me."

Lisa Kremer, reporter

At 2 o'clock in the morning, Suki Dardarian called me at home and asked me to go out the next day on the story.

Some of the guys who'd been in the avalanche were going back up the mountain to Ashford, to Lou Whittaker's bunkhouse. She said, "Find the climbers. Ask them what it was like."

I met Janet Jensen, a photographer, in the newsroom about 5:30, and we drove up together, a two-hour drive. When we arrived, the climbers were going to a restaurant nearby. And there were no other media there.

I talked to one of them and he confirmed that he was a climber and he was going up for breakfast. And he indicated that he didn't really want me coming along with him at that point.

So he went up to breakfast at this place. Meanwhile, I was trying to cover all my bases. I went around to basically everything else in Ashford that was open at that hour, which wasn't very much because it's a pretty small town, and left my card with everybody and explained why I was there. I really emphasized that I was from the local newspaper, and that it's our mountain. The mountain is a big deal for us. When the mountain's out, when the day is clear, it's a good day, and when it's not, it's another gray day.

Then we went up to the restaurant. I stopped by the climbers' table and explained that I was from *The News Tribune*. I wasn't going to be pushy, but I wasn't going to go away.

I told them, "People really want to know just what happened, because we all have friends or relatives who've climbed it and we just want to know what happened that day." And so I asked them if they'd be interested in talking about it. One of the guys still was pretty negative, but the others said that they might be willing. I said, "Would you be more comfortable here at the restaurant? I could sit down right now. Or would you rather go back to the hotel?" And they said they'd rather go back to the hotel. And I'm still looking around and there's no other media there, so I said, "OK, great, I'll meet you back there. I'll leave you alone now and I'll see you back at the hotel."

So when I got back to the hotel, I sat there on the stairs, praying that I hadn't blown this and that other reporters weren't going to show up. But you know, these are guys who've been hiking—one of their really good friends is dead and they've been in this horrifying avalanche, so I really didn't want to be high pressure.

And this guy comes down and sits down next to me, some guy I had never seen before. And I said, "How are you doing?" And he said, "Oh, fine. How are you doing?" So he sat there for a minute and he said, "I'm Curt Hewitt. I was one of the guides on the avalanche." Somebody at the hotel had told him I was here and that I wanted to talk to him, so one of the cards that I had left around town had paid off.

He started describing what had happened. His hand was swollen to about double its normal size and it was black and blue. He had four people hanging from the rope that was wrapped around his hand.

While we were wrapping it up, the guys from the restaurant showed up. We started going through it chronologically. I have brothers who climb and my dad's a former climber, so I know what a crampon and a piton are. I kept saying, "Now wait a minute. How many are to a rope?" and "You had how many to a rope on the way up and how many to a rope on the way down?" and "How steep was it?"

They started trying to describe for me how people finally landed. Allen Fedor or Gregg Swanson took a page of my notebook and sketched where everybody landed. That was key to the graphic that we put together. I brought up for them several copies of that day's *News Tribune,* which had pictures of the avalanche in it. It had pictures of the mountain and they were able to draw for me on the picture exactly where they were, and they were able to show me on the picture the tracks that they had made. They drew for me a picture of how they were hanging over the cliffs and precipices and who was hanging from whom, and they worked it all out themselves. I got a really good detailed description from them of how that all happened.

These guys were quite enthusiastic about getting all the details right. It was sort of like putting together a puzzle.

I knew we were going to want a graphic and I knew that was going to take a lot of time, so when I got back to the newsroom I started typing up the names of the climbers and I showed Roy Gallop, the graphic artist, the sketch that the climbers had drawn for me. I typed up all of the names and I typed up the short explanation that runs across the bottom of the graphic.

The first thing I did was sit down with Sandi Doughton, who was writing the story, and I told her the story. I didn't hand her notes. I just told her the story, told her what I'd heard and some of the quotes.

This was a plain old-fashioned reporting story— send out as many people as you can, use all the interviewing skills that you've got, and the writing skills. I mean there was nothing high tech or complicated about this story; it was just good old-fashioned reporting.

The purpose of our newspaper is to tell people what's going on in their community and what other people in their community are doing, and maybe it's something that they can learn from and it will help their own lives.

I like talking to people and making them explain things to me and asking really basic questions and sounding stupid and saying, "Oh, I'm sorry, I don't understand. Could you explain?" That's basic reporting.

Ninety-nine percent of the people are glad to do that. It seems to be more of a challenge to try to find a better way to explain it. Most people want their message to be clear, so they're willing to work with you on that. I mean, what's the point of talking if people don't understand what you're saying?

I was trying to put myself in the climbers' shoes so that I would have a better idea of how to approach them. And I was thinking, "OK, I've been climbing the mountain and I've being working really hard and I'm exhausted and it was the best day of my life, but then on the way down, Patrick died and it became a horrifying day." I was trying to put myself in their position and imagine how they felt so that I could approach them comfortably when I finally found them.

Deadline tip:

Put yourself in your interview subject's position and approach them in a way that's going to be comfortable for them, so that they feel comfortable talking to you.

Bruce Rushton, reporter

The avalanche happened right about the time that I make my round of afternoon calls to the various police agencies and emergency agencies. So we got fairly quick word of it from Pierce County sheriff's dispatchers.

I was out the door within 30 minutes of getting the first word of it. I grabbed a down coat and some boots from my car and headed toward the mountain, listening to the radio for any bulletins, knowing that it's about an hour's drive. I was listening to the news radio all the way up, phoning in anything that I heard that I thought was pertinent. I drove directly up to Paradise, which is the staging area where folks start their climb to the mountain. I got some of the first details from the woman working the desk at the visitors' center.

We had a room reserved at the inn at Paradise, so I went up there. I'd been told that some of the rescuers were descending, and I wanted to see them when they came down. There were no other reporters up there in evidence and so I waited around the parking lot. And then I saw the bobbing of the miners' headlights. The rescuers were skiing down the mountain after the rescue. When they got there I was fairly close, but I kept my distance. It was a very solemn moment. They were clearly exhausted. So I went back to the inn.

It's after midnight at this point. And the guys that I'd just seen come down, about four of them came into the inn and they just wordlessly went and embraced their girlfriends. At that point, I made the decision that I wasn't going to interrupt them. This was too personal. I made a note of who they were because I suspected I'd be able to get a chance to talk to them the next day. Right then was their time.

I got back to the Paradise Inn sometime after 2 in the morning and was up and dressed and outside by 6, waiting for the climbers, the remainder of that party, to come down. We knew there was going to be a news conference. I made sure I was going to get a front row seat.

It was just a zoo. I maybe asked three questions during the news conference but just sat writing everything down. Kind of like letting other people do some of my work for me. The conference lasted maybe 45 minutes.

That's when I went up and started asking all my real questions. I talked to Mike Gauthier, one of the rangers involved in the rescue, and had him draw pictures in my notebook and diagrams of exactly what happened. By observing folks and not crashing in real hard, I was able to pick up a lot of nuances.

Then I went over to the Glacier Room over at the Paradise Inn and sure enough, some of the clients who had been on the climb were there. So I talked to them. I talked to a guy who actually saw the thing start. He said it was just a tiny snowball the size of a cantaloupe.

Deadline tip:

Deadline is important, but keep things in perspective. Don't rush out like a rabid dog. Let others do as much of your work for you as you can in news conferences and things like that. As long as there's people there, you can keep asking them questions.

Have patience in the face of pressure. Don't panic.

Never ask anybody, "How do you feel?" "How does it feel?" If you talk to people in conversational tones, they'll tell you how they feel. It'll come out naturally.

Randy McCarthy, crime and breaking news team leader

The day before, we had police scanner traffic that there had been some sort of accident up there, which is always important to us because we consider that mountain *our* mountain, and we treat it just like any other beat.

We sent people up through the evening to cover the avalanche. We basically reported it 'til deadline. The story outlived the day, so we still had more to do, even after our 11:30 deadline, and we thought that we could just keep going and probably turn a pretty good story for the next day, because we had not yet gotten to the actual climbers.

We decided the simplest thing was to wake up a couple of people and send them up the mountain. We always want to know the dog's name, and how much water they put on the fire, and what's the birthday. We're big on the directions, and the cars, and how much did it weigh. It's the way people work around here.

I always tell people to ask the birth date of any subject they're doing a profile on, or anything more than the normal, because it always seems like the birth date shows up somehow in the story. It's always "the week before," or "the week after," or "the day of."

I had editors who always asked me that stuff. It's almost annoying. But it instilled in me that idea that it's easier to write something when you know more about it—the better blocks you've got to build from, the better off the structure.

Guys on the copy desk at the *Idaho Statesman* always seemed to know more about everything than I did, and made me feel so stupid if I didn't have every little fact on every little car wreck and whatnot. And it didn't occur to me until years later, when I worked with reporters who didn't know all that stuff, that you weren't allowed *not* to know every little stupid thing about everything.

They taught me to ask how many rounds were in the chamber, what the caliber was, where the bullets flew. All the colors and times and dates, when I started way back when.

It's all in the details. I'm just a nut for knowing as much of every little thing as possible, because you never know when those little strands are going to lead to bigger things.

Deadline tip:

Walk slowly through the newsroom.

I find that the crazier things are in the newsroom, if you calmly walk around and look people in the eye and nod and don't seem harried yourself, I guess it's reassuring to them. I don't know why, but the bigger, the faster things are going, the slower I roam around.

I always know that we always get it. And I have never been disappointed in what we've turned out. I know that in the back of my head, and I think everybody else knows it one way or another. Maybe they aren't confident in themselves, but they know that the guy next to them is going to pull it off. Somebody's going to pull it off. We always pull it off.

Once you have the confidence it's coming, it's just a matter of making it better.

Sandi Doughton, reporter

Usually in newspaper stories, you give everything away at the beginning, but I wanted the story to have some dramatic tension and to keep people reading. They knew in general what had happened, but they didn't know the details and they didn't know it from the perspective of the people who were there.

I decided to do it in blocks. My initial block would tell everybody the necessary things that set the dramatic tone right from the start, but give the basic information. A dramatic quote from Ruth Mahre, a quick summary of everything that happened, setting the scene on the mountain that day, and ending up that section with something to indicate how devastated these people were.

Then I would go back through that day up until the point when the avalanche hit: what the day had been like, what this class had been like that these people were in, setting the scene of them crossing this dangerous area, to describing the avalanche, then leaving them there and the guy pulls out his radio. "Mayday, mayday," he calls for help.

Then I wanted to switch the scene to some of the other people involved. I switched to a woman who was with the handicapped guy.

Wreatha Carner put in her observations, and then I took it from the perspective of Mike Gauthier, the ranger who was up on the summit.

It got a little complicated because it was very much a tangled mess up there. And we wanted to be able to explain to people who was where. It was tough in that section not to be too boring, to keep the drama up, but also to explain this complicated situation to people so they would have a picture of where these people were. The graphic helped quite a bit.

As best I could, I wanted to be able to describe how the rescue transpired, to try to give people a sense of how long this all took. We had such good stuff from Lisa Kremer and Bruce Rushton that made it possible to sustain interest.

So the last big block is basically describing how the rescue took place and the difficulty of getting Patrick Nestler down and trying to explain a little bit why he was in such a bad position and why he died.

That one was a little bit tough. A lot of the people didn't want to talk about that. It was really taken by the depiction from Mike Gauthier of the scene in the helicopter and from Lou Whittaker, how people's emotions let go and how it was this incredibly beautiful sunset scene. That seemed like a really nice way to wrap it up.

Whittaker's quote about the mountain being completely indifferent to us was just like the perfect walkoff line.

I always try to keep in mind my audience. I wanted to, as best I could, use the techniques of storytelling to sustain their interest, to draw them through it, and to create interest in the people involved.

Given the fact that there was so much coverage of this story, I was hoping to give them a different view of it. And that was something that they only were getting in snippets, like the television mike in the person's face for 10 or 15 seconds. There were plenty of little things like that, but nothing that had really pulled together all those elements into an overall narrative of what happened.

I used the cliffhanger structure to keep people reading, to keep them interested, and to keep the drama high.

In a cliffhanger, you have your characters in a precarious situation and then, boom, you leave them there and you don't automatically tell people what happened next. Hopefully, that's going to hold the reader's interest and he or she will want to find out what happened next to those people.

Deadline tip:

Don't hold back. When you have something that has so much drama to it, put your heart in it and let the drama come through. We restrain ourselves a lot in newspaper writing. Don't be afraid to feel the emotion of the story and to let that kind of carry you through.

You have to keep a clear head in view of the facts, but feeling a gut connection to the story is not a bad thing with a dramatic story.

Images on deadline

BY KENNY IRBY AND MONICA MOSES

At 2:45 p.m. Casey Madison, director of photography at *The News Tribune,* was preparing for the afternoon news meeting. What appeared to be a routine afternoon quickly changed with an emergency television report. When they heard the word "Avalanche!" the adrenaline rushed. He knew that his team would have to work together to cover the tragedy on Mount Rainier.

Immediately he dispatched veteran photojournalist and Tacoma native Peter Haley on a fixed wing plane ride to Mount Rainier's Disappointment Cleaver—the site of the avalanche. Haley had climbed the mountain before, and Madison knew he was knowledgeable about the region.

On the ground, fellow staff photojournalists scrambled to make their way to the mountain and also to cover the evacuation and medical transport of the injured to five local hospitals. It was a drill that this eight-person photo staff had "prepared for many times in our minds," Madison said.

Haley rushed to make up about a 45-minute response gap. "We only got a couple of passes before the airspace was closed down," Haley said. Inside the small high-wing aircraft, in bone-chilling temperatures at 12,000 feet, "I really did not know what I had," Haley said. "Information was hard to come by, and we did not have anyone talking to us in real time. I was shooting blind."

Two primary pictures were used in the first-day coverage. "We were saddened the next day to learn that the picture that we ran on the front page on the first day of our coverage of the ice fall was incorrect," Haley said. He found out he was in the right area. The actual slide area was "just down the mountain and across from the picture that we published on Page One."

The second photo turned out to be a critical part of the second-day coverage of the avalanche.

The day after the accident, reporter Lisa Kremer tracked down some of the climbers involved. With her

were copies of the paper's first-day coverage. "They were explaining to me how it had happened, and I kept asking more and more detailed questions about who was roped to whom, and how they'd fallen, and how they'd been attached to each other after the avalanche.

"Finally they took the newspaper from me and starting drawing on the picture and pointing out the ledges that they'd been hanging off of, because those were in the picture," Kremer said. They even used a page of

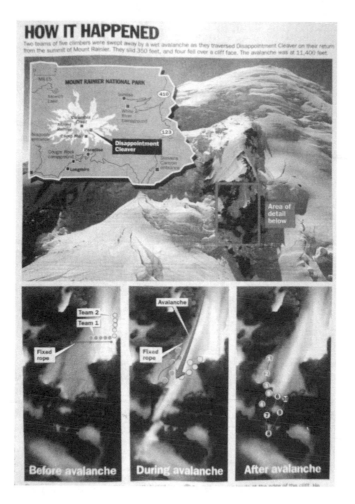

HOW IT HAPPENED

Two teams of five climbers were swept away by a wet avalanche as they traversed Disappointment Cleaver on their return from the summit of Mount Rainier. They slid 350 feet, and four fell over a cliff face. The avalanche was at 11,400 feet.

Before avalanche

During avalanche

After avalanche

Kremer's notebook to sketch in more detail about the specific locations of the climbers.

While they sketched and talked, Kremer began to see that this piece of the story would be best told as a graphic.

"It became pretty clear that the easiest way to tell that story was to give a graphic representation of what had happened, so other people could see the same thing I was seeing," Kremer said.

When she returned to the newsroom, Kremer briefed reporter Sandi Doughton, who was writing the second-day narrative, and then went to work with graphic artists Derrik Quenzer and Roy Gallop. Quenzer began to diagram the events Kremer described, using Haley's photograph as a base. For the three detail panels underneath the photograph, Quenzer worked with the image using Adobe's Illustrator and Photoshop software to simulate the movement of the avalanche and locate the climbers on the mountainside. Meanwhile, Kremer and Gallop worked on the text to be sure it described where each climber ended up.

"It was hard to explain to people why it was the middle person on the ropes who died," Kremer said. "Sandi came up with a description of the rope lying like a necklace over the cliff face and that was exactly right.

"But I think it helped even more seeing the rope hanging like a necklace on the cliff face there in the graphic."

The result of the teamwork was a wonderfully clean graphic that several readers called to say they pored over. One of the climbing guides said it clarified for him exactly how the accident happened.

"I wanted to make sure that you could read the thing very well, very quickly," Gallop said. "I didn't want people fighting to understand what we were saying."

The News Tribune offered a dramatic and comprehensive second-day package that included dramatic storytelling, a photo of the actual slide that had been uncovered in the frame-by-frame editing process, and a highly informative graphic, in addition to a correction about the photo on the front page the previous day.

"It was an incredible paper and a super team effort," Madison said. The graphic won a medal from the Society for News Design and an award in the Malofiej international informational graphic competition.

One key to the paper's powerful report was planning. Madison and senior editor Suki Dardarian were up until 3 a.m. following the first day's news, mapping out the game plan for second-day coverage. "We began storyboarding the information that we had...who was where and where we needed to be the next morning," Madison said.

Essential to their success is a newsroom commitment to telling stories simply and a real respect for each other's crafts.

"In its best form, a graphic will take some of the most technical parts of your explanation and you don't have to spend so much time laboriously going over technical details in the story," Kremer said. "A graphic can really open up the story that way, give you more time to spend on description and narrative rather than on those complicated details."

Gallop echoed that team commitment. "We rely very heavily on reporters, and we talk to them, and we encourage them to grab visuals, and get exact locations, and show us where and how things happen, because they're our eyes and ears when it comes to news. Without them, we can't really do our job effectively."

"There were no super dramatic, 'moment photos' in this package," Madison said. "Just simple but highly informative moments that everyone contributed to."

The Boston Globe

Boston Globe reporters Thomas Farragher, Stephanie Ebbert, Ric Kahn, Doreen Iudica Vigue, and Brian MacQuarrie. Not pictured is Ellen O'Brien, who was out of town on assignment. Farragher and Kahn wrote the story; the others reported from the field.

Finalist, Team Deadline Reporting

The Boston Globe is a New England institution, so when a disgruntled accountant showed up at work at the Connecticut State Lottery on March 7, 1998, and opened fire on his co-workers, the newsroom scrambled even though the scene was a state away. In all, 14 reporters and correspondents fanned out to the neighborhoods of the shooter and his victims, while writers back in Boston stitched together their findings. The result of this deadline teamwork: a meticulously reported and moving reconstruction of what has become a terrifying and familiar story in corporate America.

5 die as Connecticut lottery worker goes on rampage

MARCH 7, 1998

NEWINGTON, Conn.—He was an accountant who had a chip on his shoulder and a bayonet on his kitchen table. He lived with his parents across from a llama farm in a small beige house with a sign informing visitors: "Trespassers will be shot; survivors will be shot again."

As dawn broke over Ledyard yesterday, Matthew Beck, 35, left his folks' home—across town from the casino—got in his car, and drove 1½ hours to his job at Connecticut Lottery headquarters. At some point, he strapped a bandolier of bullets across his chest, over his gray pin-striped shirt but concealed by a brown leather jacket. He carried a 9mm pistol and a knife.

At 8:35 a.m. a co-worker at the lottery saw Beck fumbling in a storage closet.

"Why don't you put the light on?" she asked.

"I'm looking for something," he answered.

Five minutes later, Beck opened fire, mowing down four of the lottery's top brass. First was Michael Logan, 33, director of information services, stabbed and shot in a suite of executive offices. Then vice president Frederick Rubelmann III, 40, was shot. Next, Beck burst into a meeting, said "bye-bye" to chief financial officer Linda Mlynarczyk, 38, and shot her three times.

As Beck continued down the corridor, lottery chief Otho Brown, 54, sprinted ahead of him, screaming to his employees, "Run, run, run!" Later, those who survived would call Brown their hero. The lottery's security chief, who was unarmed, also yelled, "Keep running!"

Some workers dived under their desks; about 20 ran into a paint warehouse in the same building as the lottery. "Call 911; he's got a gun," someone cried. Others ran out the door and into nearby woods. One man tried to leap into the back of a truck driving by and smashed his head.

Some jumped into a trench beside the building. As they lay on their stomachs trembling, crying, and praying, Beck chased Brown past the ditch and across the parking lot. About 100 yards across the lot, Brown stumbled and fell. He raised his arms in a position of surrender: "Don't kill me, don't kill me," he pleaded. "Ah, shut up," Beck said, and shot him.

As police closed in, Beck pumped a bullet into his own right temple.

* * *

He had spent almost half his life shadow-boxing with depression and suicidal thoughts. A brainy boy brought up in a loving family on the outskirts of Ledyard, Matthew Beck lived in a rustic house set off from neighbors by a split-rail fence. Horses grazed in the back yard.

The family didn't socialize much. Joe Rezendes, who had lived two houses down from them for 19 years, never spoke a word to them. He'd see them and wave.

At Ledyard High School, Beck left few footprints. His yearbook is empty of mischievous inscriptions. Teachers remember him as a fine young man, a good student.

But as Beck entered his 20s, friends thought he had become more paranoid. At age 21, he slit his wrist but survived.

At some point, he graduated from the Florida Institute of Technology. He worked at various times as a security guard and a tax representative for the Internal Revenue Service. He joined the Connecticut Lottery's accounting division in April 1989.

Things seemed fine until the summer of '96. He was galled that his bosses started asking him to do data processing work without increasing his $45,214 salary.

By January 1997, Beck seemed depressed and delusional. He complained to a friend about his parents, his girlfriend, his job.

"Sick of life," is how one friend described Beck's mood. Even his father would later call him troubled.

As Beck rambled on to his friend on the phone, he said he was holding a knife. Afraid that Beck would turn it on himself, the friend called police.

When police arrived at Beck's apartment in Cromwell, they found a large bayonet on the kitchen table.

But Beck was gone. Later, he asked two friends to check his apartment for him. "Something strange is going on there," he said. He eventually surfaced at a friend's house.

Friends said he looked creepy after he grew a goatee and shaved his head about a year ago when his hair began to fall out.

An aficionado of guns and golf, he apparently was able to acquire a pistol permit despite his increasing mental instability.

And his frustration at work continued. Last August, he filed a grievance with the union. Angst continued to corrode him, and in October, he went on a paid leave of absence for work-related stress for four months.

He returned last week, but seemed more moody, even stone-faced.

On Friday of last week, Beck met with his union shop steward, Joseph Mudry, and Mlynarczyk, the chief financial officer, about his grievance. Beck had won the first part of his private labor battle: He wouldn't have to do data processing anymore.

But the question of back pay remained up in the air.

Twice this week he bugged his shop steward, asking him Thursday how much longer the process was going to drag on. Beck already had put out feelers for jobs outside the lottery.

This week, he reportedly was passed over for a promotion and a raise.

* * *

In Otho "Otto" Brown's Avon Mountain neighborhood in the upper-class, residential town of Avon northwest of Hartford, houses sit back 100 feet from the road and the front lawns are an expanse of pine trees and sharp shrubbery.

It's an old neighborhood that has been discovered in recent years by young executives with some money and some children. Brown had both.

Brown, a Wilmington, Del., native, was chosen president and chief executive of the Connecticut Lottery in 1993. He made $104,572 a year, and neighbors said he earned it, working long hours and returning late to his wife, Denise, their twin 8-year-old daughters and an older son.

He was looking forward to his girls' 9th birthday party Monday. The Browns were fixtures at the neighborhood association's pool in the summer, and Brown delighted in escorting his children among the crowd of angels and goblins who patroled Avon Mountain each Halloween.

When he wasn't at his desk, Brown preferred the outdoors—the roar of a motorcycle or the serenity of a sailboat near sunset.

"He was a hands-on, fair administrator," said Frank D. Brown (no relation), deputy director of the Delaware Lottery, which Otho Brown directed before he went to Connecticut. "He liked to show off pictures of the kids. This was a family man."

Early yesterday morning, Brown said goodbye to his family. And then neighbors saw him drive off quickly, a man in a hurry to get to his job running the state lottery in Newington.

* * *

The last time Linda Mlynarczyk faced death, love bloomed.

She was Linda A. Blogoslawski then, New Britain's mayor. It was 1993, and she was in a small airplane when it was forced to make an emergency landing in a Middletown cornfield. Next to her sat Peter Mlynarczyk, a former New Britain alderman.

"Facing death side by side brings people closer together," Mlynarezyk told *The Hartford Courant* in 1994. The couple married—a union her husband said made him "the luckiest man in the world."

She was a hometown girl who grew up to be mayor in a city where her Polish roots and her attention to detail made her a natural for the job.

"She was young, vibrant, intelligent—and she had a great smile," said Lucian J. Pawlak, the Democrat who defeated Mlynarezyk for the mayoralty in 1995.

Even as she exchanged one public job for another—appointed in 1996 to the lottery's $79,500-a-year post of chief financial officer—residents said she remained dedicated to local causes and the idea of marketing the city of New Britain.

"She had great ideas for this city," said Daniel Hogan, one of many who stood in clusters downtown yesterday, murmuring about the morning's murders.

For Mlynarczyk, home was in New Britain's West End section—a symbol of attainment in a working-class city. Recently married, her sandy-colored home on a wooded lot provided a bit of remove and seclusion from the busy downtown neighborhoods where she grew up.

Yesterday morning, as Mlynarczyk began her commute to work, she wound her way down Reservoir Road and past the kids piling out of a yellow school bus in front of red-brick Vance Elementary School a short distance away.

And then she continued on to lottery headquarters.

* * *

As vice president of the Connecticut Lottery's operations and administration, Frederick Rubelmann III's work life was that of the harried executive.

And his life at home was just as busy.

The father of two young children, Rubelmann was the sort of man who coached the Little League team, plowed neighbors' driveways after a snowfall, and dipped into the savings account to give his children a special vacation on the West Coast.

Rubelmann, whose $84,656 salary kept him financially apace in one of the nation's wealthiest states, lived with his wife, Mary, in a two-story home with tan siding and a porch. It's a quiet street off Route 10 in Southington, where Rubelmann, who studied forestry at the University of Connecticut, balanced the rigors of work with the pleasures of family.

"He took care of his kids and had a lot of plans for them," said a neighbor, who asked not to be identified. "What happens now to those plans?"

It sometimes was a crazy morning routine at the Rubelmann household. "Mornings were hectic down there," said a neighbor whose children used to baby-sit for the Rubelmann kids. "Lots of laughter and kidding and joking and trying to find things."

The lottery executive planned to go to the Hartford Wolfpack hockey game last night with his son, a nephew, and a sister-in-law. It was his nephew's birthday.

But first, he had to go to work.

* * *

Michael Logan, the lottery's director of information services, lived in a split-level Colonial in a modern development whose backyards are dotted with swing sets, basketball hoops, and plastic toys.

He was married and the father of two children, a neighbor said. "A good father and a good husband," was how she described him. "He loved his family."

Like Rubelmann, Logan thought lottery officials were right to fight Beck's job grievance.

Besides Beck, Logan traveled the farthest yesterday morning to reach his job in Newington, 40 miles away from his Colchester home.

* * *

At 8 a.m. yesterday, Matthew Beck walked into his office, hung up his coat, and waited.

This article was reported from Connecticut by staffers Doreen Iudica Vigue, Brian MacQuarrie, Ellen O'Brien, and Stephanie Ebbert, and written by Ric Kahn and Thomas Farragher. Contributing were correspondents Richard Weizel, Scott Schulte, and Valerie Jackson and news assistants Matt Falconer, Mike Glover, Andrew Nesbitt, Rachel Mullin, and Byron Calamese. AP material was also used.

Lessons Learned

It was just another Black Friday at *The Boston Globe*: the
day of the week when the newsroom is short on staff, long on
anticipation; the time when half the room prays to the news
gods to spare us another four-star catastrophe on Friday
while the other half dares the Big Story to drop.

And then the Earth rumbled 90 miles to the south: a disgruntled Connecticut lottery worker went on a rampage,
gunning down four top officials before blowing himself
away with a bullet to the right temple.

Because the story broke early, and there was wall-to-wall
TV and radio coverage, we decided we could best serve our
readers with a narrative. We wanted to reconstruct the hours
from the time the killer and his victims awoke on "just another
Friday morning in March" until their paths collided.

And so the reporters fanned out in the field, each carrying
a defined objective: help chronicle the carnage, profile the
victims, or find out what made 35-year-old accountant Matthew Beck tick—and why he exploded like a time bomb.

In the newsroom, the two rewrite men split up reporting
and writing duties as well, one taking the victims and the
other the perpetrator. It's always easier to write through a
clearer lens when your own hands have helped rake in the
information.

Early on, a picture of Beck began to emerge. We reached
his parents, but they were too shaken to speak. Without the
foundation they would have provided, we had to scramble
for every telling detail, like the sign that guarded their house,
where their adult son lived with them: "Trespassers will be
shot; survivors will be shot again."

A simple question about what Beck was wearing elicited
an unusual response. From medical sources we learned that
Beck's body was found with a bandolier of bullets strapped
across his chest, over the kind of gray pinstriped shirt favored
by many accountants. Rambo with a pocket protector.

From police, we found out that they had recently been
called to his house by a friend who told them Beck had a
knife and was threatening to kill himself.

The cops were helpful in describing that incident. But
what's important to them as investigators is different from
what's important to us as reporters. So we asked if there
were police reports from that day, and if the officer could

please fax them to us. Hidden in the hieroglyphic scrawl of Connecticut cops were juicy gems: Beck was sick of life. He suffered from delusions that his apartment was spooked. He kept a bayonet on his kitchen table.

From union officials and co-workers, we discovered the undercurrent of Beck's angst: He had been passed over for a promotion and a raise even though he had been asked to take on extra work he considered demeaning. Depressed and paranoid, Beck took out his anger on lottery officials he blamed for not resolving his grievance for back pay, and for other work troubles.

As police tried to shoo us from some of the victims' houses, we sensed from their ages and small-town expressions that they personally knew the dead. Rather than flee, we pumped them and others for tidbits about the bake sales and Little League games that helped define the lives now lost.

At lottery headquarters, blocked from talking to employees who had witnessed the shootings, we jotted down the license plate numbers of cars as they drove home. We then turned up at their doorsteps after an editor dispatched one of the reporters to the Registry of Motor Vehicles to trade plate numbers for addresses.

Determined to find the voice of a victim, and with deadline looming, we approached the home of a woman who had been chased by Beck. Instead of sticking a notebook in her face, we offered apologies for treading on her trauma. Surrounded by family, she told her story, a trip back to the trench where hours earlier she lay trembling and praying for her life. For her, it was cathartic.

We were freed from a conventional format and the need for constant attribution, but that forced us to report the story with more depth so that we could write authoritatively. The result: We were able to layer the woman's chilling recollections into the lead at the last moment.

Our story eased into its ending, in the same way that Black Friday had begun: "At 8 a.m. yesterday, Matthew Beck walked into his office, hung up his coat, and waited."

The Oregonian

Front row: Maxine Bernstein and Courtenay Thompson.
Back row: Field editor Quinton Smith; staff writers Brian T. Meehan,
Tony Green, and Dana Tims.

Finalist, Team Deadline Reporting

It has become a familiar, but always terrifying story: An
armed student opens fire on his classmates and teachers.
On May 21, 1998, the dateline was Springfield, Ore.,
110 miles from the newsroom of *The Oregonian,* the
state's largest newspaper. That morning, *The Oregonian*
sent more than a dozen staffers to Springfield: reporters,
photographers, a local columnist, an artist, even the au-
tomotive writer who races cars on weekends. "We did
not ask, 'Can you go,'" recalled executive editor Peter
Bhatia. "We asked, 'How fast can you drive?'" Later
that day, editors and technicians set up a small newsroom at a Springfield motel.

In the week that followed, more than 50 staffers contributed to the paper's exhaustive coverage of the shooting at Thurston High, its impact, and most of all, on
efforts to answer the most pressing question of all: Why?
They produced stories, sidebars, commentary, photos,
and extensive graphics, striving to balance the need for
speed with attention to accuracy, thoroughness, and fair-
ness. As Bhatia noted in his nominating letter, "How can
we help our readers?" was the question that guided every
coverage decision.

Methodical violence leaves 4 dead and 22 hurt

MAY 22, 1998

SPRINGFIELD—Eight minutes before the first bell Thursday morning at Thurston High School, a skinny 15-year-old freshman walked into a cafeteria bustling with 400 students and methodically opened fire with a .22-caliber rifle.

In the next few minutes, one of the nation's worst schoolhouse shootings broke the heart of this close-knit Willamette Valley mill town. Before the gunman was wrestled down by valiant students, one 17-year-old boy was dead and 23 other students were wounded. One of the injured students died Thursday night.

Police grabbed Kipland P. Kinkel, who had been arrested and booted from the school a day before on a weapons charge. They said Kinkel, a youth who often joked about killing people, fired more than 50 rounds into the crowded cafeteria.

"He just kept walking toward us with a blank look on his face," said Larissa Rybka, 16. "He just kept shooting and shooting."

Later Thursday morning, authorities discovered the suspect's parents—popular Springfield teachers William and Faith Kinkel—shot to death in their McKenzie River home 10 miles east of town. Police later evacuated seven homes in the area and warned air traffic to avoid the Chita Loop area. State police found explosives in the house and thought it might be booby-trapped.

Mike Moskovitz, a spokesman for Lane County, said residents wouldn't be allowed back in their homes until later in the night.

"You never in your wildest dreams think this is going to happen to your son, your child, in your town," said Mona Walley, 44, whose son, Jessie, was wounded in the stomach but was expected to recover. Walley said the shooter was "just an unknown face; none of the kids really know him."

Mikael Nickolauson, 17, of Springfield was pronounced dead at the scene of gunshot wounds. Ben Walker, 17, died Thursday night.

The shooting occurred as students ate breakfast and milled about just before 8 a.m. The lunchroom was especially crowded because the school library, another gathering spot, was being used for a breakfast honoring the contributions of senior boys. Students were abuzz about school elections, an afternoon pep assembly and the coming four-day holiday weekend.

Kinkel made the 20-minute drive on the winding, two-lane road from his house in a rustic subdivision called ShangriLa, where his parents lay dead. He parked off campus and walked into the east Springfield high school, clad in a trench coat and carrying three weapons and a backpack. This was the day that Kip Kinkel's crazy talk about murder and mayhem would come true.

"He walked into the cafeteria and very calmly kept walking, swiveling back and forth, and firing," said Jonathan Crawford, a 16-year-old junior who was sitting with friends about 15 feet from Kinkel. "The only thing I could think was, this can't be real."

At first, students confused the gunshots with firecrackers, perhaps a stunt to accompany Thursday's schoolwide election. But the blood and the cries of pain ignited panic.

"A girl right across from me went down on the floor with blood all over her head," said Stephani Quimby, 16, a junior. "People just started screaming and running for the doors."

Sixteen-year-old James Kistner thought it was odd when he saw Kinkel walk through a side door into the cafeteria. He knew Kinkel had been suspended Wednesday pending an expulsion hearing after he was caught with a .32-caliber pistol on campus.

"He was wearing a long trench coat, to his ankles," Kistner said of Kinkel. "He pulled a gun from inside the coat and started shooting. He squeezed off two or three rounds. I saw the flames coming out, and I dropped.

"Then he just started blazing everywhere.

"It was complete chaos. People were screaming and on the floor. Everyone hit the floor at once. Then there were tons of people running out the door, jumping over tables."

Witnesses said Kinkel was deadly calm as he shot his schoolmates, some point-blank.

"He put his foot on the back of one kid and shot him four times," said David Willis, 15. "His face was casual, like it was something he did every day."

The carnage ended when three students, including a wounded varsity wrestler named Jake Ryker, tackled Kinkel.

Shaun McGillvrey, 16, a sophomore, saw Ryker go after the gunman after Ryker had been shot. He said the 6-foot-4 wrestler shouted at Kinkel, who is 5-foot-5 and 125 pounds, and then knocked him to the ground.

Ryker was shot once in the chest and listed in critical condition.

"He's a true hero," Springfield police Capt. Jerry Smith said. "If he hadn't acted when he did, other students would almost certainly have been wounded or killed."

Ryker held the gunman with the help of his younger brother, Josh, and Tony Case, who was wounded in the abdomen.

"The true heroes are the guys who took down Kip— Jake and Tony Case," said Michael Peebles, a senior who gave first aid to several wounded students.

Peebles, 17, had pulled into the parking lot moments after the shooting. As he stepped out of his car, another student shouted that two students were lying wounded in the hallway.

The former lifeguard put his first aid training to use.

He knelt next to Walker, who had been shot in the back of the head. "Hey buddy," Peebles said, "Hey buddy. Are you OK?"

Walker did not respond. Peebles felt only a faint pulse.

"Don't leave us," Peebles said to the unconscious teen-ager. "You have to hang on."

Walker died Thursday night at McKenzie-Willamette Hospital in Springfield, according to several sources.

Within five minutes of the shooting, the first of seven paramedic ambulances arrived. Three fire engines staffed by Eugene paramedics pulled into the school's parking lot shortly after that.

Medics quickly established a triage center in the cafeteria to sort and treat the most seriously wounded students. Those most critically injured were immediately loaded onto stretchers and rushed to ambulances.

Within 53 minutes, all of the wounded had been taken to either Sacred Heart Medical Center in Eugene or McKenzie-Willamette. Sacred Heart admitted 11 students with gunshot wounds. McKenzie-Willamette admitted eight with gunshot wounds. The remainder were treated and released.

At Thurston High School, anguished parents demanded news about their children. At 8:45 a.m., Principal Larry Bentz, in a macabre lottery, read aloud the names of injured students.

The announcement of nearly every name drew screams from a crowd of 80 parents. Several mothers collapsed into the arms of their husbands. Others sobbed uncontrollably.

"My God," one mother wailed. "My God, this can't be happening."

Students comforted one another in clusters of two and three. Most knew at least one injured classmate.

Students offered a conflicted portrait of Kipland Kinkel, who took Prozac for anger management and was dubbed by his classmates as the student most likely to start World War III. Some described Kinkel as the "class clown"; others spoke about a boy with a dark side and an obsession with bombs and violence.

Students said Kinkel had threatened to plant a bomb in the bleachers at a pep assembly and once read in class from his journal about killing people.

Kinkel listened to the music of self-described Satanist rocker Marilyn Manson, presented a three-minute talk in class on how to build a bomb and gave a friend a device to break into a car as a birthday present. Students said he daydreamed about killing people as if they were in a video game. He bought a 9mm Glock pistol with money he earned doing chores around the house.

Kinkel is scheduled to be arraigned on aggravated murder charges this afternoon in Lane County Circuit Court. According to Oregon's Measure 11, he will be tried as an adult but cannot face the death penalty, said Lane County District Attorney Doug Harcleroad.

The incident prompted statements of sympathy and support from President Clinton and Gov. John Kitzhaber.

"I'd ask that all Oregonians pause today and ask themselves how we have failed as a society and to ask how this could have happened," Kitzhaber said at an afternoon news conference. "We need to ask ourselves, as well, what kind of despair drives children to make this kind of terrible choice?"

Although Thurston High was scheduled to be closed today, district officials said they would open Thurston Middle School to provide counseling to students. About 70 counselors were expected to be on hand.

Grief-stricken families filed quietly into a church Thursday night. Young people wept as church leaders read the names of the wounded. Pastor Zane Wilson of Springfield Lutheran Church lighted a candle for each wounded student, including Jake Ryker, the wrestler who helped subdue Kinkel. Ryker is a member of the church; Thursday was his 17th birthday.

"Today, lightning struck at Thurston," Wilson said.

Moans echoed from the pews when Laurie Loftsvold, another Lutheran clergywoman, asked the audience to "remember the lives of Mikael Nickolauson... and Ben Walker." Most people in the church had not realized Walker had died.

"These were all our children," Wilson said. "And they will continue to be our children as long as we remember them."

Wilson asked people not to lose faith.

"God has not moved out of Springfield," he said.

Lessons Learned

BY BRIAN T. MEEHAN

Mayhem often follows mayhem.

That is, in the way newspapers cover big, breaking stories.

Editors dispatch legions of reporters and schedule extra news meetings. Key writers vanish from the radar only to surface after deadline. Reporters who dutifully stay in touch are harried by calls from several editors. Deadlines hurtle by. First edition is a mess.

In the stories that do make the paper—next to the large house ads—separate writers spell the protagonist's name differently. Sidebars overlap and offer conflicting versions of the chronology. The best anecdotes are filed too late for publication.

During the last five years, *The Oregonian* has worked to develop a better system to handle major stories. We've blended old newsroom tactics with modern reportage in an effort to deliver a more readable report the morning after.

Our reporters file from the field but a rewrite reporter pulls together the lead story from various reports.

We have used this system to cover 100-year floods and hurricane-like windstorms.

On May 21, 1998, we launched it again after a 15-year-old boy opened fire on his classmates at Thurston High School in Springfield, Ore.

I was the "mule" on these stories. Half reporter, half editor, my job was to blend a stampede of reports into a coherent lead story that was accurate and evocative.

That I was relatively successful in the Thurston High shootings is a tribute to the outstanding work of my colleagues, because I never left our Portland office.

More than 40 *Oregonian* reporters worked on the story, including 15 at the scene. In the past, these 15 reporters would have spent a lot of time on the phone briefing four to six different editors at home base. This sort of structure disrupts Job One: helping your reporters get the story.

When gunfire pierced a Thursday morning, *The Oregonian* sent a veteran editor to the scene, a two-hour ride from Portland. Quinton Smith became the newsroom liaison. He coordinated assignments, monitored the setup of a hotel suite "newsroom," and insisted reporters make deadlines.

In Portland, we staggered deadlines so the copy wouldn't land at once, and so I could see everything while writing the main story.

I reported by phone, which grounded me in the story. I left the details of the shooting to our reporters at the scene. I focused instead on the high school and the community.

How did Thurston High differ from the other high school in town? Did its students go on to college? What programs was Thurston known for? The answers provided context and turned the high school into something less than an abstraction. It also promoted accuracy, the Achilles heel of any rewrite process.

I spoke briefly to several key reporters about the kind of detail we needed to build the main story. I read all the incoming copy and drafted a basic outline. I began writing two hours before deadline.

One of my colleagues, Dana Tims, was the designated reporter at the scene for the main story. We talked about the story's structure and its top. He filed early. I wove in material from more than a dozen sidebars.

Everyone involved understood I had the right of way. If I thought a quote or a detail belonged in the main story, I used it and alerted the editors. The system will not work if reporters and editors fight to save their best material for sidebars.

The two editors managing the story from Portland steered all the appropriate material to me but left me alone so I could write.

But the mule does more than just write. The rewrite reporter must help create the paper's style on any given story. In the Thurston High story, this began with the shooter. We quickly learned the suspect was a freshman named Kip Kinkel. He was arrested by police after being disarmed by students. Police and dozens of witnesses said Kinkel was the shooter. We waived our normal policy of not naming minors as crime suspects and identified Kinkel.

As the story evolved, I tried to ferret out the best information on conflicting elements. What time did the shooter begin firing? What caliber guns were used? How many shots were fired? Which of the victims was executed at point-blank range? By working hard at precision, we avoided some of the bad information that inevitably surfaces.

We made deadline and printed a clear, lucid account of a horrible day in Springfield. Almost a year later, the accuracy of our story holds up well.

Here are some of the key points we learned:

▪ **Use a field editor:** The on-scene editor was vital in helping our reporters do their jobs. He was decisive and supportive. He was able to quickly reassign reporters as the fast-emerging story changed. He kept Portland informed and took care of the logistics. Our reporters just ran for the story. He ensured they met deadlines.

• **Let people do their jobs:** You must trust your reporters and line editors. Communication is crucial, but you can't script out and control a big breaking story from the newsroom. Reporters must use their instincts and resourcefulness in the field. They can't spend all their time on the cell phone to a desk editor. Editors must resist the impulse to overmanage the story. If your field people are not up to the task, you either have the wrong people assigned or have not trained them properly. You can't save the day another area code away.

• **Hit your deadlines:** Without discipline, all is lost. Reporters naturally want to push deadlines, especially on a monster story. Don't do it. Set reasonable deadlines, but make reporters stick to them. Otherwise, the best stuff remains in the notebook instead of in tomorrow's paper.

• **Leave time to write:** Not allowing enough time to write is the single biggest mistake reporters make on a breaking story. The bigger the story, the worse this problem gets. Again, a news organization needs discipline on a day like this.

• **Give the rewrite reporter the right of way:** The mule gets to eat what it wants. And there's no time to argue about this. At *The Oregonian,* this system has the unqualified support of Sandy Rowe, our editor. This keeps the passing lane open.

• **There are no small details:** The accumulation of telling detail gives the story weight and credibility. What route did the gunman drive to school? Where did he park? How was he dressed? How does a 15-year-old pay for a 9mm pistol? (Answer: with money he earned doing chores around the house.)

• **Train the mule:** Don't experiment with this system on the biggest story to hit your state in a decade. You can work up to it. Extreme weather often provides training opportunities. Hurricanes along the Atlantic coast, blizzards in the Midwest, wildfires in the West are terrific ways to train for the huge story. And every newsroom needs more than one mule. Select them on the basis of experience, ability to work calmly with others, and a knack for clear writing done quickly.

On the Thurston High shootings, we wanted the lead story to accomplish a lot: describe the events, the scene, the emergency response; quickly profile the suspect and the heroes; show the community's reaction.

I wrote the piece as tightly as I could. I paid extra attention to the pace of the story; it had to move quickly to cover all the ground. I varied sentence length and used quotes as a drummer might use the cymbals. The story's brisk rhythm helped speed the reader.

The best advice I can give to any deadline writer delivering a story full of tragedy and pathos, however, concerns the story's tone. Tone will influence a reader more than any other element. Readers recognize when a newspaper exaggerates. They usually believe the press is just trying to sell papers.

With major events, a writer must be vigilant or hyperbole will creep in and ruin your story. Remain understated. When you look back on the piece, overstatement will make you cringe like a dog. It also makes readers think you are trying to make money on the bones of tragedy. Cut it out. The story will speak for itself.

J. Peder Zane
Commentary

THE NEWS&OBSERVER

J. Peder Zane sees books as a portal through which to explore the world around us. The 38-year-old book review editor and columnist for the Raleigh *News & Observer* believes books can play a vital role in today's public discourse. He uses the works of authors in his Sunday column as voices of thoughtful reflection, historical perspective, and cultural insight.

His opportunity to connect the book world with the news world took a circuitous career route. The would-be historian became a private investigator for a year. He experienced an epiphany while squirreled away in a surveillance truck, watching to see if people who claimed they had medical problems truly were injured.

"While I was doing that, it just came to me: 'Newspapers,'" he recalls. "I don't know why, except that I think there's a connection between history, which is seeing what people did and trying to explain it, and journalism, which is doing the same thing but being more active. Getting out there and being in the fray."

He wrote 130 letters to newspapers all across the country, attaching two sample stories he had made up, which he identified as such since he had no clips. He landed on *The Patent Trader,* a twice weekly newspaper in Mount Kisco, N.Y., then became an editor at *Travel Agent Magazine.* He entered *The New York Times* writing program for young reporters in 1990, where in addition to doing clerical work, he pitched stories to the various desks. When the program ended two and a half years later, he returned to free-lancing for newspapers and magazines

His 800-word pieces on popular culture—many of them on books—for *The New York Times* "Week in Review" section helped prepare him for the column he now does for *The News & Observer.* He was hired there as books editor in December 1996.

Zane scrutinizes serious and substantive literary fiction and nonfiction for messages, wisdom, advice, information, knowledge, and history that can speak to us today. He shows the synergy between the books and buzz. In his view, books can transcend the topical and speak across the years and the geography that separate us. His column, "If Mother Superior Speaks, Listen," recreates in a humorously trenchant style the interior dialogue we engage in as we encounter the normal and the incongruous. In "The Wages of Sin is Fame," Zane sears shock-jock Don Imus, himself, and us for our fascination with fame, however it comes to us.

For Zane, books talk. And we should listen. Think. And talk back.

—Aly Colón

If Mother Superior speaks, listen

APRIL 26, 1998

Be outrageous; defend the indefensible; try to convince me that fat-free tastes as good as the real thing.

At first I'm a regular Sally Jesse Raphael—sans the satellite dish glasses. I'll listen, really listen, withhold judgment, and try to see your point of view. But just when I'm ready to say, "I understand," my Mother Superior side has a habit of kicking in. Instead of patting you on the head, I'll want to smack your knuckles with a thick brown wooden ruler and say, "Cut that out."

Gender issues aside, none of this worries me. In these loopy times, when the word "inexcusable" has become archaic, a split personality is the best defense.

So it was with initial curiosity and wonder that I took a look at Tony Horwitz's *Confederates in the Attic* and Donald McCaig's *Jacob's Ladder* (both reviewed today). Though Horwitz's book is a work of contemporary journalism and McCaig's book is a historical novel, both hinge on efforts to find what was noble, admirable and courageous about the Confederate soldiers who shed their blood *to insure that millions of innocent men, women and children would remain in bondage.*

Whoops, there's Mother Superior talking—pipe down, sister; you'll get your chance.

Thwack!

"Ow."

Ahem. *Jacob's Ladder* is McCaig's epic tale of the interlocked lives of slaves and slave owners whose lives are forever changed by the Civil War. In a recent phone interview, McCaig told me that as a "Northern liberal"—he'd been an ad man in New York before moving to Virginia 25 years ago—he had to clear a big moral hump before he could write the empathetic portrayal of Confederate soldiers that lies at his book's center. They seemed unfathomable to him: horrible and evil. "I must have spent two years on false starts with this book," he explained. "Then, one day I was at a 'deer-beer party' down by the river near my home. Willie Nelson was blaring out of some pickup truck speaker, and I looked around at all my neighbors and I thought, if this were 1861, I'd be going to war with them."

Reminding me of Hannah Arendt's classic work on Nazi Germany, *Eichmann in Jerusalem: A Report on the Banality of Evil* (1964), McCaig continued: "What I learned as I researched my book was that a good many honorable and decent men and women in the South were slave owners. Slavery was a great sin, a great wickedness, but they weren't any different from you or me—how could they be? They didn't wear the mark of Cain on their arm. They were, for the most part, decent people doing the best they could in a tragically flawed system."

Horwitz underwent a similar conversion while writing *Confederates in the Attic,* which depicts the black-and-white world of modern-day men who spend their days dressed in blue and gray (mostly gray). For these Civil War re-enactors, the Lost Cause is not a blood-soaked crucible. Instead, it is a nostalgic portal, Horwitz writes, to "a time when the South seemed a cohesive region upholding Christian values and agrarian ways...[when] larger-than-life men like Stonewall Jackson, Robert E. Lee and Nathan Bedford Forrest" walked the earth. It is a balm that blows them back to a simpler era when people knew who they were and what they were. As Horwitz crisscrossed the South, he met strange birds who soak their uniform buttons in urine to give them that real old-time look, starve themselves to achieve that gaunt appearance that was all the rage at Andersonville and one Lon Chaney-type who can make himself look bloated and sallow like an authentic corpse on an ersatz field of battle.

We might dismiss these men as historically impaired yahoos as long as we include Horwitz, a Pulitzer Prize-winning reporter, among their ranks. For, as his book marches on, the lines fade between the writer and subject as he gradually cottons to the re-enactors' illusory certainties: "It restored my appreciation," Horwitz writes, "of simple things: cold water, a crust of bread, a cool patch of shade."

What do these two books tell us? It is that too much understanding, like too little knowledge, can be a dangerous thing. Undoubtedly, it is useful to acknowledge that slavery's defenders were not anomalies of evil and that their modern-day doppelgangers are simply pathetic. But we must also heed Mother Superior's warning: Do not allow that empathy to obscure your moral vision. People may display nobility and courage in the name of evil. Others may derive comfort from that cause. But, the failure to understand the evil that lay at the heart of the Confederacy is inexcusable.

Writers' Workshop

Talking Points

1) The column opens with a challenge to the reader: "Be outrageous; defend the indefensible; try to convince me that fat-free tastes as good as the real thing." How does this draw the reader into the rest of the column?

2) Note how the writer converses with himself in the column beginning with the italicized comments in the fourth paragraph. He brings the column back to the topic with the one-word sentence, "Ahem." Is the commentary-within-the-commentary effective? What does it reveal about the writer?

3) Zane discusses the conversions of the authors of the two books mentioned in his column. How do their experiences compare with Zane's "Mother Superior" stance?

Assignment Desk

1) The books reviewed are compared with Hannah Arendt's *Eichmann in Jerusalem: A Report on the Banality of Evil.* Read it and compare it with *Jacob's Ladder.*

2) Zane's moral theme is explained in the last paragraph: "Do not allow that empathy to obscure your moral vision." Write a column analyzing the opposing side of an issue about which you have a strong opinion.

Bridging the gap between words and deeds

SEPTEMBER 20, 1998

From soft-core in prime time to triple-X in the Oval Office, from the deification of the Dow Jones to the inexorable dumbing-down of culture, it's hard not to look around modern America and think: Ugh.

In this era of low expectations, when people assume the worst and get even less, it seems the only viable response to our condition is a feckless, ironic shrug that says, "Wake up, smell the Starbucks and go back to sleep."

Then along comes somebody like Curtis White to give us a kick in the cortex. A writer from Normal, Ill., White thinks that through books—yes, books!—we can still muster a little informed resistance.

"Contemporary fiction is a literature of great promise, productivity, and possibility," he writes in his new collection of essays, *Monstrous Possibility: An Invitation to Literary Politics* (Dalkey Archive, $12.50, paper, 118 pages). "It is a literature of monstrous possibility."

But White- -who has written five previous books, including the experimental new novel, *Memories of My Father Watching TV* (Dalkey Archive)—is no Pollyanna. An inexorable radical—someone who would find something to criticize even in his own Utopia—White believes that modern literature and art have rendered themselves largely irrelevant as forces of social betterment and change.

New York and commercial presses, he writes, are now largely subsidiaries of multinational conglomerates that serve their masters by churning out safely diverting books that confirm rather than challenge the way things are.

Likewise, "literary academia is wed to the status quo, [and] has little desire to understand what political power it might claim for itself." The paradox is that as "radical thinking has prospered and deepened" on American campuses, "radical activity has not."

How can we bridge the gap between words and deeds so we can mine fiction's monstrous possibilities?

White, justifiably, has little, make that no, hope that mainstream publishers will miraculously get religion. Instead he focuses on the forces preventing the cultural Left—an umbrella term covering radical/experimental/ alternative thinkers and writers—from becoming agents of healthy subversion. The bottom line: Literature has withered as a political force because it has become overpoliticized.

Through a witty and erudite survey of contemporary thought (his discussions of Jean Baudrillard, Jacques Derrida and Jean-Francois Lyotard render those high priests of the obscure nearly penetrable), he suggests that in its headlong effort to deconstruct, debunk and ultimately defenestrate traditional culture, the Left has thrown the kitty out with the litter.

The root of the problem, he suggests, is the notion that there is no Reality, but only interpretations of reality. Through this mindset, there are no timeless verities; every book, every idea, is simply an assertion of power, usually by the folks in charge. So fluid an environment creates a sticky landscape: "If there is no Real for revolution to return us to, no 'true sex' (to use Michel Foucault's famous example) for a sexual revolution to revive, then what informs resistance to what we have?" We know what we're fleeing, but where are we going?

A result of this thinking has been the rise of identity politics, which has led to the "superimposition of the political on the aesthetic." Thus "art about AIDS or racism or corporate hegemony or patriarchy," White writes, "has a de facto relevance, importance and justification quite apart from whether or not there is any artistic 'value' (let's call it) involved....Whether we acknowledge it or not, we are saying that art is irrelevant."

What is to be done?

Quoting Ezra Pound—"it's easy to go to extremes, hard to stand firm in the middle"—White suggests that even as they pound away at the status quo, writers must recognize that mainstream culture has its merits. "People are not miserable or painful to look upon who: listen to Beethoven's late string quartets; read Henry James; visit the Whitney....This is not a description of a hollow, superficial life....Let the truth be told: the yuppies are right! Balsamic vinegar tastes great."

White's solution, then, is to work both sides of the street. He is a confirmed debunker, rejecting the idea that literature is a "great tradition" of "classic works" by "men of genius," understanding it, instead, as a place where the dominant culture "perniciously administers notions of value and desire." And yet, "literature is also one of the places where administered value has been most purposefully contested."

As we look askance at our world gone awry, what White reminds us is that literature—at its confrontational, unbounded and arty best—remains the most liberating way we have to reckon with and to remake the world. By reinvigorating literature, we can revitalize our sense of possibility.

Writers' Workshop

Talking Points

1) The first paragraph begins with a long sentence followed by the one-word summary: "Ugh." Note the use of long and short sentences in this column.

2) The writer asks the question, "What is to be done?" This phrase refers to the title of a work by Lenin that set forth his political thought. Does the reference to this revolutionary work apply to the ideas in the column?

3) Zane tackles a complicated theme in this column—the purpose of literature. Note how he guides the reader through the treacherous terrain of White's arguments. How does Zane articulate his own views of White's thesis?

4) Note the literary name-dropping in this column: Baudrillard, Derrida, Lyotard, Foucault, Pound. Does this encourage or alienate the reader?

Assignment Desk

1) The writer offers a new twist to several expressions: "Wake up, smell the Starbucks," "a kick in the cortex," "throw the kitty out with the litter." Is there a way to employ such wordplay in your articles?

2) Who are Jean Baudrillard, Jacques Derrida, and Jean-Francois Lyotard? Research their philosophies and see how they bolster the arguments put forth in the column.

Only an empty memory?

SEPTEMBER 27, 1998

The second greatest crime of the 20th century is the way we remember the Holocaust, how we have turned an apotheosis of human degradation into a feel-good cause for optimism.

Every year millions of people visit the Holocaust Memorial Museum in Washington, donning its gift shop buttons that promise "Remember" and "Never Again," while touring the place President Clinton called "an investment in a secure future against whatever insanity lurks ahead."

And yet, as the *New Yorker* staff writer Philip Gourevitch reminds us in his powerful new book, *We Wish to Inform You That Tomorrow We Will Be Killed With Our Families* (FSG, $25, 356 pages), a year after the museum was opened in 1993, the United States and the rest of the world stood by as Rwanda's Hutus perpetrated a genocidal war upon the nation's minority ethnic group, the Tutsis.

The slaughter erupted on April 6, 1994, when the African nation's president, a Hutu, was assassinated— probably, Gourevitch writes, by extremists in his own entourage.

Under the rallying cry, "Do your work," the Hutus murdered 75 percent of Rwanda's Tutsis within a month. "Take the best estimate: eight hundred thousand killed in a hundred days," Gourevitch writes. "That's three hundred thirty-three and a third murders an hour—or five and a half lives terminated every minute. Consider also that most of these killings actually occurred in the first three or four weeks, and add to the death toll the uncounted legions who were maimed but did not die of their wounds, and the systematic and serial rape of Tutsi women."

Most fell from the blows of spiked machetes. But, as a survivor told Gourevitch, "'One hopes not to die cruelly. Not death by machete, one hopes, but with a bullet. If you were willing to pay for it, you could often ask for a bullet.'"

Though Daniel Goldhagen's book, *Hitler's Willing Executioners* (1996) stirred angry debate with his thesis that most Germans were complicit in the Holocaust, there is no dispute that the vast majority of Rwandan Hutus were directly involved in the slaughter. "These dead and their killers had been neighbors, schoolmates, colleagues, sometimes friends, even in-laws.... Neighbors hacked neighbors to death in their homes, and colleagues hacked colleagues to death in their workplaces. Doctors killed their patients, and schoolteachers killed their pupils."

Gourevitch traces the genocide to the racial caste system enforced by Germany and then Belgium when those countries held Rwanda as a colony. They anointed the minority Tutsis—whose features they considered "nobler" and more "aristocratic" than the "bestial" Hutus—as their puppet leaders. When independence came in 1961, the Hutus took control. In this poor and corrupt land, they perversely used violence against the Tutsis—in 1959, '61, '63 and so on through '94—to forge a fragile and fleeting unity that could only be maintained by another round of terror. "Killing Tutsis was a political tradition in postcolonial Rwanda; it brought people together."

Though the causes of genocide are specific to Rwanda's history, the world's reaction, we might hope, would have echoed the universal pledges, "Remember," and "Never Again." Heartbreakingly, Gourevitch reports, the United Nations commander in Rwanda said he could stop the bloodshed with "5,000 well-equipped soldiers and a free hand." Instead, he got the cold shoulder. "The desertion of Rwanda by the UN force," Gourevitch writes, "...can be credited almost single-handedly to the United States," which was wary of UN peacekeeping missions after suffering televised casualties in Somalia.

Meanwhile, the pro-Hutu French forces who were dispatched "supported and preserved the same local political leaders who had presided over the genocide permit[ting] the slaughter of Tutsis to continue for an extra month."

Indignation is the natural—and necessary—reaction to Gourevitch's book; to abandon our revulsion is to abandon hope. And yet, the false comfort our emotion provides should not blind us to the darker truths that

Rwanda (and Cambodia and Bosnia) reveal about how we have actually responded to genocide since the Holocaust.

I can think of no better distillation of this wrenching abyss between our empty resolve and deadly inaction than the two quotes from Holocaust survivor Primo Levi that Gourevitch uses as epigraphs.

In 1958, Levi wrote: "If there is one thing sure in this world, it is certainly this: that it will not happen to us a second time."

But by 1986 Levi had realized: "It happened, therefore it can happen again: this is the core of what we have to say. It can happen, and it can happen everywhere."

What Gourevitch—and Rwanda—show us is that memory only has meaning as a prelude to action.

Writers' Workshop

Talking Points

1) Zane doesn't describe his own reaction to the book until the end of the column. Notice how much of the column is focused on describing the book and its author's opinions and commentary. How does this differ from other columns? How is it similar to the structure of other columns?

2) The genocide in Rwanda was grisly and horrifying. How does Zane treat the details of the slaughter?

3) Absent from this column are some of the short, casual phrases and expressions Zane has used in other columns. How would this column be different if he used a lighter, more conversational tone? How does the subject matter dictate the tone of his columns?

Assignment Desk

1) Analyze your own reaction to the Holocaust, the war in Rwanda, or in Kosovo and write an essay. How does your reaction affect your writing?

2) Compare U.S. reaction to the war in Rwanda with the war in Kosovo. Write an essay explaining your reasons for the difference in response.

Psst, I've got a secret

OCTOBER 4, 1998

Psst. Come here. Closer. I want to tell you something. It's personal and rather embarrassing. Something my dearest friends only suspect. So be warned, it might make you a little uncomfortable.

OK?

You're still reading, aren't you? Of course, you are. Who could resist?

Here it is: I love gossip. Who's doing what to whom. I can't get enough of it. Tell me a really juicy bit and I might tell you I want a bar of soap, but what I'm really hoping is you'll spill some more. Dish, poop and inside scoop are like Lay's potato chips to me.

My revelation may seem a tad tame, obscenely obvious, but nowadays it is deliciously taboo. We are a nation of Geraldo Riveras who want everyone to believe we are Edward R. Murrows. We tell pollsters our top concerns are health care, Social Security and campaign finance reform, but let the networks move from INVESTIGATING THE CRISIS to those more high-minded topics, and we reach for the remote. And, what would the newspapers do without editorial, op-ed and book pages, which allow them to condemn the salacious, invasive material they print in their news sections?

I'm not ashamed to say that I'm part of the crowd that has shot *The Starr Report* onto the bestseller list. And civic virtue had nothing to do with it. I bought it because of...do I really have to tell you: The most intimate secrets of the world's most powerful man, the story Bill Clinton tried to hide from the world for eight months. A favorite scene: Clinton told Lewinsky that "he suspected a foreign embassy (he did not specify which one) was tapping his telephones, and he proposed cover stories. If ever questioned, she should say that the two of them were just friends. If anyone ever asked about their phone sex, she should say that they knew their calls were being monitored all along, and the phone sex was just a put-on."

That *is* a bit much, isn't it? I, mean, he is the president. Had enough? But don't you want to know which famous writer eats frozen peas for breakfast?

That would be J.D. Salinger, of course. If Joyce Maynard is to be believed in her book about the year-long affair she had with the reclusive writer a quarter-century ago, *At Home in the World* (Picador), Salinger also hates doctors, encouraged Maynard's bulimia and recited dialogue verbatim from *The Andy Griffith Show!*

But wait, there's more:

In *Here but Not Here* (Random House), Lillian Ross reveals the secret she and the late *New Yorker* editor William Shawn shared for 40 years: They were lovers. (The fusty Shawn liked rich food, fast cars and was a spirited lover!)

Paul Theroux portrays his mentor, V.S. Naipaul, as a bigoted, disloyal genius in his new work, *Sir Vidia's Shadow: A Friendship Across Five Continents* (Houghton Mifflin). Imagine!!!

Although those tawdry tales have a little extra zip because of the star power involved, plenty of complete strangers are eager to reveal their most intimate details —God bless 'em.

Dani Shapiro tells us how she prostituted herself out to an older man in *Slow Motion* (Random House); Lauren Slater reveals how she had to trade her sex drive for her sanity in *Prozac Diary* (Random House); and Catherine Texier lets her two children and the rest of us see what a creep her adulterous husband was—and how remarkable he was in bed—in her memoir *Breakup: The End of a Love Story* (Doubleday).

Like a Peeping Tom who has moved next door to a nudist colony, I have only one regret: so much revelation, so little time.

Of course, I know that there's no such thing as a free double latte. To invade everyone else's privacy, I have to surrender my own. I must accept that my employers can peruse my e-mail and tap into my voice mail; that bank, mall, workplace (etc.) video cameras surveil my every move; Internet companies track me on the Web; the magazines I love sell my name and address to people and causes I despise; credit companies I've never heard of hold thick dossiers on me; my supermarket records every one of my purchases—what do they make of the fact that I crave diet soda as much as coffee almond ice cream with chocolate syrup?

Slap a bar code on me, and let's just get it over with.

Sometimes I wonder, is it all worth it? The poop on them for the scoop on me?

But then, what can I do about it? And besides, who can resist?

Writers' Workshop

Talking Points

1) Note how Zane lures the reader in with the promise of personal revelation. Yet it takes him four paragraphs to reveal his own secret. What's the effect of delaying through paragraphs two and three? Is it effective? Would it be as effective if those two paragraphs were cut?

2) How much of this column is commentary on American society and readers? Do you think he really loves gossip, or is he mocking readers' love for "dish, poop and inside scoop?"

3) Note the use of all capital letters to reinforce the notion of a high-minded theme of "INVESTIGATING THE CRISIS." What's the purpose? What tone does it set?

Assignment Desk

1) The end of the column discusses the tradeoff for gossip: less privacy for the rest of us. Write a story discussing the erosion of privacy in today's environment.

2) Zane's column suggests that we all love gossip. Does his confession make you feel better about your own love for gossip? Or worse? Write your answers in a brief essay.

3) Zane uses the phrase, "free double latte," a '90s twist on the expression "free cup of coffee." Note how he retains the rhythm and rhyme of the phrase with his twist. Incorporate such wordplay in your own writing.

The wages of sin is fame

NOVEMBER 1, 1998

I confess. At times I've been "a punk," "a jerk" and a tad "arrogant," but I don't think I'm "illiterate"—judge for yourself—and I am decidedly not a "hermaphrodite" (you'll have to trust me on that).

Those are just some of the epithets the shock jock Don Imus hurled at me recently during his morning radio show. For almost an hour he blustered and raged against yours truly in response to my somewhat critical column on his Imus American Book Awards.

The funny thing is that my friends and colleagues— even my own mother, for goodness's sake—viewed this nationally broadcast abuse as a cause for celebration. People slapped my back, shook my hand, rang my line and flooded my e-mail to offer heartfelt congratulations. You see, I had been noticed by someone with real power—STAR POWER—and in modern America it doesn't get any better than that. Whether the neon light bestows insult or praise, it doesn't matter. That's J. Peder Zane. Thanks, I-Man.

But as the day wore on, I wondered: What sent Imus into such a tizzy? What angered him so much that he spoke of pistol-whipping me? Ouch!

On the whole, my column had been affirming. Commending Imus' plan to create America's richest literary prize—which will award $250,000 to four authors this December—I wrote, "At a time when only a handful of authors can make a living off their writing and when midlist authors are going the way of the dodo bird, this infusion of cash is heaven-sent."

What got Imus' goat was this brief description: "Filtering world and personal news through the smeared lens of locker-room humor that relies on racial, ethnic and sexual stereotypes, Imus has earned infamy and fortune. Having made his millions by being puerilely offensive...Imus now wants to purchase himself a little dignity, using his lowbrow perch to become a tastemaker of American letters."

You'd think that little dig would be tame stuff to the I-Man, who makes his living calling people "morons," "scumbags"—and yes, even "hermaphrodites" (not that there's anything wrong with that). But, as I thought about it, a useful distinction began to emerge, the line between honesty and truth. Much of Imus' appeal is that he seems fearless sitting behind his microphone, ensconced in that glass booth in his faraway studio. He's willing to blast everyone from Bill Clinton to delivery men whenever he sees fit. Callow and rude, he is a vent for the grand injustices and petty irritations we all suffer from time to time but are too afraid, too unwilling or too well-adjusted to voice.

In short, he seems to his millions of listeners like an honest man—just as Howard Stern, G. Gordon Liddy and other muck mongers seem to their followers. But passion is not thoughtfulness. Anger is not insight. Name calling is a mode of attack, not explanation. While honesty is the expression of how we feel at any given moment, truth can only be arrived at by exploring those feelings and seeing if they can withstand the scrutiny of reason. Imus is honest, but rarely truthful.

I riled Imus because I wouldn't play his game. I didn't try to denounce, but to explain some aspect of him. If I hadn't hit my mark—hadn't pinpointed the nagging insecurity that he tries to conceal behind his bluster and good works—he wouldn't have reacted so violently.

Since Imus has told me I was on the right track, let's peel another layer of the onion's skin. Like so many people who believe they must compromise their better sides to get ahead, a part of Imus is ashamed about how he makes his living.

Some part of him senses that he is Better Than That. And yet, despite his great success and fat bank book, he doesn't have the courage to walk away from it, to transform a program built on put-downs into something edifying.

At heart, I must admit that I know exactly where he is coming from. As he pilloried me, I wasn't so much offended as thrilled. Hearing my name spewed across the airwaves conjured small fantasies of ambition. Maybe he'll ask me to be on his program. Maybe I should call him. And so on. My distaste had evaporated. I was momentarily willing to sell out even before an offer was made.

The truth is that as American society continues to coarsen and entertainers such as Don Imus exert ever more influence on our cultural life, we will increasingly wrestle with that difficult question: Will we fall prey to the lure of celebrity, or are we better than that?

Writers' Workshop

Talking Points

1) Once again, the column starts with a confession. How does it fit into the theme of the column?

2) This column includes many side comments set off by dashes. Are the comments necessary? Appropriate? Is it clean or confusing writing?

3) Zane offers pop psychology insights into Imus's character. Do you think they hit the mark?

4) Zane mentions "hermaphrodites" with the comment "not that there's anything wrong with that," an allusion to an episode of *Seinfeld* that discusses homosexuality. Is the comment effective without knowing the reference to the TV show?

Assignment Desk

1) Listen to Don Imus's radio show and research him. Then write your own essay analyzing his popularity.

2) Zane uses his commentary on books in his columns as a way of analyzing contemporary culture. Using another medium (television, movies) write your own analysis of today's culture.

A conversation with

J. Peder Zane

ALY COLÓN: Let's start with a basic question that faces anyone who writes commentary on a regular basis. Where do you get your ideas?

J. PEDER ZANE: Let me give you a long answer. When I came down here, I'd never written a column before.

I was writing for a books page, but I couldn't just write criticism. I didn't want it to be just another review, because it *wasn't* a review, it was a column. And I didn't want it to just be, "Here's my opinion on the book," because that's what the critics were doing on the page.

I had a sense that books have become less important to the national discussion. I'd found that when I was a news journalist, I read far fewer books than I would have liked because I had so many newspapers and magazines, and even television programs, to keep up with the topic of the moment.

When I got into this job, which required me to read lots of books all the time, I was reminded of how much books actually have to say about all sorts of fleeting matters that run across the headlines. And that, in fact, books—even novels written 100 years ago—can give us a deeper understanding of Monica Lewinsky, or the Oklahoma City bombing, or whatever it is that we're talking about.

But I think that it's easy to forget that. So what I wanted to do was to write a column that would relate books to the things people are talking about. And to show that it's not just enough to read newspapers and magazines, and that books have a lot to say about what's going on, and that to be an informed person about the things that people are talking about, you need to read.

So my first approach was to relate books to the world outside of books.

The second thing was to emulate Russell Baker. He's one of my heroes and every time I read him I'm completely humbled by his skill. What I understand, of course, is that he writes the way he does and I write the way I do, and I can't copy what he does, or else I'll just be a lesser Russell Baker.

But he has a very distinctive approach to writing columns. It's the humor that he brings to make serious points. What I learned from him was you can't turn to any issue and say, "Well, now I'm going to write funny." You have to begin to have a way of looking at things that then becomes the way that you *do* look at things. So it becomes natural for you to think about things in that way.

I doubt that William Safire, when he looks at an issue, sees the funny side of it. That's not what he does. That's not how his mind works. Russell Baker has, I think, developed his mind in such a way that when he looks at something, he sees the humor in it.

So what I set out to do was to train myself to start making the connection between whatever I'm reading and whatever's going on. That becomes ingrained in me so that it's not something that I have to struggle every week to say, "How do I relate to something else?" That's the way my mind works.

The questions that I have in mind are how can I turn this into a column that will explain other things that I'm thinking about or talking about, or my readers are thinking about and talking about?

What I hear you saying is that you need to know about yourself, and your work, as a model for integrating everything that's around you and the work that you're actually reading and learning from.

What you have to do is say, "I'm going to train myself." My take on books is: "What does this say about things that we're talking about?"

Part of it, too, is just deciding what's of interest to you. What's of interest to me is how books relate to other things, and not how books fit into literary tradition.

How do you write so that you don't sound like you're engaging in sophomoric sophistry?

I read good books. I don't read trash. There's a lot of really good and challenging thinking going on, and those are the books that I want to write about. I don't want to do an injustice to those books by turning them into pabulum, and just sort of having fun with things instead of giving the essence of the ways that they may disturb how we normally think.

That said, when I first started, I tended to be a little too solemn, maybe. [Laughs] And there, again, is sort of where the Russell Baker thing fits in, and why I use him as an example. I just realized that what I was saying was interesting, but it was not engaging the reader at the level that it could.

So what I started to do was to write lighter, fun, and more creative openings. Oftentimes, I would make up a scene, or create something that brought us to the book. It served as a lead into a traditional news story of telling you what it is I'm writing about, but would have a slightly more engaging tone to bring the reader in.

For instance, one of the pieces I think that you have is "If Mother Superior Speaks, Listen."

Yes.

And you know, I wanted to write something about memoirs and about tell-alls, to see problems in this confessional culture that we have. But who wants to read a piece with some guy crying out: "Everybody's spilling their guts. Blah, blah, blah. What's happened to our culture?" Which is what I wanted to say. But I didn't think anybody would want to read that, if that's what I was saying off the bat.

So what I tried to do was to push myself to find a different way. I would say one of the things that I try to do is bring a little ambivalence into the columns. I think too often newspaper columnists are telling you, "This is exactly what I believe." They come down on one side of an issue.

I think you need to take a stand. I think you also have to have a strong voice. But I also think things are very complicated, and it's good to let readers know every once in a while that you have a little ambivalence about things, that you are thinking through things.

That's one of the things I try to do in the column. It is to not just tell people *what* I think, but to tell them *how* I think. Hopefully, as I show them, I prod them to ask themselves what *they* think about it. So the column becomes a process. It's getting people to be part of the process, to ask themselves not just to think about what I said, but what *they* think about what I'm writing about.

Also I try to construct leads that will both do the job that a lead should do, but also draw the reader in, and then through, the piece. By showing them the process I'm going through, of how I start in one place and end up somewhere else, they can see how I've arrived at where I am.

One of my teachers at Columbia, Bruce Porter, told me—and I've actually used this line in my column—that the least interesting thing you have to say is your own opinion. The most interesting thing you have to say is how you *got* that opinion.

I think that is the best piece of advice I ever got on writing, and especially on writing a column.

How do you create a voice that is both your own voice—an authentic voice—and yet is a voice they want to listen to?

When I start a new piece I say, "What am I going to write about?" Often I write about a book. So I'll figure out what I want to say about this book. Oftentimes what I do is read a book and I'll think about it for four or five days, which means that I have to have the discipline to be a week ahead.

How many books do you read in a week?

A book a week. When I read a book, I'm already figuring out what I want to say. So it makes it sort of fun, because I'm deep in the book. I'm constantly talking to myself while reading the book, which can be a little distracting.

Once I have figured out what the one idea is that I want to explore through the book, I think, "What is the one thing I want to say?"

As I'm finishing my column for the previous week, I'm thinking about what I'm going to say in the next one. I sit with that for four or five days, when I go running, or when I go driving in the car. Just thinking about it, things bubble up, so that oftentimes the first one or two takes that I had on it I get rid of.

Then what I do is sit at the computer and just say, "This is a column about blah blah." I think that it's a very good discipline, to say in one sentence whatever it is you're trying to write about, because it means that you're clear. When people can't write, it's because they don't know what they want to say. I have to be able to know what I want to say before I sit down to write.

Then what I do, once I've read the book, and figured out what's the one idea that I want to explore through the column, I figure out how to say it. I start paying attention to the reader and saying, "How can I write this in a way that will be engaging and meaningful to the reader?"

You always have to keep that in your mind. You can't on Monday not care about the reader and on Thursday say, "Now I'm going to start thinking about the reader." That always has to be part of the process, so that you train yourself to think that way.

I have to write from the top. I'll often write five or six leads, seven or eight leads.

You don't proceed to the rest until you've got your top down?

Exactly. I just don't know where it's going to go. And often what happens is, as the paragraphs pile on to one another, it suggests different thoughts to me. I'll start with the lead, inasmuch as I've already figured out what I want to say, I'll often get midway through and realize, "Oh, geez." Because the process of writing is one in which you really figure out what you want to say.

That's where it really counts. It's all well and good to be jogging and thinking about something, pushing your baby in a carriage and thinking about something. But when the words hit the paper, you really start revealing yourself, revealing to yourself what you think. Often, I'll take a completely unexpected turn in a piece.

Is that what happened with "The Wages of Sin is Fame" piece?

Yes. I wrote a piece about the radio shock jock Don Imus. I had written a piece on another topic, and he'd said some nasty things about me on the radio.

It wasn't 'til I got midway through that one that I realized what would really make that a good piece. What I really owed to the piece was to reveal my own sense of being attracted by the fantasy of what he could offer me. Not that he would have. In other words, that was not something that when I set out to write the piece that I said, "This is going to be the ending." It was something I realized that in the direction it was taking, that was the best way I could think of to make a point.

So you might do three, four, five different leads before you really start to get through the piece itself?

The lead presses you to really do bright writing. So I'll often cannibalize. Some of the leads that I've jettisoned, I'll use bits of them in the other pieces, because the lead is often where people think of the clever turn of phrase, or the bright way of saying something, and I'll often take those phrases and little pieces and sprinkle them throughout the piece—when I'm lucky.

You mentioned keeping the reader in mind. For you, who is the reader?

My reader is me. What do I feel is the most interesting and engaging way to tell a story? Pushing myself to write something that's more along the lines of what I want to read.

I think that people who are reading me, who read the books page, are interested in ideas. Another great piece of advice that my old editor, John Landman from *The New York Times,* gave me when I took this job. He said you have to "edit a page that you'd want to read."

That's the same thing with writing. I tell this to my reviewers when I'm working with them. Write what you feel and what you think. Don't worry about what the reader is going to think, because if you start putting other people into your head and writing for people, then you're not letting it flow out of yourself. What you need to do is find a middle ground where the way you write, the way that it makes sense for you and gives the

best force to your expression, is also the way that becomes most engaging to the reader.

In other words, you can't hold back. I care about
ideas, and particular subjects that the guy on the street
maybe isn't talking about every day. I want to say to
this person—because I have them for six minutes on
Sunday—is "Hey, this is why you should care. This is
what's interesting about it."

That's the reason you communicate with people. To
share your joy and your interest, or your sadness, or
whatever, about the subject at hand.

It's a balancing act. But you have to be true to yourself about what you think about things, and what you
want to say about things.

**I want to follow up on that. One of the things that
you hear often is that you need to know your readership. Know what your public is like. Know who is
in your community, so you can write to those issues
they care about.**

**I sense you're not as concerned about the com-
munity that surrounds you, and therefore do not try
to write in a way that either mirrors or communicates with them where they are.**

I think that I have the luxury of being able to spend my
time doing what a lot of people would love to be able to
do, but they have other jobs. I think about things. All the
books come by my desk, and all the newspapers and
magazines. My job is to be informed about the news in a
way that people that are not in the news business aren't.

I then have to make a judgment about what I think is
important, what I think readers will find interesting. I
think that's our job as newspeople. I think it's absurd to
say, "People who don't spend their time thinking about
things and reading up on matters, and becoming sort of
junior experts on certain things, know more about
what's really going on than people who do."

That's where we have the luxury of being able to
figure out what's really important. But part of what's
really important is what the readers are doing and
thinking about. So there's a back and forth there.

My job, I think, is to take all of that material and see
what people are doing, what they're thinking about.

So you were saying your job...

Is to see what our readers, and our non-readers, everybody else, what are they doing? So we don't create. We don't make it up. We determine what's of interest to them by seeing what they're doing. Then by using our news judgment to decide what they ought to be thinking about. What will be most satisfying to them to think about? The harder job is to tell them these things in a way that's interesting to them.

People often say, "Social Security. The public doesn't want to hear about it." Well, geez. Write about it in an interesting way. It's not impossible to write about it in a way that will make people care. That's the job. There are no boring stories. There are only boring writers.

How do you choose the books that become fodder for your commentary?

I think one of the jobs of a newspaper columnist is to get people to confront important issues that they'd rather ignore. I want to put before them things that are not often included in polite conversation.

I think that space that we have is a gift. I don't want to waste it. I want to use it for good reasons, for the reasons that make journalism such a rare and beautiful line of work. It's that opportunity to say, "Hey, let's talk about this."

That's one of the great things I love about interviewing people. You can ask them the most personal questions. I don't mean personal about their personal life, but "Who are you? What do you think about yourself? Why are you doing what you do?" Questions that never come up in normal conversation.

Likewise, the column gives me an opportunity to talk about things that I don't normally discuss around the dinner table.

So, in addition to topics like the Holocaust and race, what are the other issues that interest you?

I write a lot about the dumbing down of American culture. I write about the death of national discourse and of public life.

I mean, today everybody talks about how there's no more privacy. But actually, everything's private. There's no more public. Nothing is public. We bomb other nations. We get bombed. And nobody talks about it. All anybody's interested in is what's the latest revelation about this person's life or that person's life.

Books, and writing a column, are very public acts. They revolve around our public life. What I want to show is why we should still care about our public life.

So while I try to document how everything is being, quote, privatized, I also want to add a positive thing to it by showing people books that are engaging us on a level that we aren't normally engaged on, and how gratifying that is. How much it helps us grow in lots of different ways.

You mentioned earlier that you read good books, not trashy books. Could you elaborate a little more on the distinction between the two?

I guess what I meant by that is that a lot of newspaper coverage today is almost too reader-friendly, in the sense of books that sell well, but are not particularly well-written. These books are getting a lot more ink in newspapers, the John Grishams and Danielle Steeles of the world. Thriller writers and all that are getting a lot of that prime space.

Now, I don't know what it was like 20 years ago, but my memory of these things is that books like that generally weren't given prominent display in newspapers. We, both in the books we review and in the books that I write about, will focus not on popular fiction, but on literary fiction. We'll focus on history, good nonfiction.

I think we're cut off from history because the world seems to have changed so rapidly. I like to focus on history, for instance, to show that what happened 300 years ago has a lot to say about what's going on today. That we should be engaged with the past in order to understand the future, rather than just being absorbed by things of the moment.

So good books, to me, would be those by John Updike and Penelope Fitzgerald, works from small presses, like Dalkey Archive, instead of devoting our space to best-selling books by popular writers that are serviceable. I want to write the most interesting piece I can. That's why I read interesting books, because they give me the most material. I'm already way ahead of the game.

When I'm reading Philip Gourevitch's book, *We Wish To Inform You That Tomorrow We Will Be Killed With Our Families,* a brilliant book about the Rwanda genocide, just by telling you what's in this book I've written a good piece.

That's much harder to do with mind candy. I have no problem with them wanting to read it, but that's not what I want to use our small amount of space for. Even though that's what more people are reading, I don't think that's the job of the newspaper.

In your "Psst, I've Got a Secret" column, you talk about this huge interest we have with people's personal revelations, what's going on in their lives. You cite Joyce Maynard about J.D. Salinger, Lillian Ross on William Shawn, the *Prozac Diary.* Are those examples of books that are good books that give you a sense of how people are revealing themselves? Or is this part of your discussion of how people are exposing their lives?

Some of those books are very good. Paul Theroux's book *(Sir Vidia's Shadow)* is excellent. But what I will often do is write about books we wouldn't send out for review, that on their own are marginal, but that when grouped with like-minded books, can make a powerful point about something that's going on.

One of the things I try to do is to find the trends in books, what subjects that people are writing about, and ask: "Why are they writing about this now, and what does that say about us? And why now?" I mean, any time you ask the question, "Why now?" you often will find something revealing about yourself.

When you write your columns, do you use other people as sounding boards?

I use my wife, my mother. I can't wait 'til my daughters get older. I'll use them. I use my colleagues at work. I have editors here who are extremely helpful.

But I want to be pretty clear in my mind first, and work it through, before I start asking how they feel. You can be influenced in good ways and bad ways. I want to be pretty convinced about what I want to say before I start bouncing the idea off other people, so that they'll have to make a pretty darned convincing argument to show me why that doesn't hold muster.

But I particularly use them just to make sure that once I've written my pieces, that they're clear. I would say, "Here's the piece. What do you think?" And usually after a first draft, I'll get feedback: "Well, I don't know about this," or "This isn't clear."

One of the other things I wanted to say, which I think is important for younger reporters, is just to take every minute you can to keep going back over the piece, and seeing how you can make something clearer.

Are the type of words as important as the ideas you want to convey? I noticed in your columns, you write "...a kick in the cortex." With the Confederate re-enactors, you wrote "cotton" to re-enactors. Is that a conscious thing?

I think you need to press yourself, by saying to yourself, "I'm not going to be satisfied with just regular language."

I'm a newspaper guy. But you need to press yourself to find the most interesting way to say things. I train myself to do that. I ask myself about my word choice.

I write my columns Sunday nights. It takes me about three and a half hours to get 800 words down. Which I've thought about. That's why I'm pretty clear what I want to say.

We close on Thursday at 5 o'clock. I will then go over that piece once or twice a day. Just read it over and be thinking about it. Oftentimes I'll be driving and I'll say, "Oh. That's a good way to say that" or "That's a better way to say something."

If you can come up with two or three things that are interesting, they become memorable. They give the reader an experience they're reading something fresher.

It's my process to push myself to get interesting word choices, to go beyond verbs that are bland, that just sit there. Sometimes I overreach and look a little silly. I'd rather push myself, and every once in a while look a little silly, than to just play it safe.

Does being on the books page play a role in the way that you're able to write?

I think the books page makes a big difference. It allows me to write about lots of different things. My slot is not, "What's going on in Washington," or "local politics." My slot is books. And books are about everything.

If I get an idea for something, I can find a book that will give me the excuse to explore that.

I also think the books page probably pushes me a little bit more. It gives me license to be a little more creative in my leads, or it pushes me to test the language a little more.

Also editing the books page allows me to work with a lot of very accomplished writers. We have a wonderful group of reviewers. They've raised the bar pretty high.

In a sense, it gives you the opportunity to use words that are a little more esoteric than you would normally find in a newspaper, like "inexorable," "feckless," and "cortex"—words not commonly used in journalism pieces

It also allows me to oftentimes not identify something. If I mention a writer, I can just assume that people know who he is. I'll assume they have a certain amount of knowledge, which allows me to write quicker, because I'm not spending a lot of time identifying things. Identifiers tend to slow people down. So I can operate at a different level.

What's been helpful to you in thinking about how you write a column?

I read tons of columns. I'll read as many columnists as I can now to see how they do it. To constantly have before me the form that I'm working in. By reading lots of columns, you think more like a columnist.

What columnists stand out to you in addition to Russell Baker?

I love William Safire, his playfulness with language, the risks he will take with words, the freedom he has.

I like Michael Skube, a book columnist at *The Atlanta Journal-Constitution.* He has the most elegant style of anybody writing in newspapers today. He is serious-minded, literate, and insightful.

Then there's Joseph Mitchell, the great *New Yorker* writer. He has a clarity of style. He, to me, is the height of what journalism is all about. It is about being interesting and engaging, writing about things that matter, and showing you why.

Joseph Mitchell, besides being a brilliant stylist, writes about people and things that you never would have heard of before—and makes them fascinating to you. He's dead now, but he did this book, *Up in the Old Hotel,* which is just fabulous.

When I read him, what I take away from that is that that's our job. To show people things they hadn't seen or thought about before, and make them excited about them, and wonder how they ever got on in their lives without knowing that.

The Washington Post

Colbert I. King

Finalist, Commentary

Colbert I. King is an editorial writer for *The Washington Post* where he writes commentary on national, local, and international topics and a weekly column. Before joining the *Post* in 1990, King was a banking executive, U.S. representative to the World Bank and a deputy assistant secretary of the treasury in the Carter administration, and a U.S. Senate staff member. He has a bachelor's degree from Howard University where he did graduate studies in public administration.

Here King uses the occasion of Father's Day to craft a tribute to Isaiah King. Through the prism of his hard-working and nurturing dad's life, King reflects on current events, from the White House sex scandal to the murder of a black man chained to a pickup truck in Jasper, Texas. By the time you finish the column, it's easy to understand the familiar refrain of the author's mother: "I'm so glad Isaiah King isn't around to see this."

If my father were here

JUNE 20, 1998

Seems as though every week or so something causes my mother to shake her head and sigh, "I'm so glad Isaiah King isn't around to see this." In truth, she and the entire family would give anything to have my father with us, especially tomorrow. That's not going to happen, however, death having a way of being final. But I understand what she's getting at. Knowing my father and his values, there's plenty that would not make sense to him on this Father's Day 1998.

Of course, if Isaiah King occupied his regular place at the dinner table on Sunday, we wouldn't get through the meal without listening to his views on the Southern Baptist Convention's notion of family hierarchy. I can hear him mischievously instructing my mother—from the safety of the other side of the table—to recognize divine truth and "submit graciously" to his benevolent leadership. And I can imagine her ungraciously responding that she'll put a knot upside his head if he even thinks about letting those words pass his lips again.

My dad would have regarded the whole submissiveness thing as a hoot. Oh, he was a strong backer of the traditional family. But docility in a woman never had much standing in my family. A mule had a better chance of whistling than my father had of dominating my mother. Don't get me wrong. Isaiah King was plenty masculine. And he did his share of the bread-winning, working two jobs most of his life. But an authoritarian, calling all the shots while the obedient little wife cared for her three children? Unimaginable! In our family, it was the other way around.

Most evenings and weekends, my father was the family entertainment. He was the nurturer, teaching us about life through his dinner-table tales about the world of work and the comings and goings of the nice and notorious folk in our community. He helped give us our moral foundation. And he was, indeed, the principal provider of funds. But big deeds were the special province of Amelia King.

We all marveled—my father being the chief admirer —at my mother's ability to combine his meager wages with her even smaller earnings to feed five mouths, pay a mortgage, clothe an entire family, give local merchants their due, find a few dollars for hard-up relatives and still manage to give her husband his small weekly allotment to purchase his favorite beverage from nearby Wolf's Liquor Store. Maybe that's why the Biblical story of five loaves and two fishes feeding thousands never really made a strong impression on the King household. My mother performed miracles by the week.

But while my dad might have had us in stitches teasing my mother about the submission of women, there's no telling what he would think about contemporary America. He probably would be especially mystified by news accounts detailing the life and loves of the First Father in the White House. Time was, in my dad's day, lurid stories like those were found in plain brown wrappers sold surreptitiously from under the candy counter.

I also would be at a loss to explain what has happened to his beloved Washington, D.C. The year my father went off to glory—1990—Marion Barry removed himself from the mayor's race, boasting that he could have won if he had decided to run. Eight years later and look: same man, same script. I just wouldn't have the heart to tell my father about the ghastly years in between. He probably wouldn't believe me anyway. ("What in the world is a financial control board?")

Jasper, Tex., also would come to him as a jolt. Not that he never heard of racist brutality. After all, the year Isaiah King fathered me—1939—things were so bad for black people that the NAACP launched a campaign to obtain 1 million signatures on an anti-lynching petition calling for a halt to the very kind of cruelty inflicted in Jasper two weeks ago. Still, chaining a disabled black man to a pickup and dragging him by his ankles until his body was torn to pieces ranks as barbarism at its worst.

My father, however, would not have missed noticing that Jasper—which drew together on a multiracial basis to condemn James Byrd's slaying and put out yellow ribbons signifying unity and justice—also memorialized the ghastly tragedy in separate islands of black and white churches. And Byrd, a resident of the predominately black neighborhood of East Jasper, was laid to rest, according to the *Austin American-Statesman,* in the historically black section of the Jasper city cemetery—all of which my father would have regarded as mighty curious ways for the faithful to ready themselves for the world to come.

If my dad were here tomorrow, we would probably top off Father's Day with a drive through the District to recapture scenes from a past still dear to our hearts. We would motor through the Foggy Bottom neighborhood where he grew up and to the area over in Georgetown surrounding the First Baptist Church his mother attended. We would drive through the West End community where we lived as a family, taking in the blocks around Stevens Elementary School on 21st Street NW and Francis Junior High School at 24th and N streets NW. We would cruise New Hampshire Avenue, motor up and down 18th Street, and travel along the historic U Street corridor exploring cross streets from 15th to Ninth. He knew those sections of town like the back of his hand because he walked them as a boy and man, never owning a car of his own.

And I know—as sure as I am his eldest son—that on the drive home, my father would think about where he had been and the faces he had seen on the sidewalks and on the porches and seated at the restaurant patios. And recalling the Washington of his youth and where he and his wife had raised their three children, he would quietly ask, "Son, what happened to our people?"

My mother often says she's glad Isaiah King is not around to see these things. I know what she means.

The Sacramento Bee

Peter H. King

Finalist, Commentary

Peter H. King is a columnist for *The Sacramento, Fresno,* and *Modesto Bees.* He is a native of Fresno, attended California Polytechnic State University, and has worked as a journalist in California for nearly 25 years. He was a staff writer and copy editor at the San Luis Obispo *Telegram-Tribune,* and held summer internships with the Associated Press and *The Fresno Bee.* From 1977 to 1978, he was a general assignment reporter in the AP's San Francisco bureau and then spent three years reporting for the *San Francisco Examiner.* He joined the *Los Angeles Times* in 1982; during his 15 years at that paper he held a variety of writing and editing positions, including city editor, metro staff writer, and columnist. In 1996, he won the ASNE commentary prize for his "On California" columns.

In "A Roll of the Dice on a Fog-Shrouded Freeway," King tells a vivid survivor's story. By showing what it's like to live through a chain reaction pileup, and why drivers continue to gamble with their lives, he produces a cautionary tale that may save lives the next time fog transforms a freeway into a killing zone.

A roll of the dice on a fog-shrouded freeway

NOVEMBER 25, 1998

FRESNO—He remembers how his little boy, snug in a new yellow sleeper, was dancing in his car seat to rock on the radio. He can't recall the exact song; something by Led Zeppelin, maybe. Ten days later, some details have slipped away. Others most likely will remain in Richard Mead's memory for life. They were headed to Porterville, Mead and 19-month-old Clayton, side-by-side in a flatbed Ford, returning a house trailer that belonged to Mead's father-in-law.

A tule fog was up, but Mead would not consider abandoning the Saturday errand. His wife's father was ill. She and Clayton's twin already were at the hospital. Reaching Porterville seemed of utmost importance. Besides, the 43-year-old Clovis contractor had driven in dense fog many times before.

"I can do this," he told himself, driving on.

At the Kings River, conditions worsened—"like somebody put a pillow over the truck," Mead would recall. He eased off the gas. Other cars zipped by, disappearing into the whiteness. What happened next returns as a series of images: A truck trailer on its side; a pickup veering into Mead's path; the startled look on Clayton's face as the flatbed jerked sideways.

They were at a dead stop now. Mead looked over to his son and there, looming up through the passenger window, was "the biggest orange truck I ever saw, coming right up my tailpipe." Even now, he can see the driver's face, mouth agape, eyes startled. The trucker was staring right at him as the big rig, wheels locked, skidded toward the flatbed:

"We had eye contact. I saw the fear in his face. It looked like he was thinking, 'Oh my God, I am going to kill somebody.'"

* * *

They are a frightful phenomenon of the Central Valley, these wrenching, chain reaction pileups of 50, 70, even 100 vehicles on fog-bound freeways. Like silent movie shots of locomotives crashing head-on, they might seem—from a safe distance—almost darkly comic. However, to be caught in one is another matter altogether. "Surreal" is one way Mead describes it. "Beyond terror" is another.

He and Clayton were near the front of the Nov. 14 pileup of 74 vehicles, a wreck that left two people dead and 51 injured. And now, more than a week later, he sits in a coffee shop booth, patiently trying to re-create the experience. He does this, not to dwell on it, but in the hope—however faint—someone might be moved to stay off the freeway in the next fog siege.

He reaches clenched hands overhead, demonstrating how he gripped the steering wheel as the big rig hit. The front of the flatbed bucked skyward, its tail pinned under the truck. Suspended, Mead could only sit with Clayton and wait for what was to come. There was a screech of tires, followed by a jolt. Then another. He describes the sound of each hit:

"Screech. Bam. Screech. Bam. Screech. Bam."

He counted at least five impacts, each threatening to tumble the flatbed. Then all fell spookily quiet, the fog acting as a baffle. Engine dead, the flatbed's wipers kept up their methodical slapping. The cell phone rang; Mead could not reach it. Clayton made what his father calls a "boo-boo lip," fighting tears. "Get my baby out of this truck now," the father screamed into the whiteness. He figured they could not survive one more hit.

* * *

Hands came through a rear window to snatch the boy. Mead scrambled out, slid down the bed, and huddled with other survivors beside the freeway. They took inventory of cuts and scrapes, watched the orange rig smoke and burn, heard screeches and watched, horrified, as the northbound traffic narrowly escaped a second pileup.

Waiting to be debriefed, Mead wandered amid the wreckage, Clayton in one arm. He saw cars smashed flat; a badly wounded man being carried toward an ambulance; a woman partially covered with a yellow blanket, arms akimbo, eyes shut. He waited for her to breathe. She never did. He began to cry:

"I mean, there she was, all alone. Nobody there to mourn her, nobody crying over her. Just lying there, dead, in the middle of a freeway. Alone. I remember thinking, 'That's how fast it can go.'"

In the aftermath would come the secondary pileups of lawyers, insurance adjusters, investigators. There was a truck to be replaced, nerves to be calmed and lessons sifted. Mead now questions the wisdom of keeping freeways open in the fog. Still, he can understand the instinct to push on through the muck. You see, the night after the wreck, a call came from the hospital: His wife's father was dying. To her, understandably, getting to Porterville seemed of paramount importance. And so she headed down Highway 99 south, into fog just as thick as before. This time there was no pileup...a matter of luck, and only luck.

"That's the insanity of it," says Richard Mead, who knows.

Lessons Learned

BY PETER H. KING

More than 20 years ago, a wise and wise-cracking city editor pointed out to me that, in truth, there is nothing new in newspapers. "Innovation" often is merely a lack of institutional history in disguise. With this column, it would be a stretch to say any new lessons were learned. Rather, it was more a matter of rediscovering some old ones.

For starters, the column ran 10 days after the accident occurred. Stories can have a longer shelf life than conventional daily newsthink would suggest. People can be good storytellers—if given the opportunity. In this case, I spoke for more than two hours with Mr. Mead, the central character, asking few questions. He just sort of told the column for me, even dictating its basic structure.

The best column endings come as a surprise and flow naturally from the preceding paragraphs. As the interview wound down, Mead mentioned how his wife had been forced to drive in the same sort of fog a few nights later. His eyes showed surprise as he admitted this, as though he grasped at once that he had arrived at the largest point of all: Often, we learn nothing from the past.

Finally, the most important lesson re-learned: I got to Mead through the work of two *Fresno Bee* reporters, Matthew G. Kreamer and Lesli A. Maxwell. In the chaotic aftermath of the crash, they had the smarts and gumption to walk the entire wreckage field, carefully charting every car and victim. When I called for help, they had Mead's name and number in their notepads, remembering him as an articulate participant in the pileup. The lesson? The hardest and most important work of newspapers is done, now as always, not by publishers or editors or twice-a-week pundits, but by the reporters in the field.

The Atlanta Constitution

Cynthia Tucker

Finalist, Commentary

Cynthia Tucker is editorial page editor of *The Atlanta Constitution* and a
syndicated columnist. She is a fre-
quent commentator on the *NewsHour* with Jim Lehrer
and *CNN and Company*. Tucker has covered local governments, national politics, crime, and education, and
has reported from Africa and Central America. A graduate of Auburn University, she was a Nieman Fellow at
Harvard University in 1988-1989.

In her commentary, "Black Anti-Gay Prejudice
Adds to AIDS' Toll," Tucker draws a connection between homophobia among black Americans and higher
rates of AIDS in that community. With characteristic
bluntness and withering irony, she blasts the prejudice
of black Christian ministers, noting that "In America,
even blacks are free to be bigots."

Black anti-gay prejudice adds to AIDS' toll

MAY 24, 1998

Remember Reggie White? He is the Green Bay Packers' defensive end who found infamy by delivering a rambling speech full of odious stereotypes to the Wisconsin Legislature in March.

The right Rev. White, an ordained fundamentalist Christian minister, demeaned practically every ethnic group on the planet, including black Americans, whom he said are gifted at worship and celebration. "If you go to a black church, you see people jumping up and down because they really get into it."

Suffice it to say that White has never been to my church. If a worshiper started jumping up and down at First Congregational Church in Atlanta, somebody would dial 911.

After making that sweeping generalization, White then launched a vicious verbal attack on gays and lesbians. "We've allowed the sin of homosexuality to run rampant," White said. It is "one of the biggest sins in the Bible."

It was that attack that brought White into the warm embrace of Gary Bauer's ultraconservative Family Research Council, which recently held a luncheon to honor the football star. And it is that embrace that has compelled me to comment on White.

I tried to ignore him. Not every ignorant utterance by a grown man who is overpaid to play a child's game deserves a response. But those of us in black America who do not cotton to the sort of homophobia in which White trades cannot sit by quietly while he is held up as a hero by the religious right wing.

Homophobia is one of those all-American, color-blind prejudices, as rampant in black America as it is in white America. As far as I can tell, it also exists among Asian-Americans and Latinos. But black America pays a high price for that homophobia, in the advance of AIDS among blacks. Although we make up only 12 percent of the population, 40 percent of the new AIDS cases are among African-Americans.

Intravenous drug use accounts for 36 percent of AIDS cases among black men and 46 percent among black women, but a substantial share of AIDS cases among blacks are the result of unprotected gay sex. Though gay white men have made inroads against the disease through public education campaigns, gay black men have built few support networks, probably because they fear rejection by family and friends.

If 100,000 black lives had been claimed by a Jeffrey Dahmer, so-called black leaders would have taken to the streets. But the toll of AIDS among blacks—100,000 and climbing—has been met by indifference or outright hostility. The loudest black voices to be heard on the subject of homosexuality are homophobes such as White and Atlanta's Amos Moore.

Moore, also a minister (God help us), called together his neighbors in a gentrifying, predominantly black community in east Atlanta to protest the influx of whites, especially white gays and lesbians. Recently, Moore distributed fliers that read: "If you are concerned about the 'white takeover' of Kirkwood, come meet...to discuss how we can put an end to the homosexual and lesbian takeover of our community."

White and Moore, of course, can believe and say whatever they please. In America, even blacks are free to be bigots.

Lessons Learned

BY CYNTHIA TUCKER

In the 15 years or so that I've been writing commentary, I've taken a particular interest in writing about those ugly or destructive or ignoble patterns in black America that deserve scrutiny. Who better than me to discuss such issues as bigotry among blacks or the terrible toll of AIDS in black America?

Because those subjects interest me, I read about them a lot. I clip stories and columns about AIDS. I know the experts on AIDS, whether they're stationed at the Atlanta-based Centers for Disease Control or the National Institutes of Health. I keep up with the bigots, from Khalid Muhammad to Reggie White to an Atlanta preacher named Amos Moore.

So I guess the first lesson would be this: Know the subject well. Be intimately familiar with the topic so the writing seems authoritative. I was comfortable stating well-known facts without getting bogged down in unnecessary attribution. And I was also able to make connections between seemingly disparate trends—the rise of AIDS in black America and the insidious homophobia that enables the virus.

If I relearned any other lesson, it was this: Use a range of emotion to relate to the reader. The topic of AIDS in black America is deadly serious and a little off-putting, so I didn't want to show only anger or frustration. I tried to throw in a little humor, too, as when I related how wrong Reggie White was about the form of worship in my church.

Bailey Thomson
Editorial Writing

You could say that Bailey Thomson won the ASNE award for editorial writing by spending a summer driving his blue pickup truck around the South. On that journey of discovery, Thomson learned how other states and communities were solving serious social and economic problems that continued to plague the state of Alabama.

Thomson grew up in Aliceville, Ala., and graduated from high school there. He holds three degrees from the University of Alabama: a bachelor's and master's degrees in American history and a doctorate in communication theory. He spent 25 years as a newspaperman, beginning at *The Huntsville Times*. Before coming to Mobile, Thomson was chief editorial writer for *The Orlando Sentinel*. He also worked at the *Shreveport Journal* and *The Tuscaloosa News*.

In Mobile, Thomson headed a special team that investigated industrial pollution, work that won a national award. In 1995, he and two colleagues were finalists for the Pulitzer Prize in editorial writing for a series on Alabama's antiquated Constitution. His work has won many other state and regional awards.

Thomson also serves as an associate professor of journalism at the University of Alabama. His academic interests include the history of American reporting, literary journalism, and newspapers as an economic and cultural force. He is the author of *Shreveport: A Photographic Remembrance,* published by LSU Press.

Building upon a foundation of strong reporting, Thomson constructed a seven-part series of editorials, five of which are reprinted here, designed to instruct, outrage, inspire, and challenge his fellow Alabamians.

—Roy Peter Clark

Dixie's broken heart:
The two Alabamas

OCTOBER 11, 1998

Along U.S. 11 in Tuscaloosa County, which parallels Interstate 59, you pass the back door of Alabama's new Mercedes-Benz plant. Rising Oz-like in the distance, its white buildings shimmer through the native pines, suggesting the wizardry and wealth of Alabama's high-tech dreams.

Go east for another mile or so, and you'll see what appears to be a down-at-the-heels trailer park. Families sometimes stop there to inquire about renting. What they find, however, is Vance Elementary School. You can't see the original building from the road because 17 portable classrooms surround it.

Crowding at the school may grow worse. A Los Angeles company plans to develop a real mobile home park nearby that will attract 550 households. The prospect frightens local people—and for good reason. The county has no zoning laws to manage such growth. It can't even levy sufficient taxes and fees to pay for schools, roads and other services that newcomers will need. Still, Principal David Thompson says Vance Elementary will find a way to teach these new kids, even if he has to put them in closets.

Naturally, people who promote Alabama's image would rather have visitors approach Mercedes' front door. Five years ago, the state committed more than $250 million to attract the plant, which caused the company's losing suitors to complain that incentives had gotten out of hand. But since then, Mercedes has exceeded even its own expectations. The plant employs 1,600 people, and recently it underwent a $40 million expansion. Another 1,300 people work in satellite factories that supply the assembly line.

Alabamians can be proud because Mercedes reflects a shining moment when leadership propelled our state to the front of the class. Alabama outbid its rivals, and the gamble is paying off. Equally important, Mercedes has brought something we Alabamians rarely demand of our institutions: excellence.

This success, however, has a short reach. Just outside of the plant's fence, in the community around Vance Elementary, many people can't qualify for those high-paying jobs. They lack skills that the German auto-maker requires. Instead, they drive trucks, clerk in stores, mine coal or find other work they can do.

Along U.S. 11, within a few square miles of Mercedes' gleaming edifice, is a microcosm of Alabama. In one direction, you see the reward for decisive action and vision, as Alabama workers produce some of the world's finest vehicles. In the other direction, you encounter people struggling to get by, with little hope for good jobs. You see a school suffering from neglect and crowding, and a local government unable to manage costly sprawl.

What you see is a story of two Alabamas—one pegged to a promising future, the other trapped in the weary past.

OUR PREDICAMENT

On the eve of this century's final gubernatorial election, Alabamians deserve the full story of the state's condition. We may prefer to think of Alabama as purring ahead like one of those Mercedes marvels our workers build. But too much of our state sputters along like an old pickup truck, held together with baling wire.

The gubernatorial candidates illustrate our predicament:

Fob James, the Republican incumbent, has no plan for Alabama. Worse, he doesn't see the need for one. He prefers to deal in symbols rather than solutions. He wraps himself in the Ten Commandments, vowing to protect them. But when he was asked by a reporter to summarize those biblical rules, he couldn't do it.

Mr. James brags about the frugality of his administration. Yet during his term, Alabama has borrowed nearly $1 billion, sloshing more red ink onto the account books than during any recent four-year period.

When a study showed that Alabama had the nation's lowest—and probably most regressive—taxes, our governor whooped with satisfaction. But is it a bargain to tax giant timber companies only about $1 an acre, while saddling working people with sales taxes of 8 percent or 9 percent, even on their groceries?

Meanwhile, thousands of children start school hopelessly behind because Alabama under Mr. James squanders some of the best learning years by refusing to help more poor families secure good child care. Many more children leave school poorly prepared because Alabama has not embraced serious education reform. Such failures, when compounded over decades, help explain why our state's prisons bulge at 169 percent of capacity.

So much for the Republican hope. What about the Democratic nominee?

True, Lt. Gov. Don Siegelman occasionally talks and acts as if he might become Alabama's first New South leader. He is even willing to copy other successful governors. Unfortunately, he has picked a questionable idea as his centerpiece.

Mr. Siegelman's pitch is to impose a voluntary tax on our most vulnerable citizens through a state lottery, which would pay for college scholarships. Polls tell him that most Alabamians think a lottery is a good idea, although Baptists, among other religious groups, condemn the practice—at least publicly.

Where was Mr. Siegelman, however, during the last four years, when as the powerful president of the state Senate he could have spoken forcefully about Alabama's condition? Why was he not more vociferous in advocating fairer taxes, dramatic school reform and sound growth management?

The answer, of course, is that Mr. Siegelman wasn't about to sacrifice any of his political capital by acting like a statesman. He exemplifies the politician who works hard to win an office but then can't think of much useful to do with it.

IDEAS BECKON

Good ideas are out there. Our politicians just aren't willing yet to seize them, either because they live in the past, as does Mr. James, or they fear the consequences of sounding too bold and visionary, as may be the case with Mr. Siegelman.

These good ideas beckon at a time when the South is "all shook up," according to a new report by a think tank in North Carolina. No longer the nation's problem child, the region is an emerging powerhouse, where one out of three Americans now lives. Immigration from places like Latin America and Asia is changing the face of the South, while expanding industries are closing the wage gap with the rest of the nation.

At the geographic center of this vibrant region lies Alabama, which for a long time has claimed to be the "Heart of Dixie." But our state provides no successful model for this emerging New South. Indeed, this generation of Alabamians has failed even to elect a governor worthy of regional respect.

Rather than the "Heart of Dixie," Alabama represents Dixie's broken heart. Instead of pride and satisfaction, our state flag evokes an overwhelming sadness and regret that we Alabamians have not been the wise stewards of our inheritance. Certainly, we have failed to invest sufficiently in our greatest resource—our people.

Over the next several days, you will read in this space about some of our neighbors' good ideas. This perspective arises from weeks of travel in those states and close observation of their progress. Dozens of interviews and stacks of documents support the conclusion that Alabama has fallen dangerously behind in its thinking, leadership and results.

If our politicians fear to address matters that are critical to our future, then citizens must force the debate themselves. Later in this series, we will look at how Alabama can rejuvenate its civic culture so that democratic deliberation can replace the selfish rule of special interests and the empty posturing of demagogues.

For now, however, our state remains caught between competing versions of itself, a condition so evident along that stretch of U.S. 11 in Tuscaloosa County. Just beyond the trees glimmers the new Alabama that we would like to show the world. It represents our best thinking, our boldest leadership. But around us lies the other Alabama—the one with crumbling schools, unskilled workers, weak local governments and hurting children. It is that Alabama that haunts this election.

We have coaxed our old pickup about as far as it can take us. Bring on the ideas.

Writers' Workshop

Talking Points

1) The writer compares the state of Alabama to a car. Why do you think he chose a car for the comparison? Note how he continues the comparison throughout the editorial. Is it effective or does it lose its punch with too much repetition? Why?

2) Numbers tend to bog down writing. Are they effective in this editorial? Note how they are included.

3) In this opening editorial of the series, the writer explains the premise and theme of the series. Is this necessary? How effectively does he follow through in the other editorials?

Assignment Desk

1) Rewrite this editorial as a news story about conditions in the state and its prospects. Can you keep the symbolism and powerful writing of the editorial?

2) Analyze economic conditions in your own state. As Thomson used a car for comparison, what would you use? Write an editorial based on your research.

Hogs at the door

OCTOBER 12, 1998

Ray and Barbara Stevens had only $76 when they married, but they vowed to own a farm one day. They worked, saved and eventually bought and cleared 250 acres in St. Clair County, where they raise cattle and operate a wrecker service at Ashville. They built a brick home and added a swimming pool.

Then in 1991, the Stevenses' dream collapsed. A neighbor moved about 5,000 hogs next to their property. The family has lived with a nauseating odor ever since. "We can't even raise our windows," says Ray Stevens. "We can't hang clothes on the line." When their granddaughter, who is now 13, visits, she often won't go out and swim because of the stinky air.

St. Clair has four such hog farms now, and dozens more may be on the way as big corporations transform pig parlors into pork factories. Thousands of animals packed tightly together produce the equivalent of a small city's waste. But the stuff doesn't go into a sewage system. It flows into open pits, which belch odoriferous clouds that may drift for miles. Even worse, these waste pits can break under a heavy rain, fouling streams and lakes with pollution.

Such disasters have inspired tougher laws elsewhere. So now more corporate operators are moving quietly into Alabama. Our state doesn't control animal waste unless farms channel it into public waters. Regulators won't restrict a corporate farm just because neighbors such as the Stevenses don't like it.

In St. Clair and other targeted counties, people beg for help. Can't local officials stop this threat? That's why people elected them, isn't it—to protect the health and property of decent, hard-working folks?

Yes, but here's the catch: Alabama's state constitution denies counties the right to govern and tax themselves. Instead of "home rule," Alabamians have despotism from Montgomery, which forces local leaders to ask the Legislature for authority to do virtually anything. That's why 40 percent of legislative business concerns local matters.

As a result, counties can't control nuisances, even when they may threaten citizens' health. Only three counties have even limited zoning power to guide development in rural areas, where about half of Alabama's growth is occurring. There's little to stop a hog farm, a junkyard, a racetrack or some other objectionable business from elbowing into a residential area.

But the absurdity doesn't stop with land use. Consider these typical cases:

▪ Residents in Mobile County's Twin Lakes subdivision watch their yards turn into ponds during heavy rains as runoff from nearby parking lots and other development floods in. But the county can't require adequate drainage for new businesses and homes.

▪ Tuscaloosa County now has its deeds in a computer data base. Title companies, lawyers and others are willing to pay for online access to that information. The revenue could help pay the courthouse bills. But the county clerk can't sell that access because the Legislature hasn't authorized the service.

▪ About 3,000 people are moving to Blount County every year. Development is gobbling up farmland, swamping schools with new students and packing roads with traffic. It's only fair that this growth pay for the services it requires. But Alabama doesn't give county officials the tools they need to raise adequate revenue.

Why does Alabama hamstring its counties when neighboring states consider government closest to the people to be the most effective? One reason is that special interests such as the Alabama Farmers Federation— Alfa for short—lobby hard with generous campaign contributions to keep home rule out of the state's constitution. These special interests resist reasonable rules for land use so they can do as they please—right down to building a hog farm across the road from a home.

These same interests and their legislative toadies make sure local governments can't impose fair taxation. Result? Owners of agricultural and timberland pay the nation's lowest property tax rates.

Alabama is asking for more messy problems unless citizens demand the right to home rule.

SOUTH CAROLINA'S ANSWER

Just such an uprising happened in South Carolina in the early 1970s, when local people changed their state constitution to allow self-government. Before that reform happened, South Carolina's local laws were even more backward, if that's possible, than those of Alabama. In a typical case, the local legislative delegation supervised its county's affairs. These legislators even wrote the local budgets and approved them in the state Capitol.

But in 1973, reformers managed to put the issue of home rule to a vote of the people. This event occurred after a commission worked to overhaul the state's constitution, which was as antiquated as Alabama's present document. Overwhelmingly, citizens said they wanted stronger local government; thus, a more democratic era began.

New voting laws made this transition to home rule even more necessary. Legislative districts began to cross county lines to ensure fair representation. That districting change meant a legislator might not know enough or care enough about a county's affairs to make wise decisions. All the more reason, then, to give local people the right to govern themselves.

Home rule restricts legislators to passing laws that affect the entire state. They can no longer single out a community or county for special action.

Naturally, South Carolina's legislators resisted giving up their local power, and they still find ways to meddle, especially on taxes. But because reformers persisted, county and municipal governments now can manage their communities' growth and provide services their people need.

Indeed, home rule came just in time. South Carolina is the country's 10th fastest-growing state. As in Alabama, most of the growth occurs in urban counties, such as Spartanburg along Interstate 85. There, a traveler passing the giant BMW plant and other industries can feel the economic pulse throbbing.

This rapid growth has created big problems. For example, Spartanburg saw junkyards sprout in outlying neighborhoods, threatening property values and peace of mind. But unlike their Alabama counterparts, Spartanburg's leaders could take action. They passed an ordinance to control these nuisances. They had home rule backing them up.

MISSING LEADERSHIP

But where is the leadership that would champion home rule in Alabama, giving urban counties the authority to manage their growth and address difficult problems? The leadership must begin with a governor and legislators who are willing to risk their political futures by doing what's right for local government, even if that means incurring the wrath of special interests. Alabama's citizens deserve to govern themselves locally just as people elsewhere enjoy that right.

In 1901, the state's constitutional convention was debating whether to hand legislators control over local government. Big landowners and their industrial allies wanted to concentrate power in Montgomery and restrict democracy. John A. Rogers, a delegate from Sumter County, rose to challenge these "Big Mules."

"I would like to know if there are men sitting here in this convention who think that their people have exhausted their senses in sending them here," he said. "Why is it that these people can select such fine representatives to the Legislature and yet it is feared that they won't be able to select satisfactory County Boards...?"

The question rings true nearly a century later as we struggle to correct the error of that convention. Yet the recent example of South Carolina raises hope. If that state's citizens can overcome the lords of privilege and march forward under home rule, then so can Alabama's.

As Ray and Barbara Stevens might warn you from behind their shut windows, our collective failure to act invites the hogs to frolic.

Writers' Workshop

Talking Points

1) Note the alliteration of such phrases as "pig parlors into pork factories." Find other examples and discuss their impact on the reader.

2) "These same interests and their legislative toadies make sure local governments can't impose fair taxation. Result? Owners of agricultural and timberland pay the nation's lowest property tax rates." What is the effect on the pacing of the paragraph with the one-word sentence sandwiched between the longer sentences?

3) "Industries can feel the economic pulse throbbing." Is this phrase effective or overworked?

Assignment Desk

1) How much authority does local government have in your community? Write an editorial about whether that system is effective.

2) This editorial includes a 100-year-old quote that summarizes the problem. Look for ways to include such comprehensive research in your writing.

Suffer the little ones

OCTOBER 13, 1998

Two governors—old South and new.

In Alabama, Gov. Fob James squirmed, dodged and lied to avoid higher tobacco taxes. Result? Lightly taxed companies aren't accountable for the horrific cost their tobacco inflicts on Alabama citizens.

But Florida, under Gov. Lawton Chiles, has forced Big Tobacco to pay restitution. What's more, Florida is investing that money in the next generation, rescuing children not only from smoking but also from poor health, abuse and neglect. The payoff will be healthy, productive workers who'll keep Florida competitive for good jobs.

A similar vision drives a coalition for children in Alabama, whose members include judges, district attorneys, legislators, civic leaders and other concerned people. They want to spend $85 million a year on a group of programs known as Children First. Alabama would secure the money by either assessing or taxing tobacco companies. In turn, this investment would generate another $45 million in federal matching dollars.

Last spring, the coalition sensed victory, but Big Tobacco's hired guns ambushed supporters in the House Rules Committee. The lobbyists' maneuver delayed action long enough for their flunkies to strip away the tobacco tax. The Legislature went on to approve the programs, but it provided no immediate money to pay for them.

Gov. James was in the thick of the dirty work. "He's run the dagger in our back every chance he's gotten," lamented a veteran of this fight.

The governor's disgraceful behavior occurred after he had promised Attorney General Bill Pryor and others that he would support the tobacco tax for Children First.

Mr. Pryor and a bipartisan coalition managed to salvage a promise from the Legislature that the children's programs would receive the first $85 million a year from Alabama's share of any national settlement with tobacco companies. The settlement is no certainty, of course. Big Tobacco recently foiled Congress' attempt to levy more taxes.

Meanwhile, Gov. James was soon talking about diverting any potential settlement share to pay for college scholarships. This treachery came from a man who had the gall to declare 1997 as the "Year of the Child."

With a national tobacco settlement still uncertain, voters can consider what Gov. James' perfidy so far has denied Alabama's children, a fourth of whom live in poverty:

▪ More than 100,000 children won't get health insurance, because their families can't pay for it without state help.

▪ Thousands of children will languish on long waiting lists for subsidized child care.

▪ Growing numbers of juveniles in trouble won't receive adequate treatment and supervision.

The consequences of such inaction will cost many times more than what Children First proposes to spend on prevention. For example, advocates for these programs argue that every dollar spent immunizing children against diseases such as measles saves more than $10 in treatment costs later.

With the failure to pay for Children First, Alabama perpetuated its worst old ways. Big interests, such as tobacco companies, prevail in Montgomery, while the poor and the weak suffer. No wonder that a national comparison ranks Alabama at the bottom in efforts to help children from poor families.

THE FLORIDA CONTEST

Now, let's consider what's happening elsewhere—and what visionary leadership can do for a state.

Gov. Chiles is Florida's best granddaddy.

After retiring from the U.S. Senate, he ran for governor in 1990, vowing to help Florida's mothers and children. He refused to take the special interests' money, limiting campaign contributions to just $100. That independence showed in 1997, when he wrested from the tobacco companies an $11.3 billion settlement for Florida—money the Legislature is now investing in kids.

At the end of his second term, Gov. Chiles looks upon a remarkably better state for its youngest citizens.

Much of the improvement owes to his tenacity as their greatest champion. Contrast some of Florida's legislative action in 1998 with Alabama's shameful surrender to Big Tobacco:

• By combining federal and state dollars, Florida will provide health insurance to an additional 254,000 children.

• The state will hire about 200 new investigators to fight child abuse.

• Another 23,900 kids will get quality child care—a lifesaver for working parents who can't afford to pay the full cost.

Such victories crown this governor's leadership with a lasting legacy, as healthy and educated kids grow up to be successful parents themselves. Indeed, more of them are alive today because Gov. Chiles fought to reduce infant deaths.

Under a program Gov. Chiles sponsored called Healthy Start, women receive nursing care for themselves and their infants, breastfeeding instruction, parenting classes and other help through a network of community agencies. More than a million mothers and infants have received help, and Florida's mortality rate has dropped 16 percent since 1992 to beat the national average.

Like Gov. James in Alabama, Gov. Chiles used his 1997 legislative address to extol children—but the Florida leader's words meant something. He educated his listeners about how the first three years of life can set a child's future, good or bad. This time is critical, he said, because new research shows how fast a newborn's brain develops.

At birth, the brain has about 100 billion neurons. By age 1, that figure explodes to 1,000 trillion. Talking to children, showing them games, even playing classical music to them during these first years can make a difference of 20 IQ points—an astounding implication for the state as it struggles to provide good child care for mothers who are leaving welfare for work.

HOME-GROWN INSIGHT

How ironic that much of the research Gov. Chiles cited was conducted at the University of Alabama in Birmingham, under the guidance of child-development experts Craig and Sharon Ramey. Their acclaimed work over the past 30 years demonstrates how high-quality health care and child care pay extraordinary dividends in stimulating toddlers' brain development. With sufficient intervention, even children who have a high risk of failure can enter school and keep up with their more fortunate peers.

Without extra help, Craig Ramey warns, such children often never catch up, and schools tag them as slow learners. "We can't expect special ed to reverse a lifetime of inadequate experiences. It can't make up for what the children have missed," he says.

Gov. Chiles grasped this great insight from scientific research and saw the potential to break the cycle of poverty and neglect that has bedeviled our region. "Education must start at gestation," he told Florida's legislators.

If only Alabama had such leadership and common sense in its governor's chair. Or if only there were more legislators willing to pull the voting lever for what's right, rather than jerk at the ends of the lobbyists' strings.

Writers' Workshop

Talking Points

1) The writer uses powerful language to describe the effectiveness of the governor: "disgraceful," "perfidy," "gall." Does the reporting support the editorial's tone?

2) In this and other editorials, the writer uses bullets to summarize the reporting. Is this effective? Is there another way to present the information?

3) In the last paragraph, the writer uses opposing verbs with punch: "pull," "jerk." Does it effectively summarize the editorial?

Assignment Desk

1) These editorials include great depth in their reporting. List the sources for this one as an example of the degree of research needed.

2) Rewrite this editorial focusing solely on the problem in Alabama. Is it more effective with the information about Florida or less effective?

A shameful legacy

OCTOBER 16, 1998

*Unless whites vote on June 2, blacks will
control the state...Vote right—vote Wallace.*

— Advertisement, 1970

Our youngest voters don't remember the racial hysteria
behind George Wallace's comeback victory over Gov.
Albert Brewer 28 years ago. They might laugh at how
the Wallace camp's crude doctoring of photographs
depicted Brewer arm-in-arm with Black Muslims
Muhammad Ali and Elijah Muhammad.

After all, that stuff's just history, right?

If only it were behind us, and we could rejoice that
white Alabamians no longer succumbed to the kind of
demagoguery that cost them the only New South governor our state can claim.

But these young people—along with the rest of us—
saw last June that the racial sin of the fathers remains
upon the land. Supporters of Gov. Fob James, desperate to defeat Winton Blount in the Republican primary,
pulled a George Wallace.

Just before the vote, 300,000 fliers blanketed mail-
boxes, in response to Birmingham Mayor Richard
Arrington's endorsement of Blount. The flier showed
Blount between the black faces of Mr. Arrington and
attorney Donald Watkins. Just so you wouldn't miss
the message, the Watkins photo was an old one from
when he sported a fluffy Afro. The message? Mr.
Blount would sell out the state for black votes.

The headline that announced Mr. James' subsequent
victory might have read, "Race Trumps Reason." As
the governor's former adviser, Tom Perdue of Georgia,
lamented afterward, "I didn't know how deep racial an-
imosity ran in Alabama. I also didn't realize the depths
Fob James would sink to keep his job."

Race-baiting persists in Alabama because our leaders have not cultivated an ethical politics. Too often,
they pursue power for its own sake, rousing prejudices

and fears to win, but weakening democracy in the process.

Fault also rests with the voters. They have failed to create a civic culture that values honest discourse and rewards politicians who do the right thing. Within this ethical and civic vacuum, special interests will rush to spend upward of $70 million this year in hopes of influencing the elections. Often, it's impossible to track this money to the source and hold contributors accountable. Alabama's weak campaign laws allow influence peddlers to hide contributions by swapping money back and forth among myriad political action committees, many of them run by hired-gun lobbyists.

Lt. Gov. Don Siegelman, who is Mr. James' Democratic opponent in the November governor's race, is no babe, either, when it comes to exploiting weak campaign laws. The latest report shows his campaign account bulging with more than $3 million, much of it donated by trial lawyers, unions and other friendly interests. No wonder Mr. Siegelman has not distinguished himself as a champion of campaign reform. He's part of the problem.

Must the selfish always rule while the virtuous perish? Or can we infuse our democracy with the energy of an involved electorate?

For inspiration, we need look no farther than Louisiana.

LOUISIANA'S VICTORY

In 1995, the Bayou State's voters demanded—and won—higher ethical standards from their politicians, reversing a dark period of corruption and sleaze. They also elected an activist governor, Mike Foster, who has championed reforms such as better schools. Organizers behind this movement vow there is no returning to the state's bad old days.

Louisiana's problems sound familiar. For example:

▪ Special interests owned the Legislature, throttling reforms such as local-option voting on gambling. At one point, the Senate president handed out checks on the floor from a powerful lobbyist.

▪ Politicians openly accepted public contracts and engaged in other conflicts of interest. Legislators refused to toughen ethics laws, even as the public grew disgusted with the spreading corruption.

252

- Voters lacked confidence that politicians could deliver better schools or reduce crime. Moreover, citizens linked a weak economy to unethical politics. At one point, four in 10 respondents said they would leave the state if they could.

A group called the Council for a Better Louisiana became a catalyst for expressing this discontent. Long active in reform efforts, the council borrowed a strategy that had promoted grassroots democracy in Charlotte, N.C. The Louisiana innovation was to apply this participatory model to the entire state, with the glorious goal of transforming the political culture.

First, the council conducted long interviews with about 1,600 citizens to determine what they wanted and expected from their state government. Then it used this knowledge to create the "People's Agenda" for the 1995 elections.

Many of the citizens' priorities addressed the malaise that had festered under the weak leadership of Louisiana Gov. Edwin Edwards. For example, citizens demanded the right to vote on term limits for officeholders. They wanted to stop part-time politicians from awarding themselves retirement pensions and other benefits. They called for a ban on political contributions from gambling interests.

Before the Council for a Better Louisiana stepped forward, voters had been unable to shape such concerns into a coherent program. Politics had degenerated into impersonal media campaigning, often with nasty results, as politicians bloodied one another with short television commercials after polling for hot-button issues. Missing was deliberation that could focus campaigns on significant problems.

The council provided voters with an alternative that put them in charge. Its volunteers asked candidates to address the People's Agenda, beginning with concerns about corruption. Soon, many of the politicians were campaigning for the agenda's reforms.

Next, volunteers took the agenda's issues directly to the people by distributing more than 100,000 voter guides. With this information in hand, voters could quiz candidates directly or call telephone hot lines to determine where politicians stood. Speakers spread the agenda's gospel down to the smallest hamlets, proclaiming that the state's electorate was in the mood for major changes.

Newspaper editorials trumpeted the cleansing effect of this grassroots movement. *The Times* in Shreveport, for example, declared, "Louisiana could enter the 21st century with new politics predicated on public service rather than personality, power, greed and—inevitably—corruption."

Most remarkable is how so many of the politicians, once elected, worked to complete the People's Agenda. The new Legislature, in contrast to its predecessor, passed a tough ethics law, along with term limits. It also gave citizens a bigger say on gambling. And the reforms continue. This fall, for example, voters will decide whether to put community colleges under a new governing board.

Nowhere is the contrast between old and new more vivid than in the governor's office, where Mike Foster has delivered handsomely on his promise to improve education. Under the often-absent Mr. Edwards, Louisiana had drifted into despair and cynicism. Mr. Foster, with the help of new legislative leaders, has reversed that course and become one of the South's most popular governors.

ALABAMA'S SHAME

Louisiana's civic movement promotes the politics of hope. It seeks to create a new civic culture—one in which citizens can change their system and participate fully in building their communities. By contrast, our politics in Alabama asks little of citizens and expects them to remain passive in face of intolerable practices. Where is the outrage, for example, when:

▪ Gov. James refuses to sign a promise that he will campaign ethically, although many other candidates have embraced the pledge?

▪ Public employees who serve in the Legislature vote for their own pay raises and even for their institutions' budgets (a blatant conflict of interest)?

▪ Legislators award themselves up to $60,000 each to pass out as grants in their districts just before election time, using tax money to woo voters?

Such outrage, if channeled into citizen power, could purge Alabama of such shameful practices. It could even inspire the drafting of a modern state constitution, which could address critical issues that Alabama's politicians prefer to ignore—matters such as fair taxation and efficient government.

Indeed, a convention would allow our generation to atone for the racist sins perpetrated by the state's present constitution, which in 1901 stripped black citizens of their right to vote. Although Congress and the federal courts have since corrected that injustice, racism still stalks our politics, distracting us from our citizenship.

Let us lay down that burden—and be a free people at last.

Writers' Workshop

Talking Points

1) The writer uses questions throughout the editorial. Are they effective? Would declarative sentences have the same effect?

2) In some ways, this editorial attacks voters in the state—and the newspaper's readers. When should editorials use such a tone?

3) The writer says the lieutenant governor is "no babe, either." What does that mean? Is it effective?

Assignment Desk

1) How are race relations in your community? Write an editorial outlining your position and include a plan of action if you think one is needed.

2) Research the political career of George Wallace. Write an editorial about him and your view of his legacy.

Our new century

On the eve of the 20th century, 100 years ago, Alabamians looked confidently upon a dawning New South.

A vanquished people no more, they had trod the road to reunion. Their young men even fought alongside sons of Yankees to free Cubans from Spanish tyranny, while their statesmen in Congress, such as Sen. John Morgan, helped shape what would become the American Century.

Although many Alabamians were poor, they lived in a rich state. In the north, the Tennessee River watered fertile valleys. To the south, a splendid port welcomed commerce. A belt of black soil girded the state's middle, while a mountain range from the east deposited coal, iron ore and limestone—the raw materials for Vulcan's forge.

No matter how tumultuous its past, Alabama seemed poised to fulfill the prophecies of boosters such as Atlanta editor Henry Grady, who saw a New South rising from the Civil War's ashes. And as the South rose, Alabamians expected their state to soar also into this new era of prosperity and enlightenment.

At least that was the dream—a century ago.

In our time, we behold as did our ancestors a rich and promising land, but one that has changed almost beyond recognition. Modern cities have developed, along with universities and industries, so that Alabama's urban places now resemble those of its former conqueror. In the countryside, the farmer is mostly gone, replaced by the long-distance commuter, traveling highways that bind our civilization.

In the haste to exploit this bountiful land, however, we have often left it scarred and cut over. We have been careless with pollution, unwilling to address its damage out of fear that cleaner air and water might cost jobs. More recently, we have failed to manage runaway growth, which sprawls into rural areas with costly abandon.

Likewise, we have not cultivated a responsive democracy. Too often, the majority has forsaken political wisdom for the demagogue's rant. Without vision, our state perishes under the rule of special interests, who buy influence with political contributions.

CITIZEN POWER

But the democratic spirit has a remarkable resilience. It draws its strength not from rank or privilege but from the noble calling of citizenship. Once aroused and properly armed with powerful ideas, citizens form the greatest army the world has seen.

This week, we examined in this space five good ideas from our neighboring states. We sought to learn how these states have improved their civic life. None of them has met with unqualified success, and sometimes reforms require a generation to show results. But in important and inspiring ways, these neighbors have laid a foundation for the next century.

Let us briefly review some of their accomplishments:

▪ South Carolina has pushed democracy down to the grassroots by allowing counties to govern themselves under home rule. Local government now has tools to manage sprawling, costly growth and to protect residents from threats such as corporate hog farms and junkyards.

▪ North Carolina has made good teaching central to reforming its schools. The state encourages and rewards achievement, while intervening to counter failure. The state seeks not only to improve its teachers but also to encourage bright and dedicated people to enter the profession.

▪ Florida has put children at the top of its agenda, investing heavily in preschool programs that encourage later success. As Gov. Lawton Chiles proclaims, education begins at gestation, and his leadership has taught Floridians the common sense of building healthy young bodies and inspiring inquisitive minds.

▪ Mississippi has created a rational and economical system of community colleges, each working in tandem with the others to provide academic and vocational preparation. Through special tax districts, citizens help support their local campuses, contributing to their success rather than merely benefiting from their presence.

- Louisiana has undergone a virtual civic renewal, reversing its plunge into corruption and despair. A citizens' organization inspired voters to create a new public agenda—one that would show the way out of the political wilderness.

These achievements show how motivated citizens can move mountains. When will we in Alabama do the same?

Alabamians often bemoan the fact that our state, virtually alone within the region, has never elected a New South governor. Since North Carolina's Terry Sanford provided the model of such enlightened and pragmatic leadership in the early 1960s, state after state has found governors in the same mold. By contrast, Alabama has mostly elected men who lifted their fingers to test the wind rather than thrusting out their chins to lead.

It's hardly a surprise, then, that many public schools teeter on failure. Children of working families lack decent health care. Colleges resist rational governance. Ugly sprawl devours our countryside. The shameful list goes on. And still we do not learn. Too often, our political choices remain a lesser of two evils, rather than competing visions of greatness. Such is the dilemma with our gubernatorial election next month:

Don Siegelman, the Democrat, presents himself as a moderate alternative. Yet he is strictly an old-school politician who cozies up to special interests that have stuffed his campaign account.

As lieutenant governor, Mr. Siegelman presided over the Alabama Senate for four years. During that time, he blocked or failed to support good ideas that would have moved Alabama forward. The Legislature did not reform the public schools. It did not fix the unfair tax system. It did not close loopholes in campaign finances. It did not wring a settlement or higher taxes from big tobacco companies. It did not rein in runaway civil justice awards. The list goes on.

Yet Fob James, the Republican, is no answer, either. If anything, he might act even zanier once he is re-elected and cannot succeed himself.

Already, Mr. James has attempted to liberate Alabama from compliance with the Bill of Rights, while resurrecting chain gangs, Confederate flags and threats of resistance to federal authority. Is this the direction we want to go—backward? Mr. James would take us there if given an opportunity. These reasons explain why this newspaper chooses not to endorse in the gubernatorial election. Neither Mr. Siegelman nor Mr. James has shown himself to be worthy of high office, although thoughtful voters must choose between them.

AT THE CROSSROADS

We have stumbled to the crossroads of century's end, with too little to show for such a long journey. It is not enough, however, to bemoan lost opportunities. We must raise expectations for public life and hold politicians to a high civic standard. Only then can Alabama's democracy aspire to a politics of hope and accomplishment.

In Alabama, we can lag behind our neighbors, or we can stride forward with good ideas of our own. It is a decision we dare not delay, for things are moving too swiftly in the world for hesitation.

Indeed, bold action in one instance brought our state its finest recent accomplishment: a Mercedes assembly plant of global distinction. Yet we have not shown a similar willingness to raise the rest of Alabama to that level of excellence.

You can see the results along U.S. 11 in Tuscaloosa County, where the gleaming Mercedes plant meets crumbling Vance Elementary School. One image evokes a magic future, and the other a flawed past.

Perhaps some time in the next century, with the help of good ideas and strong leadership, these images will blend into a new Alabama—one worthy of being the Heart of Dixie. But we have miles to go before that happens.

Miles to go, and a broken heart to mend.

Writers' Workshop

Talking Points

1) Note the rich description of the area in the third paragraph. Which words make this paragraph powerful?

2) This editorial is a call to action. Does it inspire and motivate readers?

3) The writer cites a litany of failures with the same phrase: "It did not...." Does repetition make the paragraph stronger or weaker?

Assignment Desk

1) Siegelman was elected governor in the election. Research his effectiveness as governor and write an editorial about his time in office in a tone that matches these editorials.

2) The writer uses the language of the Old Testament in this editorial. For example, he adapts the Bible verse, "Without a vision, the people perish," to "Without vision, our state perishes." List books that have influenced your writing and provide examples.

A conversation with

Bailey Thomson

ROY PETER CLARK: Why is there such a tradition of excellent, powerful editorial writing in the South?

BAILEY THOMSON: Melville once wrote, "To produce a mighty book, you must choose a mighty theme." And here in the South, we've had mighty themes of racial injustice, poverty, popular revolt. So we have a lot of material to work with, and those experiences create a lot of passion in Southern writers.

Sometimes, events have presented themselves in such a way that no reasonable or compassionate writer could turn away. For example, in 1956, Buford Boone was confronted with mobs running wild in the street here in Tuscaloosa over the attempted integration of the university.

And he courageously faced down the mob through his newspaper and appealed to the common decency of his fellow citizens. He didn't ask for that assignment, but when the great moment of truth came, he was ready. I read those editorials today and I still get a sense of awe at how simple and direct and powerful they were.

What other writers have influenced your writing?

Well, if we could continue along the editorial line, one writer I continue to read is William Allen White.

From Emporia, Kansas.

Indeed, a place that otherwise would not have been on anyone's journalistic map. Yet, through his sheer talent and commitment and energy, he turned himself into a national figure. But more important, his writing has a lasting quality to it that one doesn't often see in journalistic writing.

I guess my favorite all-time editorial is one he wrote called "What's the Matter with Kansas?"

What appeals to me in that particular piece is the controlled anger that he had, the passion for reform, the commitment to where he was, and the determination to be heard. But in terms of the voice, the piece has a rhythm to it, a bit of irony, and draws the reader in to deliver the message. One thing in particular I like about it, Roy, is that there's no mistaking that this is one writer speaking to his readers; this is not committee work.

I see. But is it an unsigned editorial, or is it a signed column?

My guess is in his newspaper, everyone knew when he wrote; it didn't matter whether he signed them or not.

And I like that. I think the important thing is that the writer is speaking from his heart and mind, and readers sense that.

In editorial offices, what is the relationship between the individual voice and what we've come to think of as the institutional voice of the newspaper?

I like writers who maintain an independent voice, regardless of what they're writing. They may be writing the institution's point of view, but they are still writing as one journalist to the audience. They're not trying to say, "Here I am, a group of six people. Listen to us."

A lot of editorial writing not only speaks for the institution, but it has that institutional feel about it. I don't find it to be appealing, and I think a lot of readers are turned off by that sort of all-knowing, corporate-type voice.

Now can you describe for me, Bailey, the voice that you were striving for in "Dixie's Broken Heart"?

I want to give a little background. I knew the positions of the newspaper on these vital state issues. I not only knew them, I helped shape them when I was editorial page editor of the *Register,* so I didn't need to have an editorial board telling me how to write these pieces. I have worked with some of these people for many years, and we were very comfortable with where we stood on the issues.

So when I went out to do my reporting and then my writing, I approached it as I would approach any writing project. And when I sat down to write the pieces, I wrote them as if my own name were going to appear over them in a byline, because they were essentially my pieces.

Now what I tried to do was to speak with the authority that comes from having immersed myself in these issues for a summer. And I think when you have done as much reporting as I did, your voice has more confidence. I believe it was Hemingway who said, "I always try to write on the principle of the iceberg. There is seven-eighths of it under water for every part that shows." And the great advantage that the newspaper gave me was to put me on the road and let me answer the many questions I had and then to allow me to write these pieces in my own style, in my own voice.

It's a voice of a native son who has lived through a lot of change in Alabama over the last 50 years, and a voice of frustration that we have not done more with the resources and gifts we have. And like many people of my generation, I speak with a voice of considerable anger that we continue to miss opportunities. But in all of this writing, I tried to remember who I am and to speak to readers as if I might be sitting across from them, having a conversation or a dialogue with them.

What would you be drinking?

Well, it depends on the time of the day. If it's in the morning, I would be drinking a lot of strong coffee. We don't go in too much for hot tea down here, but if it was at noon, we might have a glass of iced tea.

Sweetened, of course, no?

Well, with lemon. There's a certain art to getting that just right and you don't want somebody, once you've got it right, to be refilling your glass and messing it up. But as the clock went on toward 5 o'clock and the whistle blew, then we might switch to something that has a little more of a lubricating effect.

OK, fair enough and well said. Let's shift down from voice to the reporting. Tell me the story of your

pickup truck's journey. Where did you go, how did you work, to what ends, and what was of particular value to you?

First, I work on an eight-and-a-half-month contract, as do other professors here at the university, and therefore, I am free for the entire summer to work where I please. And for the last two summers—in fact the two summers since I have been in the academic world—I've gone back to my old newspaper, the *Mobile Register,* and worked full time for the paper, been on the payroll.

The first summer, Stan Tiner, my editor at Mobile, had me do an investigative series that took me to Nicaragua, and I spent a good part of the summer down there and produced an investigative report. We won some recognition for that. The second summer, though, I made the proposal for this series to Stan. Along about April or May, I was listening to the debates of the Republican primary—there really wasn't much of a Democratic gubernatorial primary—and I became so disgusted with the level of the rhetoric and particularly with the ad hominem attacks that the candidates were launching. And I remember driving home one night thinking how little had changed and how we seemed to be absolutely stuck in time. I was really quite depressed over it, because I had come back to Alabama in 1992 and decided this is where I wanted to spend the rest of my life.

So I talked to Stan and I said, "Here's how I would like to spend my time working for you this summer. I think that other Southern states have moved ahead of us. And in fact, I know they have in certain key areas that interest us. What if I go and spend a lot of time doing on-the-ground reporting, talking to as many people as I can, and, more important, seeing for myself the results of their progress, their reforms? Then I want to come back to Alabama and compare our experience with that of our neighbors."

Stan Tiner is one of the great editors in this country, and my proposal really appealed to him because he knew at heart that I'm a reporter, as he is, and he sensed that we weren't going to get the story any other way of where Alabama stood vis-a-vis its neighbors than to get outside of Alabama. In fact, one of the things that Stan and I agreed upon is that we are too insular in Alabama, we are too resistant to outside ideas.

So Stan, being the kind of editor he is, said, "Let's do it." I also had the support of the publisher, Howard Bronson, who is very committed to substantial reform in Alabama, and the editorial page editor, Frances Coleman, who had been the deputy when I was serving in that chair.

So with the support of those three people, I began mapping out a summer's work for the *Register*. And I went on the newspaper's payroll as soon as school ended here in May and hit the road soon afterwards. I had time to do a lot of telephone calls in advance and line up my interviews and to also amass a large stack of reports and newspaper clippings and other secondary material. So that by the time I cranked up the GMC pickup around the first week in June, I had a lot of background material already in my computer. What I needed to do was see the lay of the land firsthand.

What color is your pickup?

It is a 1993 deep blue pickup. And I got a great break. I found a camper shell for it, used, for $500, slapped that on, and I was able to carry a lot more equipment and an ice chest and that sort of thing, so I could stay on the road for long periods of time.

And I thought about taking my border collie with me. John Steinbeck is one of the writers I greatly admire, and occasionally I reread his book *Travels With Charley*. As you know, Roy, he had a poodle with him named Charley, a very well-behaved poodle. And I thought about taking my border collie, but she's a little too demanding. I'm afraid while I would be doing interviews, she would be bringing a tennis ball and saying, "Just one more time, please."

What's her name?

Lyn. With some reluctance, I left Lyn at home, and I also left my wife and daughter to keep the home fires burning; so I set out on a solitary journey.

Did you do it all at once?

No, I drove on my first trip through Georgia and did some stopping off there and reporting. And then I went on to South Carolina and to Charleston and then to the middle part of the state and then on up to the Spartanburg area. And then from there, I drove over to Raleigh and spent a good bit of time in the capital.

And I will digress for just a minute. The only scary time I had on the whole trip was that I had an opportunity to hitch a ride on an airplane, a small airplane, to fly from Raleigh to Charlotte to hear Secretary of Education Dick Riley, who was doing a town meeting on education. And by this time, I had met the chairman of the state board of education in North Carolina and was familiar with a lot of the players in education in that state.

And so they invited me to join them, the chairman did, and we got in this small, well, this two-engine plane and took off in the middle of a storm. And the storm got worse and worse and I suddenly noticed that this normally loquacious school leader had quit talking and everyone had turned ashen. I realized at that point that I may be paying too big a price for this story. And also on board was the head of the North Carolina community college system. So I could just see the headlines: "Leading School Officials Die in Crash, Unknown Reporter Aboard, as Well."

But we managed to make it over there and had a great session with Dick Riley, and of course, I met a lot more people from around the state involved in education. So just by being there, sort of showing up in North Carolina, I got to see a lot of action. I had tremendous cooperation in all of the states where I went. People seemed eager to share their successes and their failures, too, with me.

I wonder if that's sort of an underutilized reporting tool, that is a sort of venturing out from the home front to find out how other communities handle analogous problems.

Well, what I try to do is an old-fashioned technique called immersion reporting. And I've set aside lots of

time and I never try to get in a hurry. I always leave myself open for the unexpected moments, such as that plane
ride. And I try to be completely transparent in my motives. I tell people I'm coming there because I've heard
about some aspect of their state and I want to see it for
myself, that I don't have any preconceived ideas and I
don't really have any agenda, other than to see it for myself. And I try to talk to all sides; I particularly try to talk
to people at the midlevel and below, because I find these
are folks that too often we don't talk to enough.

For example, I wanted to see how a school was op-
erating after it had been taken over by the state in North
Carolina. So I just went to the school and met with the
team that had gone in there, but I also met with some of
the teachers who had been there and I interviewed the
principal. So I got a lot of different perspectives. But
that took an entire day, not counting the travel time.

I don't know how you can get that kind of perspective over the telephone, and particularly long distance.
It just doesn't work very well.

**Implicit in what you just said is maybe a critique of
editorials that are written from the desk rather
than from the road.**

Well, I would make it a little broader, Roy. I think too
much journalism today is being done over the telephone. In fact, I heard a wonderful expression, 1-800-
journalism, that we as journalists are getting too
accustomed to calling 800 numbers and getting the req-
uisite expert on the phone and being satisfied with that.
And of course, it's a very cheap way to do journalism,
not only in terms of travel time and money, but in terms
of reporters' time. So I would say that a lot of journalism is being inhibited by the fact that newspapers are
not investing enough in getting their reporters not only
out of the office, but out of the city and out of the state.

I think traditionally, editorials have not been written
in this fashion, that they have been pretty much
deskbound type activities. One reason is the sheer volume of editorials that many papers expect of their writers. If I had one reform that I could institute, it would
be to cut down the number of editorials we write and
increase the quality.

The other thing that I think is interesting in your reporting strategy and your writing strategy is that you've not only identified a set of problems that the state is confronting, but because you've ventured out, you've been able to offer a set of potential solutions.

One of my main objectives in writing this series was to show Alabamians that we can do it. I encounter a lot of cynicism about Alabama and about our seeming refusal to address long-standing and serious problems. I attribute a lot of this to the failure of leadership over a long period in our state's history, but particularly during the Wallace period and its aftermath.

So what I wanted to do most of all was to show Alabamians good, solid examples of where leadership made a difference in other states. Now, one, I never made the claim that the other states had achieved perfection. They haven't; they're still working on their problems. And number two, I never said that we could do it just exactly the way the other states have done it. Rather, we had to find our own way to solving these problems.

But what I wanted to show was that states with very similar histories, very similar sets of problems, had approached them differently from the way we had approached them in Alabama—or refused to approach them—and they had had positive results. So in doing this, I wanted to show Alabamians that, A) leadership can make a big difference, and B) that nothing is permanent in our political and civic life, that we can effect change and that we can escape the legacy of past failures. Those were the main objectives behind this series.

I want to talk about some of the strategic issues in the writing, Bailey. And that is that the way in which you move back and forth from specific examples and cases to larger issues and problems of policy and politics. Can you talk about that a little bit? In other words, we begin at the Mercedes-Benz plant, then we go to Vance Elementary School.

Well, my overall strategy was to rely on the oldest principle of writing that I know about, and that is you *show* and don't *tell.* I wanted to take my readers as if by the arm and to show them the situation in Alabama and to create strong images and, through those images, to communicate the passion and the importance of these issues for them, not just for other people.

Give me a couple of examples of what you mean by images. What would be an example of one?

Yes. Well, if you wanted to look at the very first piece, you see Mercedes-Benz, which I've described as emerging Oz-like from the interstate. That new plant is—to many Alabamians—the kind of future that they would like to have, that is to say good paying jobs, high skills, producing products of worldwide appreciation, of excellence. The M Class vehicle, for example, has been voted recently as the finest utility vehicle. It's known for its superb workmanship, high quality, performance. So that plant represents a lot more than bricks and mortar; it represents the kind of future within the global economy that many Alabamians hunger for. So I wanted to make maximum use of that.

But almost within the shadow of this plant is another image arising from a little elementary school that has 17 portables, that is in fact so overrun with portables that many people coming to Vance looking for work mistake it for a trailer park. And its ramshackle nature I compared to an old pickup truck. Let me back up and say that school, in many ways, reflects the other side of Alabama, which is where we've not invested enough in our people, we've not had enough respect for education, and the result is that that part of Alabama looks like an old pickup truck.

So you've got a different image there, one of a struggling school trying to do the best it can, but on insufficient resources, manifested by the very appearance of the school itself.

I guess I want to challenge, respectfully, the notion that what you're doing, Bailey, is showing and not telling. Because it seems to me it's more like, to use the old kindergarten phrase, that you're doing some showing, you're doing some telling.

Well, in that piece, I think you're right, you've got a combination. Maybe a better example of where I tried to take readers and show them something would be in the second piece where I wanted to show readers why the failure to give local government sufficient power in Alabama could directly affect their lives. And I had been to South Carolina and seen that state struggle to give local governments more power and they had had some good results.

But I came home and I thought, "This is a huge issue, but how am I going to interest people in local government?" And the thought occurred to me, "What I need to do is to show them what can happen when local governments don't have the power to pass zoning legislation." So I went to a county north of Birmingham where several large hog farms had moved into areas that essentially are becoming bedroom-type communities. And I attended a heated meeting where local townspeople were trying to organize to sue these large corporate hog farmers. Then I went and talked to several of the families individually and sat in their living rooms. And out of that emerged a vignette in which I tried to use what I would call a half scene, sort of a small scene of a family that had poured its life savings and work into this home and small farm, only to see it become a nightmare when a big hog farm moved next door.

Through that sort of writing, I hope to trigger a response in the reader to say, "Hey, that could happen to me."

Is it fair to call this a series?

Absolutely. It was conceived and written as a series. It began on a Sunday and ran through Saturday and then was reprinted under the title, "Dixie's Broken Heart."

Tell me what it takes to—you've hit what it takes to *report* such a piece, but when you come back from your journeys and you've got your stacks of papers and reports, if I had a video of you organizing your materials, what would I see?

One of the things I've learned after a long time in this business is the absolute importance of good note taking. I do that several ways. First, I write everything down and then I retype all of my notes and store them in a database called "AskSam." It's a wonderful database for writers.

So every day when I would finish my note taking and my interviewing and whatever I was doing, I would immediately sit down and retype all of my notes. Then I would put them into this database where I could sort them. So for me, it's crucially important that the reporting produce notes that can be read three or four months from now or even three or four years from now with good results.

I also keep a daily journal—have done that for a long time—and I would put many of my impressions about my trip into my journal.

And so I was doing a lot of writing every night, every day that I was working on the project, of simply getting the notes right. And then I would try to answer any questions I had then and not wait until later.

So you were writing early and often, rather than waiting until some point in the future.

Yes, I was committing everything I found to long notes, with the result being that while I published probably 10,000 or 12,000 words, my notes must be in the 30- to 40,000 word range. So that was the reporting side I did first. And I make a big distinction between reporting and writing because they are distinctive activities and each needs its own space and time.

Then it was only after I had satisfied myself that I had done all of the reporting that I began to actually sit down and map out the seven editorials.

Did you map them out?

Well, the first thing I did was I went back and reworked all of my notes and then when I felt I had them in good order, I printed them all out. And then I took all the notes and put them in a big, oversized black binder and organized them by the topic. I then began reading and thinking about the subject using all of this background.

And here's where I had miscalculated a little bit. I thought I could write these pieces more quickly than I did. I thought once I had all the reporting, that the writing would flow pretty quickly. But I think something we writers have to always remember is that we have to give ourselves plenty of time for all of this material to soak in and to get the thinking right.

So I began to chart out how I wanted to do the series and particularly the kinds of vignettes, half scenes, anecdotes that I wanted to use to tell the story.

And then after I had in my mind where I wanted to begin with the series and where I wanted to end, I began to come back and write the editorials one at a time.

So before you began to write one at a time, you had a sense of the global structure of the series.

Right, and that took longer to develop than I had originally thought. But fortunately, we wanted to get the series in before the election.

Now tell me, Bailey, what do you think was the impact of these editorials?

The newspaper gave these editorials a wonderful display. Each editorial took half a page, which included an illustration, and so for seven days, readers saw a very different editorial page. The editorial appeared across the entire top half. So right away, the paper signaled it had something important to say here.

In the traditional format, we got letters and telephone calls from people who read them and appreciated the fact we were devoting this much space to these important issues.

But I learned something anew about public opinion, and that is one series will seldom have a dramatic effect. It contributes to a long-standing effort of a newspaper to stand for what's right and what's good. When you make a big commitment to a series like this, I think it builds up your credibility. And the second thing I learned is that if you do good work, you need to reprint it, you need to pull it all together in one format and then redistribute it. There are two ways we did that. First, we did the traditional reprinting of the editorials in a handsome booklet and distributed several thousand copies to anyone who wanted them first and then particularly to leadership groups in the state.

Alabama has a lot of leadership classes at the state level and at the city level, and several of these have now used my series as primers for reform. And I've spoken to these groups, as I continue to speak around the state, on these issues. Another audience was business and civic leaders who belong to an organization called the Public Affairs Research Council of Alabama. I think their mailing list is around 2,500 and PARCA sent a copy to each of its members.

So wherever I go now to speak to groups, people say publicly they've read my series, they want to recommend it to other people. We still get calls for lots of the reprints. So I'm really sold on recollecting your material and making it accessible to people long after the editorial series has run.

Now the second way we can do this today is through web pages. This has opened up a whole new dimension of giving material a long life.

I'm again impressed by the necessity of always doing your best work, always continuing to advocate forcefully what you believe, and then being patient and understanding that no series is likely to change things overnight. It's simply going to contribute to a long-standing effort.

Do you consider yourself a fast writer or a slow writer?

I'm a slow writer, but I'm trying to write more in bursts of quick creativity. I'm having to discipline myself to stay on the creative track long enough to get that first draft down. I fight the impulse all the time to let the critical side of my brain intervene, take over, and gum up the works.

Do you consider yourself a confident or an anxious writer?

I'm a confident writer when I have invested enough time in my reporting and research. When I have done all that I can do to understand the subject and to interview all the people I need to talk to, then I'm a pretty confident writer. And one thing I try to do is never rush a piece before I have that confidence in all the facts.

Do you write the lead first?

Well, sometimes I go ahead with a lead I'm not happy with simply to get my thousand words a day that I try to get. But it all flows much better if the lead can crystallize into what I'm trying to say or show what I'm trying to say. So I spend a lot of time thinking about my lead and thinking about how I want to start a piece. Sometimes I have to come back and redo it, but I do find, particularly with newspaper writing, that the lead is indicative of how the piece is going to turn out. So I put a lot of time on it.

You sound from the allusions you've made in our interview that you're well read, that you've got a connection to literature. So tell me about your reading life and its relationship to your writing life.

Well, like a lot of journalists of my generation, I've been a voracious reader for all of my life and I've read across many genres. In the early part of my education, I read more history because I was a—I took—my first two degrees were in American history and from the time I was in my teens, I was fascinated with Southern history. And so as I look around my shelves at home, many of the volumes are on that subject, in particular books by C. Van Woodward and George Tindall.

But I was also heavily influenced when I was young by what I called scholarly journalists and a good example is W.J. Cash. I first read his book when I was a freshman here at Alabama. I was simply astounded that anyone could seemingly get it all right.

The Mind of the South?

Yes. And that book, probably more than any other, helped launch me as a journalist because I understood through reading Jack Cash that one could draw on all the scholarship and also one's own experiences, and present something that's compelling to a general audience. Cash and his generation of Southern writers were among my early models.

I read some more impressionable work, too, such as James Agee's *Let Us Now Praise Famous Men,* which described a sharecropper family not very far from where I grew up. And growing up in the '60s, I saw a lot of the older traditions of the South firsthand. I became absolutely enamored of all things Southern. When my reading would turn to literature, even then, I often sought out Southern writers. I read Robert Penn Warren's *All The King's Men* with great fascination. The narrator, Jack Burden, was a newspaperman who had studied history but gave it up because he found it too awful. I began to envision myself as being like these great writers or great characters. I mentioned earlier that I like Steinbeck and I was so influenced by a lot of his realistic work, such as *The Grapes of Wrath.*

And then as I was coming along, there was a lot of good journalism going on in the South, and I would read accounts of the civil rights struggle and all of that showed me how journalism could be so immediate and it could cover such universal subjects by covering the particular. So I was shaped both by the scholarly works I read as a pretty serious student and graduate student and also the journalism.

In the last few years, I have come to do much more reading in nonfiction and, in fact, have come to teach literary journalism. And so I have been most impressed with how writers have adopted long-standing literary traditions and techniques and applied them to writing about real life—for example the use of scenes and dialogue and the extensive use of metaphor and image and the building of detail upon detail, as John McPhee does in his wonderful works. I've soaked up a lot of those techniques.

I guess the only thing I've done differently with this series is that I've tried to first push the reporting as far as I could push it, and also to apply some of the best writing techniques I know to a form that can be pretty stuffy.

Paul Greenberg

Finalist, Editorial Writing

Paul Greenberg is the editorial page editor of the *Arkansas Democrat Gazette,* which he joined in 1992 after presiding over the editorial page of the *Pine Bluff Commercial* for three decades. In 1981, he was one of the first winners of the ASNE editorial writing award and was a category finalist in 1996. Among his many other honors, he was awarded the Pulitzer Prize for editorial writing in 1969. He is the author of three books, and since 1971, his column has been distributed by the Los Angeles Times Syndicate. He has a bachelor's degree in journalism and a master's degree in history from the University of Missouri.

When Greenberg takes somebody on, as he does President Bill Clinton in a column on *The Starr Report,* the dissection by this veteran commentator is surgical, precise, and anything but bloodless. It leaves a reader grateful that someone else is the object of Greenberg's withering scorn and pitiless analysis.

On first reading: *The Starr Report* and its discontents

SEPTEMBER 16, 1998

Here are some first reactions on reading *The Starr Report*—yes, the who-o-le thing plus both rebuttals from the Clinton camp, before and after. We've got to tell somebody, just to get a few things off our mind, and chest, and stomach:

▪ There is scarcely a noble or elevating thought expressed in this whole, dreary encyclopedia of mendacity. Except by the occasional innocent victim—a Secret Service agent or somebody like Betty Currie, the president's secretary and foil.

▪ It's not that our president and suspect-in-chief fails to express human sympathy, understanding, compassion, forgiveness....On the contrary, he is a vast reservoir of those qualities, but he seems to reserve them all for himself.

▪ For any Southerner, even one not familiar with Faulkner or Flannery O'Connor or Richard Wright or Robert Penn Warren, the indelible stain in Bill Clinton's testimony is his treatment of Betty Currie. In the official proceedings, she's the president's secretary and an employee of the United States government. If this were a novel, she would be the faithful black servant whom the white boy misleads, involves in his mischief, and who winds up paying the cost. It's an old, old story.

It's one thing for the president to have lied to the Sidney Blumenthals around him and then send them out to lie for him; those hacks signed up for this kind of treatment. It's another for Bill Clinton to take a faithful servant and an honest, God-fearing woman aside and plant his own version of events in her mind, and then sit back while she testifies under oath. Suppose she had repeated those false recollections as her own sworn testimony? She would not only have jeopardized herself at law, but risked her immortal soul.

If there were still a South, any man who did such a thing to a lady would be shunned by decent people till he could recognize the enormity of it—and make full amends. Just think of Betty Currie's legal fees by now, let alone the stress, the anxiety, the testifying, the tug of loyalties, the mob scenes she's been put through. And yet Arkansas' own David Pryor isn't organizing a Betty Currie Defense Fund, is he? His heart goes out to Bill Clinton.

▪ What possible defense could there be for such behavior? The president's legal team explains that he spoke to Betty Currie privately only "to test his recall." Why? He knew what had happened between him and Mme. Lewinsky; Mrs. Currie could only have had her suspicions. Did he call her aside to test *his* recall, or to shape *hers?*

▪ Monica Lewinsky comes across in this report and entire library of drear not only as a child but as a spoiled, greedy, calculating, threatening child. To call her a child is to give children a bad name.

▪ *The Starr Report* is necessarily salacious (meaning pornographic) but not in the least titillating (meaning erotic). It's got about as much romance as one of those Army sex manuals. When it comes to quenching sexual desire, reading *The Starr Report* is more effective than taking a cold shower.

▪ The report had to go into anatomical detail. There was no other way to counter what might be called the Embarrassment Strategy. It's worked in the past. For whenever Bill Clinton wanted to deny an affair, a dalliance, a sexual episode, he would do so in general terms for political purposes, trusting that ladies and gentlemen would inquire no further. It would be too embarrassing. But it turns out that Kenneth Starr and his legal team are not paid to be ladies and gentlemen but to investigate. They did.

▪ The president's testimony quoted in this report—first in the Paula Jones case and then, God save him and stop him, before the grand jury investigating him—may represent the latest apotheosis of the clinton clause. It's no longer a little escape hatch in every sentence. It has become an entire language of its own. It is a language in which answering questions "accurately and fully" means not answering them accurately and fully; sexual relations are not sexual relations; and a woman can have sexual relations with this president while he is not having sexual relations with her. It's a whole, Clintonian newspeak in which good's bad today and black's white today and day's night today and anything goes. Lewis Carroll would understand, or at least his Humpty Dumpty would:

> "When *I* use a word," Humpty Dumpty said, in rather a scornful tone, "it means just what I choose it to mean—neither more nor less."
> "The question is," said Alice, "whether you *can* make words mean so many different things."
> "The question is," said Humpty Dumpty, "which is to be master—that's all."

And hasn't Bill Clinton always been a master of words? He can use the same phrase to mean one thing legally and another politically till it comes to mean nothing at all.

Now an even greater spectacle than the birth of an indecipherable language awaits. The American people are about to see sober and respectable citizens, some of them not even lawyers, defend or at least condone the practice of perjury, at least if it in any way involves a sexual relationship. (Or, in Clintonspeak, a non-sexual relationship.)

Call it the Clinton Defense, or maybe the Clinton Exclusion, which is what it will be called if the president beats this rap. For what happens to Bill Clinton will affect more than Bill Clinton. Anyone accused of perjury or suborning it, obstructing justice or witness tampering, will surely want to consider the Clinton Defense. And courts and juries will have to.

To judge from the polls—which is, we grant you, a low and contemptible habit—this is just what enlightened liberalism may be reduced to in the next few weeks. For a great number of Americans appear convinced that the president lied under oath, but don't think it's a crime, or much of a crime, or a high crime and misdemeanor, or just don't care very much.

At this point it occurs that what happens to Bill Clinton isn't all that important compared to what's happening to the rest of us. A precedent is being set in law and well beyond the law. For the American people are on trial here, too. And we will see just how seriously we still take the law, and truth, and justice. And honor. We will see whether those old words have much meaning any more, or have they, too, been reduced to clinton clauses? For in these polls is mirrored the whole, clintonized culture.

A man need not be serious to be dangerous. And it's more than possible that this talented but really quite ordinary huckster, this carrier of meaninglessness who always manages to survive, even thrive, while one crony after another meets disaster, may finally have succeeded, not by design or malice or intention, but just by the easy, contagious sway of his own ad-hoc bumbling, in corrupting a whole society.

Lessons Learned

BY PAUL GREENBERG

There are many ways to write an editorial. I once drew up a list of 37 of them. This editorial, "On First Reading: *The Starr Report* and Its Discontents," represents only two of those methods:

The first is to know your subject, which means digging into it, reading about it, following it, living with it. Which was easy enough in the case of L'Affaire Lewinsky. The challenge would have been to escape it. Now a voluminous report months in the making had come out, and there was no alternative but to read every single legalistic word.

There was no way around it. The writer has to immerse himself in the text he's commenting on—so the reader won't have to. This is what we're paid to do, the service we're hired to render: to know as much as we can about the subject we've presumed to pontificate on.

But it must never sound like pontification. Here is where the second method comes in. After reading the text completely and carefully, after highlighting passages that look like promising grounds for comment, after making marginal notes, after storing some things in your head that will come in handy later, and after discarding most of all that once you get to the writing, and after sleeping and dreaming on it, the art and fun begin. You may find yourself following the logic of the words and feelings rather than any premeditated outline. Things fall into place, and, yes, occasionally out of place, but we all know writing is rewriting.

Call it exegesis, for what is an editorial but the news after somebody's had a day to think about it? Jews have a word for biblical commentary: *midrash.* These are the stories we write about The Story. So do editorial writers write about the news. Or at least we should, instead of just repeating yesterday's and tacking on a moral. In that way we bring our own values and experiences, our own juices and crochets, to bear on the values represented in the news.

In reading *The Starr Report* in all its unedifying mass, some incidents leapt out—like the president's relationship with his secretary, Betty Currie. It could have come straight out of a Southern novel. It was a plot, a story, an experience, a relationship that would be familiar to anyone in these latitudes. And it could be easily explained with striking effect to anyone, Southerner or not. All one had to do was point out how the story in the news matched the familiar archetypes, and the truth of it all would not only emerge but surely sink deep into the reader.

The writing was fun. It was like explaining a feeling. It came like a flash, but only after the hard, slogging work had been done in reading the report. After that, it was a matter of picking and choosing which portions promised the deeper, more rewarding insights for the reader. And discarding any cheap, obvious, partisan points.

And so, point after point, I overlaid the news story with an interpretation. And what might now seem prescience in light of the past year's events was all highly predictable to anyone who A) immersed himself in the story, and B) thought about it in terms of his own values, the characters' absence of values, and the values the writer shares with his readers.

The result was a *midrash* on the news, an exegesis, a combination of dull work and imaginative grasp. It should all seem so obvious, so simple, scarcely needing to be said—once it has been said. William Allen White once said a good editorial says something everybody knows, but nobody has said before. Or as Robert Frost said of poetry: It doesn't have to be obvious to be said, but once it is said, it should be obvious.

It helps to write *midrash* if you're aware of the values you're using. If you know where you're coming from, it's easier to get wherever you're going. Your instincts will lead you if you let them. I once jotted down the qualities we strive for in our editorials here at the *Democrat Gazette*. The list keeps getting longer, but it begins: "Quality. Character. Integrity. Candor. Arkansas roots, Southern tone. Tradition. Conservative but not predictable. Literate. Fair—mercilessly fair. Thoughtful...."

It might help editorial writers if we tried to think of the qualities we would like the reader to associate with our editorial opinion, and keep them in the back of our minds when approaching a bear of a subject like *The Starr Report*.

There are many ways to write editorials. A very few almost write themselves. Most require a combination of dull preparation and then imaginative flight.

The New York Times

Howell Raines
Finalist, Editorial Writing

Howell Raines is editorial page editor of *The New York Times.* Before taking over the editorial page in January 1993, he served as Washington editor, chief of the *Times*'s London bureau, and deputy Washington editor. He joined the *Times* in 1978 as a national correspondent in Atlanta. Raines had been political editor at the *St. Petersburg* (Fla.) *Times* and *The Atlanta Constitution.* His journalistic career began in 1964 with *The Birmingham Post-Herald,* and he also worked for *The Tuscaloosa* (Ala.) *News* and WBRC-TV in Birmingham. Raines won the Pulitzer Prize in feature writing in 1992 for "Grady's Gift," a personal reflection that appeared in *The New York Times Magazine.* Born in Birmingham, Raines received a bachelor's degree from Birmingham-Southern College and earned a master's degree in English from the University of Alabama. He is the author of an oral history of the civil rights movement, a novel, *Whiskey Man,* and *Fly Fishing Through the Midlife Crisis.*

His editorial, "Bill Clinton Speaks, a Little," reflects the canny insights of the political reporter and the cold judgment of the editorialist. Composed on deadline, it analyzes the president's five-minute address to the nation about his four hours of testimony to Kenneth Starr's grand jury—equal mixtures of historical import, scathing review, and trenchant phrase-making.

Bill Clinton speaks, a little

AUGUST 18, 1998

If a grudging admission of sexual indiscretion with Monica Lewinsky and another angry attack on Kenneth Starr can fix his Presidency, then Bill Clinton finished his five-minute address to the nation last night in good shape. But by our lights, Mr. Clinton let slip a vital chance to give a healing report to the nation and to begin the task of rehabilitating his character in the eyes of the public. Instead he went for the time-tested blend of minimal confession and contained tantrum that got him elected twice, but will not make him a leader who will be missed once he leaves Washington.

By his lawyer's account, Mr. Clinton used another vintage technique during more than four hours of grand jury testimony, refusing to answer questions that did not suit him. The outcome is hardly satisfactory for those who had hoped he would meet this challenge in a less characteristic way. Too much of a too-short speech was devoted to another blast of the familiar dichotomous blarney. His touching admission of lying to his wife was coupled with the insulting contention that his earlier denial, under oath, of a sexual relationship was "legally accurate."

To be sure, the President's situation is poignant. The country, through no fault of its own, is watching the unfolding of a family tragedy. But the nation also has a right to answers for the questions underlying the investigation of a duly appointed independent counsel. Is this President, who has now admitted giving misleading testimony under oath and in the television dismissal of "that woman, Miss Lewinsky," to be believed now, when he says he did not try to obstruct justice? We can sympathize with the Clintons' human pain and the injury inflicted yesterday on Mr. Clinton's dignity without sharing his view that he has discharged his obligations with secret testimony and a cryptic speech. Especially troubling was his call on the American people "to repair the fabric of our national discourse." He is the leader of the American family, and it is his job—

indeed, a test of Presidential leadership—to repair that fabric.

What an opportunity was wasted last night in that regard. But from the moment the 42d President walked into the Map Room he was in a confrontation with a force far more insidious than Mr. Starr, the independent counsel. In that hallowed room, Mr. Clinton was also confronting the habit that has driven—and haunted—his political career in an almost addictive way. His habit of stonewalling, of misleading by omission or concealment or fabrication or failure of memory, has been the source of virtually all this Administration's troubles.

For the past seven months the stonewall has crumbled faster than Mr. Clinton, his wife and his lawyer, David Kendall, could patch it. The full truth is a potent weapon but it is not one Mr. Clinton is used to handling, even in the most personal settings. We do not yet know what rendition of the truth Mr. Clinton spoke with the grand jury. For that reason, only he knows at this moment whether he can climb out of this mess by grasping the lifeline that Senator Orrin Hatch has repeatedly thrown him. Mr. Hatch, a Republican and chairman of the Judiciary Committee, was insulted by the attack on Mr. Starr, but he still seemed willing to help Mr. Clinton provided that no evidence of serious illegalities emerges, and, in his view, "that's a big if."

Indeed it is, for the American people as well as for Congress. The investigation of subornation of perjury and other obstruction issues must continue, and Mr. Starr ought to move quickly to conclude it. Mr. Clinton said last night that he did not lie or counsel others to lie or destroy evidence. If that is so, the case will conclude quickly and favorably for him. But nothing now known about the grand jury testimony or revealed in the speech warrants abandonment of that inquiry.

This is an odd moment in political history, but not a frivolous one. Here was a man of compassionate impulse and lofty ambition who went to Washington with every imaginable political skill except one. He seemed to think he was immune from a rule that leaps out from any reading of modern Presidencies. Everything comes to light sooner or later. Mr. Clinton cannot stop the process of revelation in which he participated yesterday. By and by, we will see entire the lineaments of his fate and his standing among the Presidents.

It can never be what he and the nation hoped, for he long ago chose to manipulate the narrative of his political life in such a way as to cripple trust. What we will know in time, of course, is whether he has so falsified his conversation with the American people that he could not, even in the hour of his greatest peril and through the simple agency of truth, position himself to receive their forgiveness.

Mirta Ojito
Covering the World

She says she's shy, but Mirta Ojito has covered major stories around the world and won several awards. She was a member of the award-winning *New York Times* team that covered the plight of deaf Mexican workers enslaved in Queens. During her early years as a reporter, Ojito covered stories on Cuban troops in Angola and a tense situation with Cuban detainees in Atlanta.

Ojito is a staff writer for the *Times* covering the immigration beat. She was born in Havana on Feb. 10, 1964, and came to the United States with her parents and sister when she was 16. Her dream was to be a journalist, but the challenge of learning English convinced her to try a different major at Florida Atlantic University in Boca Raton.

Then, an article in the school newspaper about Cuba enraged her. She responded with a nine-page letter that she took to the newspaper office. The editor offered to publish her letter as an article, pay her $10, and give her a byline. Thus Mirta Ojito became a journalist.

She earned a bachelor's degree in communications in 1986, graduating with honors after serving as editor of the student newspaper. *The Miami Herald* hired her, and for the next nine years she alternated between the *Herald* and its sister Knight Ridder paper, *El Nuevo Herald.* She joined *The New York Times i*n August 1996.

Ojito's winning stories were part of the coverage of Pope John Paul II's visit to Cuba in early 1998. She won in a new catagory, Covering the World, that helps readers understand international developments that affect and change their communities and lives. Her editors describe her stories as viewing "Cuba through the prism of time to see how people's lives have been altered under the government of Fidel Castro."

—Karen Brown Dunlap

Cubans face past as stranded youths in U.S.

JANUARY 12, 1998

Raquelin Mendieta cannot cry. Maria de los Angeles Torres cannot send her daughters alone in a plane anywhere. And Antonio Garcia, married for 31 years, cannot stand to be apart from his wife for even one night.

They are grappling with the legacy of the darkest period in their lives, the time in the early 1960s when, as children, they were sent alone from Cuba to the United States by parents who feared Communism.

The three were among 14,000 children who in the span of 21 months—from December 1960 to October 1962—were flown out of Cuba under a plan developed by the Roman Catholic Church in Miami and the United States Government. Under the plan, which for a time was kept secret from the Cuban Government as well as the American public, the State Department gave a young Miami priest the extraordinary authority to allow entry, without a visa, to Cuban children age 6 to 16.

Some of the parents who sent their children away were underground fighters seeking to topple the Government of Fidel Castro, who took power in January 1959. Others feared that Mr. Castro, who had closed all Catholic schools and confiscated church property, planned to indoctrinate children in special schools. And other parents simply thought that having children living in the United States would guarantee them a quick visa later.

Known as Operation Pedro Pan, in a bilingual reference to the boy who never grew up, it is the largest child rescue ever recorded in the Western Hemisphere. It is also one of the saddest chapters in the history of Cuban immigration to the United States.

The family separations were to have lasted only a few months—whenever the parents obtained visas to travel to the United States or Mr. Castro was ousted, as many Cubans at the time expected. But the Cuban missile crisis of October 1962 abruptly ended flights to and from the island, leaving the children stranded on the other side of the Straits of Florida.

Many remained under the care of the Catholic Church for years. They were sent to foster homes, orphanages and even homes for delinquents in 35 states. By the time they saw their parents again, they were grown women and men, already married and with children. Some of the families were never reunited.

The children of Pedro Pan, as they call themselves, now live quiet lives all over the United States. Most are successful men and women who managed to put painful memories behind as they learned English, became United States citizens, got an education, started families and worked hard. They are bankers and hairdressers, writers and teachers, artists and builders.

Only recently, with their children as old as they were during the operation, and as they have reached the age of their parents when such decisions were made, they have begun dealing openly with the memories of their lonely childhoods.

Some, particularly those who were separated for a long time, say they paid a very high price for their freedom and resent their parents' actions. Others say they are forever grateful for their parents' sacrifice. But however they view the decisions made long ago, the children of Pedro Pan are united today in a fraternity of shared pain. They all carry the scars of a truncated childhood.

"Over all, it was a good thing because it saved us from Communism," said Mr. Garcia, who is now 50 and a car washer in Miami. "But I have told my mother, and I know it pains her, that I would never do to my own children, if I had them, what my parents did to me."

Ms. Torres, a political science professor at DePaul University in Chicago, came to the United States alone when she was 6. She has spent six years researching the operation and is particularly interested in the role of the United States Government. Ms. Torres said she believed that people in the Government viewed the children of Pedro Pan as a perfect cold war propaganda tool.

"There were people involved who had their own sinister motives," said Ms. Torres, who is now 42 and the mother of two girls. "They wanted to create panic, to scare the middle class into disaffecting from the revolution."

Ms. Torres wants the Central Intelligence Agency to allow her to see the files that she is sure hold details of the Pedro Pan operation. So far, the C.I.A. has denied knowing of the operation. Today, Ms. Torres plans to file suit to force the agency to release whatever information it has. Anya Guilshes, a spokeswoman for the C.I.A., said the agency had no comment about Operation Pedro Pan.

The operation started in December 1960, when James Baker, the headmaster of an American school in Havana who has since died, met with the Rev. Bryan O. Walsh, a Miami priest with the church's social service agency, and told him that parents in Cuba were concerned about their children's welfare. The two agreed that if Mr. Baker could get children out of Cuba with student visas issued by the United States Embassy in Havana, the Catholic Church would take care of them.

When the embassy closed shortly thereafter, in January 1961, Father Walsh turned to the State Department, which gave him blanket authority to issue visa waivers to children 6 to 16. Older children had to undergo security clearances before they could travel.

Father Walsh sent the waiver forms to Cuba, often in diplomatic pouches. The forms were filled out for the children, who were then allowed to travel to the United States. When the organizers in Cuba ran out of forms, they falsified them.

With some exceptions, the children of Pedro Pan say they are grateful to have grown up in this country, but they also wonder what their lives would have been like if they had not been separated from their parents.

"It is not all as rose-colored as one may think—we carry around a lot of pain," said Elly Vilano-Chovel, a 50-year-old real estate broker in Miami and a founder of the Operation Pedro Pan Group, which was created in 1991 to help children who are orphans and refugees.

What frustrates so many Pedro Pan children is the twist of fate of 1962, when the flights were canceled, leaving a trail of broken families and troubled lives.

"That is the irony of it," said Ms. Torres, who began her research when her eldest daughter turned 6 and she started to question what could possibly have driven her parents to send her abroad at such a young age. "This operation was conceived to avoid the destruction of the Cuban family and ended up creating so much suffering."

Monsignor Walsh, now 67 and director emeritus of Catholic Charities, says he knew the children were lonely and sad without parents. But he said the church had done everything possible to make them happy and keep them safe. In all these years, Monsignor Walsh said, he has heard of no child who was mistreated.

"I know it was sad for them, but I have no regrets," said Monsignor Walsh, who still lives in Miami. "How can I? All I did was to take care of children who were alone. Ultimately, the decision to send them was made by the parents, who assumed the separation would be short-lived."

Ms. Torres, who was separated from her family for four months, considers herself lucky. Others, like Jorge Viera, a 50-year-old banker in Miami, had a much tougher time. Mr. Viera, who was sent when he was 14, did not see his parents for 25 years and then only briefly, when his parents visited him in Miami. They returned to Cuba, where they died two years ago.

"Basically, I lost my parents when I was 14—the family, as I knew it, ceased to exist then," Mr. Viera said, adding that he understands why his parents sent him alone and feels only admiration for their courage.

In Mr. Garcia's case, his parents feared for his life because he had started to rebel against the Government. He was sent at 15 and was separated from his parents for five years. When they finally arrived in 1967, he stood in front of his mother and she did not recognize him. Mr. Garcia's mother, Maria del Carmen Garcia, now 71, sobbed on the telephone as she recalled that day.

"I sent a boy, a nice child who never spent a night outside his home and I found a man with a mustache and a girlfriend," Mrs. Garcia said, adding that in the years she was away from her son, she contemplated suicide every time she went to the docks.

"I would look to the water and think, 'This water that separates us can bring us together.' But my faith in God did not allow me to do anything foolish."

Mr. Garcia, who married at 20, said that although he lived with a kind family while he waited for his parents, he would always miss the time they could have spent together. Fifteen years ago, he said, he suffered a nervous breakdown and the memories of his adolescence came rushing in. He cried all the time.

Others have had different reactions. Enma Baron, a 53-year-old perfectly composed and impeccably coiffed wine importer in Manhattan, begins to cry at the mere mention of the five years—from 17 to 22—she lived without her parents. Ms. Baron calls them "the dark ages" and refuses to discuss them. When her parents immigrated to the United States, her mother had become mentally ill and her father, a doctor, was crippled and could not work.

Ms. Mendieta, who left when she was 15, was sent to a home for juvenile delinquents in Dubuque, Iowa. She was accompanied by her sister, Ana, then 12.

She told of living a nightmare surrounded by violent girls who had committed crimes. Ms. Mendieta said nuns had forbidden her and her sister to speak Spanish, hit them when they misbehaved and once locked her in a dark closet when she cried hard. Ms. Mendieta, now 51, is an accomplished sculptor and the mother of five who said she had a large family, in part, in an attempt to replicate the family she lost.

Mr. Viera, the banker, refuses to go to Cuba to see his only brother because to see him would open up old wounds, he said.

"I have healed—I have moved on," Mr. Viera said. "It would be too painful."

And Luis Ramirez, a childless contractor in Newark who is 44, recently lost a chance to become a foster parent because he decided to return a little girl to her mother after two months.

"In the end, children belong with their parents," said Mr. Ramirez, who was sent alone when he was 8 years old and did not see his parents for two years. "Ultimately, she would have held it against us."

Yet, despite the pain, many Pedro Pan children say they would do what their parents did, given the same circumstances. Although their parents' worst fears never materialized—children were not taken from their homes by the Government in Cuba—growing up there in the '60s and '70s would not have been easy for them. It would have meant not being able to openly practice their Catholic faith and, for children of people who opposed the Cuban Government, a life of ostracism.

"Our parents gave us choices in life," said Yvonne Conde, a 47-year-old freelance writer in Manhattan who was separated from her parents for eight months when she was 10 and is now writing a book about the program. "Over all, I think it had a positive effect in our lives."

But even Ms. Conde said she was somewhat weary of people who assert that the operation was positive because so many of the Pedro Pan children are now leading productive, successful lives.

"Those are the ones we know about, the ones who want to be known," she said from her apartment on the Upper East Side. "They send their business cards and fax their resumes. But I often wonder about the ones we don't know about. What are their lives like?"

Writers' Workshop

Talking Points

1) An unlikely trio is described in the lead, leaving the mystery of their common tie until the second paragraph. How effective is this structure?

2) The writer's own life was interrupted by her move to the United States. Does this affect the tone of her narrative?

3) The article ends with a quote. Why do you think the writer chose it? What effect does it have?

Assignment Desk

1) Try to locate others who were part of Operation Pedro Pan. How do their stories compare with those in this story?

2) This story is organized by each person's personal experience. Rewrite this by weaving their experiences together. Which structure works better?

3) Rewrite the ending without using a quote.

Four decades of revolution bring Cuba full circle

FEBRUARY 1, 1998

HAVANA—For 39 years he has worked hard to build a better society for his own children and for all the children of Cuba. At 73 he still works as an organizer of the elections that every two years guarantee the permanence of the government he helped bring to power in 1959.

Pictures of him with Fidel Castro dot the walls of his comfortable apartment in the upscale Vedado district, and his frayed olive green uniform—the one he wore without fail for 13 years—hangs in his closet. He still rattles off the achievements of the revolution in health and education. When Mr. Castro speaks, he listens with pride.

Yet Serafin, the only name he would allow for publication, says he is an anguished man. "I look around and I see the needs of my people, how they must struggle to survive every day, and it fills me with sorrow," he said.

Serafin's quandary is common these days in Cuba as old revolutionaries and diehard Fidelistas come to terms with the failure of their dreams. From their posh apartments in Vedado and the area known as Miramar, those who helped make this revolution look around in horror and see what the country has come to: Many parents must scramble to feed their children, some sick people die for lack of medicines, young women marry foreigners for a chance to leave the country, old people line up in the morning to buy newspapers they can re-sell, and children as young as 8 gravitate to tourist spots asking for handouts.

WELCOME TO LATIN AMERICA

In many ways, Cuba today is not unlike any other underdeveloped Latin American country. True, children go to school and do not sleep in the streets. But there is class division (those who have dollars and those who do not). There is prostitution (young women throw themselves at tourist cars). People rummage through garbage for everything from spare parts to plastic containers. Some of the potholed city streets resemble rural roads. Large families of two or three generations squeeze into tiny, dilapidated apartments. And there are a lot of needy, unhappy, rundown, desperately sad people.

In these conditions, it is tempting for Cubans to look for solace in comparisons with, say, Peruvians or Mexicans. At least here, the Government guarantees some basic needs (rice, beans, sugar and, occasionally, toothpaste) and free doctors' care for all.

But the people who made the Cuban revolution, who for the most part genuinely believed they were building a better world, know the revolution was supposed to be much more than that. The country was not supposed to just survive, but to prosper. It was not supposed to alienate its best sons and daughters, but to convert ordinary citizens into social idealists. And finally, after all the years of scarcities and slogans, it was not supposed to depend, once again, on the Yankee dollar.

This is perhaps the cruelest failure of the revolution for people like Serafin, who believed Mr. Castro could liberate them from dependence on their huge northern neighbor. That dependence was what Mr. Castro blamed for Cuba's troubles 39 years ago—the regime of the dictator Fulgencio Batista, the reliance on American sugar markets that kept Cuban peasants poor, and the domination of Havana's tourism, gambling and prostitution by American mobsters.

Yet today, despite the United States embargo, officials acknowledge that the economy's pillars are dollar-based: tourism and "remesas," the dollars that Cubans abroad send home to relatives and friends. Half of Cuba's people– most of them in Havana—have access to dollars, either because they are paid in them or because they receive them from abroad.

With the return of the dollar, any hope of achieving the old revolutionaries' tattered ideals is buckling under the weight of all the concessions the regime has had to make in order to survive since the crumbling of the Soviet bloc.

In the last few years, the hotels have filled with tourists who snap pictures of dilapidated buildings, and the nights have reverted to a debauchery that recalls the 1950s. Teachers who taught Russian have been retrained to teach English, and young doctors and engineers bribe hotel managers for jobs serving food in dollars-only restaurants.

And the schism that separates the classes is deepening: Those who have dollars eat meat and have toilet paper; those who do not go without proteins in their diet and use pages of old textbooks for their sanitary needs. There are people in Cuba who carry only dollars in their pockets. There are others who have never seen one.

WELCOME TO 1958

In a twist of fate or bad planning, these were some of the very conditions that fomented the Cuban revolution in the 1950s. The revolution set out to eradicate ills it attributed to capitalism: poverty, inequality, illiteracy, diseases, prostitution. With Soviet help, it made enormous strides in education and health care. But it was never able to fully accomplish all of its goals. The children of government officials always lived better than the children of ordinary workers, and the economic crisis began even before the Berlin Wall fell.

In important ways, the Cuban revolution is hardly alone. Throughout the Soviet bloc, the most common—and, in the end, perhaps the most fatal—failure of Communism was its inability to turn ordinary human beings into loyal new socialist citizens. Here, after almost four decades of indoctrination, most people, including the children of old revolutionaries, are dissatisfied by the government's failure to deliver material security. The welcome to the Pope last week demonstrates that Marx did not become the only source for ideals.

The desires of today's youth, it seems, are not so different from those of people who were young here in 1958. Like people everywhere, Cuba's young want to raise families and prosper. If that is impossible in Cuba, many want to leave for a land of greater individual opportunity.

Five years ago, Serafin's oldest son was sent to prison for trying to leave by boat. Serafin finally visited him after eight months. "It was very difficult," he said, swallowing hard. "I think he made a mistake."

Although pained by Cuba's situation, some old revolutionaries stubbornly cling to their ideals. Very few admit they made a mistake. And they probably cannot. At 73 or 65, to declare the revolution a failure would be to renounce their life's work.

Reality, though, is sometimes impossible to ignore. Carlos, a 65-year-old man who fought against Batista then went into exile and returned when Batista fell, cannot accept any criticism of either Mr. Castro or his revolution. He was the only person interviewed who gave his full name. But his daughter asked him to withhold it for fear of reprisal against her. A 35-year-old former biology teacher, she rents half of her one-bedroom apartment and sells cigars on the side. Both activities are illegal without licenses. She and Carlos avoid politics when they talk; yet, when she can, she drops a few dollars in her father's wallet.

Many Cubans, of course, blame the United States embargo for their problems. But even that argument rankles old revolutionaries because to hang Cuba's fate solely on its ability to trade—and with the United States at that—reeks of the dependency mentality Mr. Castro set out to eliminate.

WELCOME TO WORLD TRADE

Economists trained here now acknowledge that few countries can survive economically without trading with their neighbors. But even that simple thought has required a shifting of the collective Cuban mind. People born after the revolution never had to worry about market conditions or the value of the dollar.

Now, there is a long list of applicants for a new M.B.A. program at the University of Havana, and people flock to English and marketing classes. The dollar has become so much a fact of Cuban life it has at least eight names: *fula, guano, guaniquiqui* and *varo* (all slang for money), *peso, verde* (green), *chavitos* (coins) and, of course, *divisas,* the official term, which means foreign exchange.

A woman who lives in Miramar takes solace in the fact that her husband, a respected official who believed deeply in socialism, died eight years ago, right before the worst times began. Since then, two of his children have left Cuba. Two more would like to go.

"As much as I miss him, I know that what happened was the best thing that could have happened," she said, drying her tears. "If he were alive today, I don't know what my husband would have done, but I do know that he would have been incredibly sad."

Writers' Workshop

Talking Points

1) Examine the authority of Ojito's writing in the second section. Note how she helps the reader feel and see the state of today's Cuba in the last two paragraphs of that section. What makes her writing so effective?

2) Compare this story with Ojito's story about children in Cuba. With which group do you feel more sympathetic?

3) The writer's life changed dramatically because she was exiled from Cuba. Do her stories betray any political bias?

Assignment Desk

1) Interview some older residents in your community. Write about how they review their lives.

2) Write a story about political refugees in your community, with a focus on how children's lives are affected.

A sentimental journey to *la casa* of childhood

FEBRUARY 3, 1998

HAVANA, Feb. 1—This is the moment when, in my dreams, I begin to cry. And yet, I'm strangely calm as I go up the stairs to the apartment of my childhood in Santos Suarez, the only place that, after all these years, I still refer to as *la casa,* home.

I am holding a pen and a reporter's notebook in my hand and, as I always do when I am working, I count the steps: 20. In my memory, there were only 16. The staircase seems narrower than I remember, the ceiling lower.

Perhaps I have grown taller, perhaps my hips have widened with age and pregnancy. I am buying mental time, distracting my mind from what I am certain will be a shock.

After 17 years and 8 months, I have returned to Cuba as a reporter. I am here to cover the visit of Pope John Paul II, not to cry at the sight of a chipped, old tile on the floor.

The last time I went down these steps I was 16 years old and a police car was waiting for me and my family downstairs. They had come to tell us that my uncle, like thousands of other Cuban exiles who had returned to Cuba to claim their relatives, waited at the port of Mariel to take us to Miami in a leased shrimp boat.

It was May 7, 1980, the first days of what became known as the Mariel boat lift, the period from April to September 1980 when more than 125,000 Cubans left the island for the United States.

That day I left my house in a hurry. The police gave us 10 minutes to get ready and pack the few personal items we were allowed to take: an extra set of clothing, some pictures, toothbrushes. Everything else, from my books to my dolls and my parents' wedding china, remained behind. There were dishes in the sink and food in the refrigerator. My underwear in a drawer and my mother's sewing machine open for work.

Since then, I have often thought about this house, remembering every detail, every curve and tile and squeaky sound. The green walls of the living room, the view from the balcony, the feel of the cold tiles under my bare feet, the sound of my father's key in the key-hole and the muffled noise from the old refrigerator in the kitchen.

A stranger opens the door and I tell her who I am and what I want. "I used to live here," I say. "I'd like to take a look."

Surprisingly, she knows my name. She asks if I am the older or the younger child who used to live in the house. I say I am the older as I look over her head. Straight into my past. My home remains practically as we left it, seemingly frozen in time, like much of Cuba today.

There, to the right of the bedroom's door, is my father's handiwork—two glass shelves he screwed into the wall—and my mother's set of orange and green glasses. Later, I learn that no one ever drinks from those glasses. If they break, the new owner of the house tells me, they cannot be replaced. Under the shelves is my bookcase, painted a fresh coat of dark brown. A carpenter friend of my father's had built it for me when I was a little girl.

My books are gone, though. When the Cuban Government declared a few years ago that it had entered a "special period" of shortages and books all but disappeared, she took my books to the school where she teaches. I am pleased to hear that. It is a much nicer fate than I had imagined.

One book remains, *Captain at 15,* by Jules Verne. I want to take it to New York with me, to show it to my son. But I do not say anything and the yellowing book remains there, inside the bookcase. My mother's pots and pans are in the kitchen. The old wooden ironing board remains where it always was, behind the door to the patio.

The dining set is exactly the way it was, except the table is covered by a plastic tablecloth and I do not feel the coldness of the beige Formica when I sit at the table as I used to. A painting of red, white and yellow hibiscus that always hung over my sofa bed is still in the same spot in the living room. It was painted by one of my mother's cousins, who now lives in Florida.

This is a strange feeling. I knew I would face my childhood by coming here, but I never expected to re-live it as I am doing now. I go out to the balcony and then, as if on cue, I hear someone calling out my child-hood nickname, "Mirtica! Mirtica!"

For a moment, I do not know who is calling or even if the call is real. It sounds like my mother calling me for dinner. But it is the neighbor from the corner who looked up from her terrace and somehow recognized me. I wave faintly. I want to stay in this apartment for a long time. I want to be left alone. But I cannot. It is no longer my home.

The Jiménez family now lives in the house. He is a truck driver, just as my father was. They have a 15-year-old son who sleeps on a sofa bed in the living room, just as my sister and I did. The Government gave them the apartment a few months after we left. Their own house, nearby, had been badly damaged in a hurricane.

They were shown three apartments, all in the same neighborhood. They settled in ours, they said, because it seemed the nicest. It does not seem so nice anymore. It is rather small, smaller than I remember. The floor tiles are porous and lackluster and chunks of plaster have fallen from the ceiling. There is no light in the liv-ing room, because nowadays in Cuba light bulbs are luxury items. But it is home. And, yes, I cry.

Despite their warm welcoming, I am acutely aware of what the Jiménezes may be thinking. For years, one of the propaganda campaigns that the Cuban Govern-ment has mastered is that of instilling in ordinary Cubans the fear that exiles in the United States want to return to the country to recover the homes and busi-nesses they lost when they left the country.

There is even a television short that mocks the Helms-Burton Act, a law intended to strengthen the United States embargo against Cuba, that warns Cubans to watch out for people like me, returning exiles.

I have no interest in my former home and whatever furniture still exists there, other than a purely senti-mental one. But I do not know what the Jiménezes are thinking. They are, however, extremely generous with their time and space. They serve me coffee. We discuss the good features of the apartment, as if this were a real estate transaction. They tell me they love the old American refrigerator, a white Hotpoint that, miraculously, still stands.

I roam through the house as if it were my own. When, upon leaving, I apologize for the inconvenience, Mr. Jiménez tells me: "Don't mention it. This is your home."

I knew this would be an emotional visit. Before I mustered enough courage to go up to the apartment, I had walked through the neighborhood. As my father asked me to do, I visit *la bodega* and search for Juan, the Spaniard who once owned it and, after it was confiscated by the Government in the early years of the revolution, remained there as an employee of the state.

He is retired now, but I find him helping out at another bodega, and we chat. I take a picture for my father as he stands behind the counter with a pencil balanced behind his ear, as he always did.

I walk the streets and find faces I recognize. I approach some; others approach me because, they tell me, I remind them of my mother. Some even call out her name, which is also mine, from across the street: "Mirta, what are you doing here? You've come back?"

They tell me who died and who left. The son of my sixth-grade teacher lost a leg in a bicycle accident. My next-door neighbor left for Spain with her son, Pepito, to claim an inheritance. The musician from downstairs died of bone cancer; his daughter married an Italian and left.

The downstairs neighbors returned to the province where they were born. For years, she was the president of the watchdog neighborhood committee; he wore a green olive uniform, a military man forged in the mountains of Sierra Maestra with Fidel Castro and later trained in the Soviet Union. Their two children left for the United States.

My old neighbors tell me how they live, how they survive, as one woman put it. They make sweets at home and sell them in the street. They receive money monthly from the United States. They steal from the Government. They save and scrape and work very hard just to put food on the table every day.

The old movie theater is gone, demolished two years ago because it was crumbling with age and disrepair.

Another theater has been condemned. The front door is covered with bricks. The hardware store is now a Government office. The glass of the windows broke years ago; crude wooden boards cover the empty shelves. The streets are unpaved and full of potholes. Workers rip them open to fix water or gas pipes and then do not have the materials to finish the work.

In a way, I'm reporting the story of a neighborhood, a typical one in Havana. But I'm also reporting the life I never got to have. Through their stories, I see what my life could have become. I search for parallels. I imagine myself as my neighbors.

What would have become of me? Could I have become a professional like the two girls from the corner who now teach? Would I have left in a raft like my next-door neighbor? Or perhaps I would have gone crazy, like the woman across the street, Regina, who could not recall my name after years of electroshock and pills. Her husband was accused of counterrevolutionary activities in 1979 and executed by a firing squad.

Had I stayed, would I have talked to a returning neighbor the way they talk to me? They tell me about the sadness of their lives, their husbands, their lovers, their misguided children, their ungrateful relatives, their never-ending litany of needs: bread, toilet paper, sanitary napkins, underwear, freedom.

Because I left, and because they know I will leave again, I become a depository of their penury. They are happy I have returned, glad that I remembered. A woman gives me a rose from her garden; another, two lithographs from an old book of paintings and a silver cross that has been in her family for years.

The Jiménezes give me a plastic bird that hangs from its beak from a wooden stand and, more important, our old soap holder, a white enamel piece from Poland that my mother always kept in the patio.

Down the block I find a man I never knew before. He stops me and asks if I am a foreign journalist. I say yes. "I want to ask you something," he says. "Perhaps you know. Why is it that children can no longer eat breakfast in the morning?" He is 70 years old and has lived in the same house for 44 years. His grandson goes to my old school, down the block. It is the man's birthday and, he says, he cannot even buy a bone in the market to make himself a soup. I get a lump in my throat and wish him happy birthday.

I cross the street to the school and ask to see the library. It is here where I became a reader and, therefore, I think, a writer. I hardly recognize the place. The marble columns are there, but the bookcases lean precariously to the side. The books are dusty and yellowing.

I ask for the French literature section, but there is not one anymore. The librarian tells me that last year she received only two books, copies of *La Edad de Oro,* by José Martí. The year before, none. In fact, except for those two books she does not remember the last time she got a shipment. Children now use the library as a classroom.

After a second visit to the apartment, I leave. And I leave exactly the way I left almost 18 years ago, profoundly sad, surrounded by friends and neighbors, people glad that I remembered them, unselfish people who are happy that I left and live better than they do.

Who says that Cubans are divided by politics or even by an ocean? In Enamorados Street, at the foot of a small hill called San Julio, my home and my people remain.

Writers' Workshop

Talking Points

1) In this story we see Ojito's apartment through the eyes of a young girl and the eyes of an adult woman. What techniques does she use to see her former home from both perspectives?

2) The writer barely quotes the family currently living in the apartment. Yet they are an important element of the story. How does her treatment of them intensify the emotions you feel while reading the article?

3) How does the writer help the reader see what might have been had she remained in Cuba? Which passages help us see the path her life might have taken?

4) One name is missing in this story—Fidel Castro. Is it understood? Does the writer reveal her opinion about Castro's effect on Cuba?

Assignment Desk

1) Revisit a place you used to live. Write an essay about the memories and emotions that trip stirs. Take careful notes about physical details.

Divided loyalties tugging at Cuba's children

FEBRUARY 18, 1998

HAVANA—More than eight years after the cold war melted in the rubble of the Berlin Wall, the children of Cuba continue to dive under desks in schools all over the island.

The drills serve to reinforce the most pervasive ideological lesson in Cuba's schools: that the United States is evil and that Cubans must always be ready to defend themselves.

That old message, fashioned after the Bay of Pigs invasion and the missile crisis in the early 1960s, is fed constantly to children here even when there are no tensions between the United States and any other country, as there are with Iraq now.

But it is an especially poignant message today when most families in Cuba have relatives in the United States and when, faced with enormous economic difficulties, the Cuban Government has allowed dollars to circulate freely on the island.

Nowadays, when children come home from the war drills, they slip on shoes bought with dollars sent by their grandparents in Miami or, in some cases, they work odd jobs catering to American tourists to earn dollars themselves.

In the mornings, William José Díaz, a 12-year-old Pioneer who is in eighth grade, swears to defend the Cuban flag against "los Americanos." In the evenings, he rushes to open the doors of tourists' cars. He works outside Pain de Paris, an expensive bakery in Vedado. Most nights, he makes at least $2. When someone handed him $1 recently, the boy rushed home to buy bananas for dinner.

Years ago, it was easier for parents to keep their children blissfully unaware of both their true political feelings and the hardships they went through. But now, with the country's economy in chaos, even young children know that once they turn 7 they lose the right to buy milk.

They know that the Government issues only two school uniforms during elementary school—one in kindergarten and the other in fifth grade. And that they are no longer able to buy toys because the Government did away with the yearly ritual of selling toys to children on the 26th of July, the anniversary of the beginning of Fidel Castro's armed uprising in 1953.

The contradictions of their young lives—hearing one message in school and another, radically different, at home—confuses some children. Their teachers want them to fight the Americans; their parents want to join them or, at least, to get some of their dollars.

"Mom," a 7-year-old girl recently asked her mother, "if William Clinton is so bad, why do we want to go live with him?"

Trusting their children and thinking them ready to absorb contrasting messages, many parents openly discuss their beliefs in front of them and even mock the revolutionary slogans and songs they bring home. But then they ask their children to keep it to themselves.

Some parents fear that their children will be ostracized if their teachers know that they live in a non-revolutionary home. Parents who make a living in what the Government considers illegal activities—renting a room or selling cigars without a license—also fear that, if their children talk, the Government may confiscate their goods, fine them or, in some cases, jail them.

The burden of living in two distinct realities affects some children in psychological and physical ways. Teresita, a 14-year-old ninth grader who lives in Old Havana, said she had never told her best friend that her parents desperately want to leave the country.

She has also never told anyone that, when the doors are locked, her mother rants against President Castro, blaming his Government for the scarcities in their home. Two months ago, Teresita began to shed the hairs of her arms and legs. The doctors told her that she lacked some essential vitamins in her diet; the mother thinks it is a result of stress.

A 52-year-old writer who insisted on being identified only by his first name, Angel, cannot stand a song praising the revolution that his 9-year-old daughter has been singing lately. He tells her to stop and his daughter obeys. The mother, worried about her daughter, intercedes.

"You want your children to be a full member of the family, to know how you feel about everything," said the mother, a member of the Communist Party who long ago grew disenchanted with the revolution but outside the home pretends to be as enthusiastic as ever. "But I worry sometimes how all this is going to affect her and how much contradiction she can really absorb in her young mind."

Yet the girl's mother, in a fit of anger, recently ripped to pieces her red Communist Party ID and threw it out the window. It was her daughter who ran three flights downstairs in a panic to retrieve the picture from the sidewalk so that no one would ever know what her mother had done.

While Angel helps his daughter with her homework, he systematically deconstructs everything she has been taught at school. She is now learning about José Martí, a 19th-century patriot who fought to free Cuba from Spanish colonialism. In Cuba today, Martí is also regarded as the intellectual precursor of the revolution. Angel tells his daughter that Martí would never have supported Mr. Castro's Government. The little girl giggles and rolls her eyes.

But there is very little that parents can do to shape their children's education. In a country with no private schools and compulsory education until ninth grade, parents are forced to send their children to state-run schools. They also have no say about the curriculum and, more and more these days, very little about their children's extracurricular activities.

Some parents try to exert control by taking their children late to school to avoid the morning ritual where students salute the flag, sing the national anthem and repeat revolutionary slogans. Others are turning to religion, hoping that lessons in catechism will open their children's minds to other points of view.

The Roman Catholic Church is taking full advantage of it. To make the shift easier for the children, it is incorporating some of the messages children hear in school into Sunday sermons. It is not unusual for priests now to somehow link Cuba's patriots to religion.

At a recent Mass here, Jaime Cardinal Ortega Alamino drew cheers from his mostly young listeners when he reminded them that the full name of Antonio Maceo, one of Cuba's most revered martyrs, was

Antonio de la Caridad, a clear reference to Cuba's patriot saint, Our Lady of Charity.

Priests in some churches are also enticing children to attend Mass and catechism classes through a system of bonuses and rewards. Children receive bonuses for every Mass and catechism class they attend. Once a week, they can exchange the bonuses for gifts like gum, clothing, pencils and toys, all donated from churches abroad.

"They get things they want and need and we get an opportunity to show them the church's way," said the Rev. Jesus Maria Lusarreta, a priest at La Milagrosa, where more than 400 children attend catechism weekly.

During his five-day visit to Cuba in January, Pope John Paul II referred to Cuba's youth in two of the four Masses he held. At the first, in Santa Clara, some parents nodded in silence when the Pope said, "Parents must be acknowledged as the first and foremost educators of their children."

But it is difficult for parents to heed the Pope's words. Elementary school children go to school here from 8 a.m. to 4:20 p.m. On Saturdays, they often return to school for sports or political events. Sometimes they sleep over in the school to await so-called Domingos de Defensa, Sundays of Defense, days in which the children practice what it is like to be under attack and receive their lessons in a bunker.

Marta Pérez Herrera, deputy director of Pepito Tey, an elementary school in Old Havana, said that, beginning in third grade, children are trained by members of the Revolutionary Armed Forces, who teach them everything from patriotic symbols to military moves. At a recent practice session in a park, uniformed men were training young children to march as one.

While the children marched, a 16-year-old girl in tight pink shorts stood in a corner a few blocks away eyeing foreigners. The girl, Yanel Noa, said she dropped out of school because she did not want to work in the fields, a requirement for all students in high school.

Had she continued in school, she would have become a dancer, she said. For now, she lives off the charity of a special friend: a 32-year-old married American man who often travels to Cuba loaded with cash.

Writers' Workshop

Talking Points

1) Why does the writer choose to focus on children to tell the story of Cuba? What does she lose or gain from such an approach?

2) Analyze how the writer depicts the duplicity of life under Castro—how one must publicly support the regime, even while privately criticizing it.

Assignment Desk

1) This is a story about a government system, but it is told mostly through individual anecdotes and observations. Use this approach to tell another story.

2) What similarities exist between children in Cuba and children in the United States?

A conversation with
Mirta Ojito

KAREN BROWN DUNLAP: What led to your personal piece on returning home to Cuba?

MIRTA OJITO: I've always thought about going to Cuba, but I never really asked for a visa, except once. I wanted to go as a former resident returning to visit relatives. That time they denied my visa. Returning was something that I wanted to do badly as a reporter, too, but I wasn't part of the foreign desk. I didn't cover Cuba. I was a general reporter, so I wasn't going to bring it up.

Then the *Times* regional editor, Carl Lavin, said, "Why don't you try to go to Cuba? I'm sure the foreign desk would love for you to go. Just apply for a visa. Wouldn't you like to do that?" And I said, "Yes."

A team of staff members was traveling to Cuba to cover the visit of the pope. And I knew someone else was going to follow the pope around. I wanted to write a story about children who are taught one thing in school and then go home to other beliefs. And I also knew that I wanted to write a story about the countryside, which was something that I was very curious about.

I wanted to do a story about a neighborhood or a block. I would dedicate four or five days to this and write a really intimate story about how people live. I was talking to the editor, and we discussed going to my old neighborhood. I was actually thinking that would save time because there I wouldn't have to earn the confidence of people. They would remember me.

It was Andy Rosenthal, the foreign editor, who said, "I think it'll be a wonderful piece, but I think you ought to make it into a first-person story." So I did.

The story tells a little about how you approached the assignment, but explain how you prepared to return home.

I really wanted to avoid going to my neighborhood the very first day because I thought I was going to get too emotional and I wanted to write sort of a curtain raiser about how churches were preparing for the pope's visit. Before I left, I called the archdiocese in Cuba looking for an interesting church. I didn't want it to be in old Havana, because that's where all the journalists always hang out, and I didn't want it to be in Vedado, which is another neighborhood where everybody always goes. I wanted it to be in a neighborhood off the beaten path, just one church that nobody ever writes about.

The woman quickly understood exactly what I was trying to do, and she said, "Well, you know, there is this old church in a neighborhood called Santos Suarez and I think you'll love it."

Of course, that was my neighborhood church. I gasped. I said, "Oh, no, not that church," and she said, "That's really the best. It's a very wonderful place. You'll like it."

You visited the neighborhood before going to the apartment. When you finally went in, to what degree were you the reporter visiting a house, and to what degree were you a 16-year-old returning home?

To the degree that I took notes on everything, I was a reporter. I took notes while I was talking to them, I took notes while I was going upstairs, I took notes constantly. I wrote down whatever was different about the house. I think that I wrote down everything as a way to keep my emotions in check. I wrote a lot of notes. It was overwhelming there for a while.

When I walked onto the terrace, I was 16 years old. I was completely transported back to my childhood, and I burst into tears. I could see the view of my neighborhood as I used to see it when I was a child. When a neighbor looked up and saw me and called my name, I just cried. It was awful. It was very, very sad.

What drew the tears? Were you angry?

There was never anger, just emotion. One reason I think the piece touched a lot of people is because everybody can identify with the idea of going back home. You don't have to be a refugee, you don't have to be an exile or an immigrant. If you're from Louisville,

Ky., or from Duluth, Minn., and you go back, you get emotional. You see your old friends, the old streets, the schools. Maybe you remember an old boyfriend. Just the idea of going home brings tears, because you really never can go home again. The cliché is true. It's this whole idea of what you lost, which is, in fact, your childhood. It's emotional.

How did you plan the personal essay?

This is sort of a bad example for an interview on writing because I have no idea what went into the piece. I just sat there and did it and sent it in. There were no thoughts, no preparation, no outline, no notes other than the ones I took while in the house.

But, to a certain degree, I'd been writing that story for 16 or 17 years. I had always dreamed about going back and I always knew that I would go to the apartment, and I always knew that it was going to be emotional. I just didn't know that it would end up on the front page of *The New York Times.* But the story was rehearsed for many, many, many years.

I wrote it as the very last thing I did in Cuba, the very last, and it was published when I was already in New York. I wrote it in one sitting, pretty much, and I just sent it in. I think whoever got it that weekend probably didn't know what to do with it. They held it until the top editors came back Monday. And I think it ran either Tuesday or Wednesday.

I've called this a personal essay. Did you think of it that way?

I kept referring to it as my first-person story.

Your editors said this is one of a very few personal narratives ever to appear on the front page of *The New York Times.* Many journalists are taught not to put themselves in stories. What are your thoughts about personal pieces?

No one ever told me that while I was in school, but I did learn that through my training on the job. I can only tell you what I like to read, and I love to read news. I love to read anything; but first-person stories or columnists stand out to me.

I used to read all of Anna Quindlen's columns in *The New York Times*. And I think a lot of people like to read them, too. As long as personal pieces are not self-serving and they're done professionally, and they really touch on a bigger point—a greater truth—I think they're fine.

Say a little bit more about when personal essays are appropriate for journalism.

Well, I can only say it through examples. If you have some kind of disease, for example, and you have gone through a particularly different experience, or if you know that a lot of other people are going through the same thing you're going through. I don't understand why, in order to avoid writing a first-person piece, you must keep yourself out of the story if you've become part of it. That seems to me an artificial barrier.

What was the reaction to your story about going home?

Oh, God! The reaction to the series was good. The reaction to that particular story was completely overwhelming. When I came back, I had about 66 phone messages, about 88 letters, tons of e-mail, and today, more than a year later, when people find out I was the one who wrote that piece they say, "Oh, my God, you're the one who wrote it!" It's just been an incredible reaction.

Cuban-Americans were definitely touched by it, but so were others: people who had never been to Cuba, or who didn't care about Cuba but could totally relate to the experience of going back home. I got calls even from Canada and Texas. It was really wonderful. People tell me that it helped them see what's going on in Cuba in a different light and it helped them understand the human drama of leaving your home and of separations and of the economic situation in Cuba now much more than anything else they have read before or since. And if my story did that, that's good.

What does it mean to you as a writer? What did you learn from this experience?

That people fundamentally want to read about other people, and I think people do like first-person stories, just like I do. Those are the ones I remember.

In my career, I've written two stories that some people remember. This is one. The other was in Miami, another first-person story. Those two really hit some sort of nerve.

What was the other story about?

The other was very, very early in my career. In fact, it was my first assignment when I switched from *The Miami Herald* to *El Nuevo Herald.*

Cubans detained in prison in Atlanta were rioting because Cuba had reached an immigration agreement with the U.S., and they were going to be deported.

The newspaper sent me to cover it. The paper opened with that story. And I had been a reporter for all of three months. I was 22 or 23 years old, so it was very intense.

After I was there for about 13 days, prison officials picked two reporters to actually witness the signing of the agreement inside the prison. We had all been outside the prison; we had not been allowed in.

Of the two reporters that the Bureau of Prisons selected, one was from the Associated Press, because they felt that a pool reporter was needed. But the detainees had demanded somebody who spoke Spanish and could understand their point of view. I had been pestering the BOP people since the day I arrived because I really wanted to go in there, so one man came to me and said, "Would you like to interview the detainees and see the signing of the agreement?" And of course I said yes.

Bill Rose, who was then the national editor for *The Miami Herald,* was there; and while the AP reporter and I waited to go in the prison, Rose would come over and talk to me. We were there for about seven hours before everything was coordinated and we could go in.

Rose came over about every half-hour. I can understand the poor guy now. Here he has the one reporter who's being picked to go inside the prison, and it's somebody who's 23, and it's her first big assignment ever. All I had been doing was police blotter stories.

So Bill must have been very, very nervous and tried not to show it, to his credit. He would come over and say, "Remember, there are only three things you need to know in journalism: details, details, details."

After I covered the story, my editors wanted me to write a first-person piece about the experience of going in the prison and witnessing the signature. So I did, and a lot of people remember that story.

Let's talk about your story, "Divided Loyalties Tugging at Cuba's Children." You have a nice way of going from the general to specific details in your writing. Here's an example:

"Years ago, it was easier for parents to keep their children blissfully unaware of both their true political feelings and the hardships they went through. But now, with the country's economy in chaos, even young children know that once they turn 7 they lose the right to buy milk."

How do you get the specific details, and how do you get them in stories meaningfully?

I really just take down everything. Most of the time I don't use everything because it's just not relevant; but there are some stories that need details because the details make the story. Frankly, I don't struggle too much with deciding on details. I do what feels right to me. At a certain point, it's almost as if the writing tells you what to do. There's a certain pause after you make the generalization, and you just know it's crying out for you to show the point with details.

A deputy foreign editor, Susan Chira, once told me, "You have a lovely style. The only thing I would ask you to remember is that the reader can only take a certain amount of detail." Take down the details in your notes if you must, but don't write them all. That was, of course, good advice.

Here's another issue writers face. When should you present people in news stories without fully identifying them? You make reference to, and sometimes

quote, a number of people who are not fully identified. You wrote this:

"Mom," a 7-year-old girl recently asked her mother, "if William Clinton is so bad, why do we want to go live with him?"

A nice set-up, and a really nice quote, but neither the girl nor her mother is identified. How do you decide when a person needs to be identified?

Well, in Cuba, it's just very difficult, and I think reporters, editors, and the readers have accepted that people in Cuba feel very nervous about giving their full names, employment, and neighborhood information. Sometimes people would give me names and I'd wonder if they were being honest. A lot of people have very common names, like Pedro Gonzalez. There could be a hundred Pedro Gonzalezes.

I try to avoid using unnamed sources, but it's sometimes impossible to avoid in Cuba and perhaps in other places, too. I have had that experience with undocumented immigrants in New York City. And we respect that, too. The reason for using someone in a story who is not fully identified has to be very strong.

In the next story: "Four Decades of Revolution Bring Cuba Full Circle," you start with a 73-year-old man and end with a woman talking. But in between, *you* really tell the story. It's told in your voice.

You say, "But the people who made the Cuban revolution, who for the most part genuinely believed they were building a better world, know the revolution was supposed to be much more than that." How do you develop voice in stories?

First of all, this wasn't a news story. This was a "Week in Review" piece. It's supposed to have a certain voice. It's supposed to be more analytical than a regular news story.

Two, to develop the voice, you have to know the subject inside out. You have to feel totally comfortable. Even though I was born in Cuba, and I know Cuban history, and I know a lot of what's happening because I've kept in touch with people for 20 years, and I'm constantly interviewing new arrivals, I still had to study. I cannot tell you the number of books and articles and things I read before I went to Cuba.

What led you to write the Operation Pedro Pan story?

I had known about the situation most of my life. The story is well-known to Cubans in South Florida. When I learned that one of the women from Pedro Pan was planning to sue for CIA records on the operation, I planned to write a brief. I mentioned this to my editor, and she wanted to know more about Pedro Pan.

You took an ethical risk as you asked people about a painful part of their past. How were you guided in your approaches?

Most of them were willing to talk. I just asked questions and they told me what their lives had been like. One woman didn't want to talk about it, so we talked about other things. After a while she began to talk about it. Since then, she has reconnected with her heritage. She has become involved in Cuban-American activities.

How important was your background to these stories?

Oh, totally. There are certain stories there that I had never seen anyone do. I knew about the children's story, because I went through that. So I knew some of what I'd find as I began the reporting. On the other hand, I learned things that I didn't expect. That is always the best part about journalism.

You mentioned Chira's comments on your style. How would you describe your writing style?

I don't really have a style, to be honest with you. I just try to write as clearly as I can. That's very important to me. It's very important to me that nobody has to read a sentence again, because I don't want to have to do that when I'm reading. I always approach my pieces as a reader more than as a writer. Will I want to read it? Is this something that I'm bored with? If I'm bored, forget it.

Why did you become a journalist?

Well, you know, it's really interesting. As a child, I was always a very good reader, and I thought I could write, and I would write little things like poetry. I was also very curious. I remember I was at the home of my mother's friend. This woman seemed so sophisticated to me. She was a single woman and she always had a lot of interesting people to her house, lots of reunions.

I was fascinated by it, so I would ask a lot of questions of her guests. One day she turned to me and she said, "You know, you should really be a journalist." And I said, "What's that?" And she said, "Somebody who likes to read and write and ask questions, like you do." What's interesting is that she used the word "journalist" instead of "reporter."

What difference does that make?

It seemed like a big, sophisticated word for a 10-year-old. She said, *"periodista."* She didn't say *"escritora,"* which means "writer." She didn't say *"reportera."* She just said *"periodista."* I liked the sound of it, so when people asked, "What do you want to do when you grow up?" I just continued saying, "I want to be a journalist."

She gave a name to what was in your heart.

Exactly. She now lives in South Florida. Throughout my career, whenever I've gotten a job or made some achievement, I've told her, "You know, you were the one who guided me." I don't think she realizes how important her words were.

What does being a journalist mean to you?

I'm a very shy person. I mean, I'm not one who talks to strangers in elevators. But when I pull out the pad and the pen, I just become a journalist.

And who is that?

Well, it's somebody who really has a job to do and who will probably stop at nothing to do it. It's someone who is completely focused, and is not embarrassed or shy. If I am, I'll hide it well. I just do it. I do my job.

How did you become a journalist?

When we came here from Cuba in 1980, I did not know a word of English, and I thought I'd better forget my dream. Journalists have to read and write and ask questions properly. I thought I'd never be able to do that. I spent the first two years in college majoring in psychology. Then I was invited to write for the school newspaper after I responded to an article on Cuba.

What happened to the language problem?

Well, it wasn't there. I was writing school papers in English and I was getting straight A's. I had scholarships. The problem was obviously in my mind. I mean, it was definitely there when I arrived, but in five years things had changed and I hadn't realized it.

There was something else that happened while I was in college. I used to go to my professors the first day of school and say, "I'll do the work, I'll do everything, but please don't ask me to speak in class because I don't speak English." And everybody bought it. All the teachers said, "OK, thank you for sharing that with me." And I would just sit there and nobody would ask me anything, and I would do my work and get straight A's and go home.

Then one day I went to a sociology professor, Dr. Jackson, and I told him, and he said, "I have no idea what you're talking about. You just said that in English to me. So you are going to speak in this class." The very next day he asked me a question, and I started to speak.

How did you land a job at *The Miami Herald*?

When I graduated from Florida Atlantic University in December 1986, I sent out about 16 letters to different publications and television and radio stations in Miami, looking for a job. I was 22 at the time.

And *The Miami Herald* offered me one. They were
the only ones who wrote back, actually. And they offered me an entry-level job working 27 hours a week
at Neighbors, which is one way to get started, or it
used to be.

And then I was lucky enough that two or three
months into that job, *El Nuevo Herald* asked me to
move there for a full-time job and better pay, so I went.
And that was really good, because I got to do everything. I was national/foreign/local reporter within two
months, because there were only about seven of us on
staff. From then on I went back and forth between *The
Miami Herald* and *El Nuevo Herald* for nine years.

**And how did you grow as a journalist during that
period?**

I recently looked through a box of my work from *El
Nuevo Herald* and I was surprised at the variety of it—
and the volume of it. I was looking back at the early
evaluations, and they all talk about how I could write
three or four stories a day.

The work was intense because there were so few of
us. When there was a trip, they usually would send me.
I went all over the U.S., to Angola because Cuban
troops were there, South and Central America, and to
Geneva to cover the Human Rights Commission of the
United Nations. They were discussing human rights in
Cuba, so I went three or four years in a row. News
could happen anywhere in the world, and if it had a
Miami connection, I had a chance to go.

**What were the differences in writing for *El Nuevo
Herald* and *The Miami Herald*? You shifted from
Spanish to English, but were there differences in
your writing or approach to stories? Did you think
of your audience as different? Did your style change
when you went between the papers?**

No, only the language changed. If you write clearly, it
really doesn't matter which language you use. The
readers were the same, because 50 percent of the population in Miami was Hispanic and most of them were
Cubans. I have never gotten as much reaction from my

work as I did when I was at *El Nuevo Herald.* I think people felt very much like it was their paper, a community newspaper, and they definitely let us know what they thought.

Why did you leave Miami?

I went to an annual meeting of the National Association of Hispanic Journalists in Washington, D.C., in 1994. *The New York Times* used to have wonderful cocktail hours at those conventions, and so everybody would go. I was there and saw David Gonzalez, who is now a columnist at *The New York Times.* I knew him from his years reporting from Miami for *Newsweek.* We were talking and he said, "Let me introduce you to my boss." His boss was Gerald Boyd, who at the time was metro editor of *The New York Times.* Now, he's assistant managing editor.

When David introduced Gerald, I was going to say my name, but Boyd said, "I know who you are." He proceeded to tell me all about my life and my career. It turned out that several people who had also worked with me at *The Miami Herald,* but who were now working at *The New York Times,* had told him about me. He said, "You're the kind of person we'd like to have at *The New York Times.*" Then they started to call me for interviews and clips and that sort of thing, and it took a long time, but I finally moved to New York in 1996.

What was your beat?

I was a general assignment reporter and for a while I also worked in the Queens bureau. And then I returned to the metro desk as a GA. Then I went to Cuba, and after I returned, I started covering immigration. That's what I'm still doing.

What were other steps that enabled you to move from one large newspaper to another?

I've never had a plan. There was no plan or scheme behind any of this. I never thought I would work for *The New York Times,* I never wrote a letter, and I never sent my clips until they asked me to. Things just sort of happened in my career and in my life as well. The only important step I've taken in my career is sending 16 letters out seeking a job when I graduated from college. Everything else evolved.

How did you learn to write?

I'm still learning. Well, I think I learned to write by reading. That's the first thing. To this day, I continue to be more of a reader than a writer.

What do you read?

I read everything, whatever I can get my hands on. I just finished reading *Black and Blue* by Anna Quindlen. But I read everything from the classics to current books. So I think I learned through reading, especially English. I never learned the ABCs in English. It's a weird process to learn to write a language as an adult. Reading helped.

Who were your mentors?

There were always people I admired at *The Miami Herald* and *El Nuevo Herald*. Fabiola Santiago was my first city editor, and then managing editor. She was the one who sent me to Atlanta to cover the prison story. I recently saw notes that she has sent me through the years, and I was reminded that she taught me everything.

I remember in particular that she was very good, and is still very good herself, with leads. I remember when I was really young and I was traveling to assignments all over the world, I would call her at whatever hour and I would say, "You know, I'm trying to say this," and she would just automatically help me write the lead. I nicknamed her "The Leading Lady."

What do you do to improve now? How can established journalists keep getting better?

I'll tell you something that I did at the beginning that impressed Fabiola when she met me. The first time she edited me, I took notes, and I never made the same mistake again, she says. I no longer take notes when I'm edited, but I try not to make the same mistake twice.

Now that you are an award winner, do you still listen to editors?

Oh, God, yes. I listen to good editors. Let me see if I can say this politely. Sometimes you have to trust your instincts. Editors are people, too. If you're lucky, you have very good editors. I do. I have very good editors now. Sometimes you're not that lucky and you don't fully trust your editors, so you have to strike a balance between what your instincts tell you and what your editors tell you.

I have not always agreed with everything my editors have done. Sometimes I've made changes because in journalism they're not only editors, they're also the boss. So I sometimes have done things I didn't agree with.

But if you trust your editor, it works. Recently I turned in a piece that just didn't work. Two very good editors who are working with me said, "This doesn't work; this is the way to do it." And they said the magic words that made the piece come together. They were absolutely right, so I made the changes.

What's your advice for writers who want to listen to editors and do their best work, but their editors can't help them? The editors don't know or can't articulate what's wrong.

They've got a problem then! Well, if they tell you the story doesn't work but they don't know exactly what's wrong, then you have to keep trying until you get it right. I find that sometimes the best way to deal with that is to not do anything to the piece for a while, if you have the time, to just leave it alone, think about it, and see how else you could approach it.

Are there others ways that you know when you've done your best work with a story?

Yes. There are certain things that happen that you really have no control over. The first-person story is an example. It was not a struggle to write. It just flowed out of me, and I had very little to do with it. It was one of those things that you do, and then you're finished. When I finished it I called my husband in New York and read it to him. While I was reading it to him, he was crying, and I was crying.

So I felt there must be something powerful there. But I didn't realize it as I was writing it. And even when I sent it, I was a little uncertain. I didn't know what to think. You send a piece of your soul and you hope that somebody understands and that it makes sense to them. That's how it was.

StarTribune

Eric Black

Finalist, Covering the World

Eric Black has been a staff writer for the Minneapolis *Star Tribune* since 1977. His newspaper series about the history of the U.S. Constitution, the Arab-Israeli conflict, and "Rethinking the Cold War" were all published as books. Black has written for *The Washington Monthly* and *The New Republic* and authored books about the background of the ethnic conflicts in Bosnia and Northern Ireland. He was an American Political Science Association Congressional Fellow and a John S. Knight Fellow at Stanford University.

Black specializes in pieces that provide historical context for current events. The article reprinted here was the sixth installment of "Say Shalom, Somebody," a seven-day series he wrote after accompanying a Minnesota delegation on the occasion of Israel's 50th anniversary. In it, he contrasts a Holocaust survivor's story with the delegation's struggles to reconcile the notions of collective and personal guilt.

Converging at the Holocaust

JUNE 18, 1998

JERUSALEM—"The Holocaust is an awkward meeting ground for Jews and gentiles," says Rachel Korazim, a Holocaust educator. It can easily lapse, she says, into the assumption that Jews are there to represent the victims of this hideous crime and gentiles the perpetrators.

This morning, we will visit Yad Vashem, the Holocaust museum in Jerusalem. Korazim is speaking to the small, mostly gentile group invited by the Jewish Community Relations Council of Minnesota (JCRC), and so she gives us an advance tour of this awkward meeting ground.

Those who were not the victims of such an atrocity could be divided into those who perpetrated it, those who stood by and did nothing and those who tried to intervene against it, Korazim says.

These last are known in Jewish Holocaust lore as "righteous gentiles." She tells us of a tree-lined pathway at Yad Vashem called the Avenue of the Righteous Gentiles, where each tree bears a plaque with the name of one of the non-Jews who tried to save some Jews.

* * *

Ben and Reva Kibort of St. Louis Park went through the Holocaust separately, as children. They come to Yad Vashem this day together, as survivors.

"This was the worst thing they did," Reva Kibort says. She is standing in front of a photograph showing naked, female inmates being herded along by armed, mocking soldiers. "They degraded us so. How could you find the spirit to resist?"

Ben Kibort, a child of Siauliai, Lithuania, had just turned 13 in 1939, had just become Bar Mitzvah and had received from his parents a new bicycle, a beautiful German import. Then the Germans came and took away his bicycle

Of course, they took away much more. They took away his family's comfortable home, took away his mother, took away his youth and almost took away his life. Kibort spent four years in Holocaust hell. But he considers himself "one of the lucky ones" because he got through the ordeal, together with his father and brother.

At Yad Vashem, Kibort sees a photo of the typical jam-packed sleeping quarters of the inmates. "Three to a bunk, that's just how it was. Me, my brother and my father, all in one bunk."

Although he grew to his adult height, Kibort dwindled to 85 pounds by the end of the war. But because he and his family remained healthy enough to work, the Nazis kept the Kiborts in labor camps—not the death camps.

The war was ending and the U.S. troops were closing in. The Nazis closed the death camp at Dachau. The Kiborts were working at nearby labor camps. One day, a detail of German soldiers marched them out of camp and across the countryside, looking for a place to finish them off.

Kibort recalls that the leader of that detail had found what he considered a good place to shoot his prisoners. But the mayor of the nearby town ran up and told the officers that he didn't want the American troops to find the bodies of a bunch of freshly killed inmates in his territory. The troops relented and marched the inmates to some farm buildings where they spent the night. The next morning, one of the inmates was shouting that the guards were gone. They had fled in the night after learning that the Americans were only hours away.

The Americans showed up and provided the human skeletons with their first square meal in years. Kibort ate himself into the hospital.

Before she was taken away from her husband and sons, Kibort's mother had told the family that whoever survived should contact her uncle Jake Edelman in Buffalo, Minn. Kibort told the Yiddish-speaking GI who interviewed the survivors about the uncle. The GI sent word to Rabbi Albert Minda of Temple Israel in Minneapolis, who, it turned out, knew Uncle Jake well. When the reply finally came, the Kibort men learned the wonderful news that Kibort's mother had also survived. They were reunited in the chaos of post-war Europe.

The displaced persons camps were hotbeds of Zionism. The British, who ruled Palestine, were not opening it to survivors of the camps, but there were ways to sneak in, or try anyway.

Kibort recalls that he and his brother wanted to go, but his parents preferred the relative certainty and prosperity of America. The United States wasn't taking all comers, but thanks to the sponsorship of Uncle Jake, the Kiborts would have priority.

So at age 21, having been robbed of his teens, deprived of education, being transported to a place where he didn't know the language or the customs, Kibort started life over as a Minnesotan. He got a job as a shipping clerk in a company based in Minneapolis called Kaufman Knitting. He learned the language, he met and married Reva—herself a survivor of the Warsaw Ghetto and the camps who lost both parents in the Holocaust. They have three children and eight grandchildren. He learned the business and now he owns the business.

Kibort made me promise that if I wrote anything about him I would say that America is the greatest country in the world.

* * *

It was strange—perhaps a writer's conceit—to begin the list of things the Nazis took from Kibort with a reference to his bicycle. Here's why I did it:

Kibort is not reticent about the Holocaust. This is his sixth visit to Yad Vashem. Every year, he and Reva participate in the Minnesota observance of Yom Hashoah, the day of Holocaust remembrance. He even visited Auschwitz a few years ago and stood in the gas chambers. He didn't feel upset, he says, but almost triumphant, as if he wanted to shake his fist defiantly and tell the Nazis that this was one Jew they didn't get.

But when he made his first visit to the U.S. Holocaust Museum in Washington, D.C., he went into a room that represented the room of a young Jewish boy in pre-Holocaust Europe. In that room was a bicycle. And Kibort says that at the sight of the bicycle, he wept until he took refuge in the washroom to compose himself.

* * *

While I've spent the day with the Kiborts, the JCRC group has had its most intense discussion of the week on the issue of collective vs. individual responsibility. Based on interviews after the fact, here's what happened:

After Rachel Korazim's presentation about how Jews and gentiles might discuss the Holocaust, Katherine Kersten, columnist, Catholic and director of the Center of the American Experiment, delivered a spirited objection to what she took as an invitation to all gentiles—except for the righteous few who risked their lives—to feel guilty about the Holocaust.

Kersten said she does not feel personally responsible for nor guilty about the Holocaust. She didn't work at a death camp, she's not a Nazi, she wasn't even born at the time.

She was bothered by Korazim using the word "Christians" to describe the group that had committed the Holocaust more often than "Nazis" or "Germans." She so disagreed with the implication that those who failed to resist the Holocaust share the blame with its active perpetrators. It's too easy for us, with our safe lives, to judge them for not risking theirs, she said.

By all accounts, Kersten's remarks rocked the group. The others had been entranced by Korazim. Lyn Parker, the Minneapolis business consultant, said her life had been permanently altered when she first learned of the Holocaust. She had sworn never to stand idly by in the face of anything similar, no matter the personal risk. Korazim's emphasis on the righteous gentiles made sense to her as encouragement, not as a guilt trip.

Patricia Hampl, the writer and the group's other Catholic, said that "2,000 years of Christian history, which included many episodes of antisemitism, obviously contributed to the Holocaust, and some sense of collective responsibility for the Holocaust has to be incorporated into our view of ourselves as Christians."

Mary Easter, the Carleton College dancer-choreographer, said she had no trouble judging those who tolerated the Holocaust in the silence. Easter, the only black member of the group, wouldn't even be on a trip like this if not for those who stood up against hatred. "If we sympathize too much with those who were weak, we risk dishonoring those who risked everything."

The conversation continued, less intensely, through the week. Kersten, the only conservative on a bus loaded with liberals, kept clarifying her point, fitting it into larger, more ideological context.

Part of the essence of liberalism, she said in one such conversation, is to promote collective guilt feelings about a historical event and use them to justify a favored collective policy to solve some contemporary problem.

"The idea of collective guilt dilutes the guilt of those who are truly responsible," she said. "And it makes a hash of the idea of personal responsibility. If all are guilty, then, in an important sense, none are guilty."

The Rev. Peg Chemberlin, executive director of the Minnesota Council of Churches, believes in collective responsibility and privilege—that the greater a group's privilege, the greater its responsibility. In her journal, Chemberlin reflected on the day's events:

"Do I have an invisible privilege as a non-Jew that allows me to pay attention [to the Holocaust] when I want and walk away when I want?"

She wrote about weeping, together with Ann Bitter, president of the Minnesota Children's Museum, at the haunting Yad Vashem exhibit devoted to the lost children of the Holocaust. "Is it self-indulgent for us to cry?" Bitter asked her.

"Only if that's all we do," Chemberlin replied. Her journal entry concludes: "Our anger and pain are redemptive only if we keep vigilant. About what? So much, but surely for the children, for all the children. Palestinian children? 'Never again.' And yet it is happening to the children as I write. Weep, but act. Weep and act."

Lessons Learned

These essays are supposed to be titled "Lessons Learned" but I suppose this one might be better called "Lessons Unlearned."

Coming up in the newspaper business, we learn many rules and norms about the appropriate way to write a newspaper article. They tell us how our craft defines "objectivity," what it considers to be "the facts," what is "newsworthy," and how to write about it in newspaperese.

But sometimes, it is refreshing for the reader—and the writer—to unlearn some of those rules; to write and see and think in less predictably jounalistic ways.

The norms probably would have told me not even to go on the trip to Israel that led to the article "Converging at the Holocaust." It meant accepting an itinerary that was planned by a Jewish group, which might be called a sin against journalistic objectivity. Traipsing around Israel with a bunch of Minnesotans might seem too provincial. If the *Star Tribune* wanted to make a big deal about Israel's 50th anniversary, the norms would suggest we plan our own trip, book our own interviews with the newsmaker-types, and follow the newsiest angle wherever it led.

There's nothing so wrong with that impulse, of course, except maybe that dozens of world-class news organizations with permanent Middle East bureaus would be doing those stories. In my midlife humility, I no longer think the world needs me to explain Israel to it, or to deliver the solution to the Arab-Israel conflict, or to put a human face and a Minnesota angle on the suffering of the Palestinians.

But the opportunity to visit Yad Vashem, the Holocaust museum in Jerusalem, with a couple of Holocaust survivors who now live in a Twin Cities suburb would at least be something that wouldn't duplicate the wires. And the idea of riding around Israel with a busload of gentile Minnesota civic leaders, and to eavesdrop on their discussions, might even give some of our readers—themselves mostly Minnesota gentiles—access to some of the reactions they might have if confronted with the story of Israel at 50.

Or maybe not. Anyway, I went. The Kiborts generously shared their life stories. I was horrified to have to edit it down to a quick summary of Ben's incredible journey and to have to exclude all but a reference to Reva's equally heart-breaking and inspiring tale. The generally congenial busful of civic leaders erupted over the question of Holocaust guilt. Those discussions gave me an opportunity to dwell for a few paragraphs on some themes I felt were among the deepest of the story I was trying to tell, themes of collective identity and collective responsibility.

In writing the story, I unlearned a couple of other lessons. Journalists are supposed to keep themselves out of the story. In writing a paragraph that said: "Kibort made me promise that if I wrote anything about him I would say that America is the greatest country in the world," I violated that norm. But writing the paragaph that way seemed more honest and less dopey than writing: "'America is the greatest country in the world,' Kibort said."

That was the paragraph in the story that elicited the most comments, mostly from people who thought it was funny. But the next paragraph was the one that a friend and colleague of mine said made him cringe. The offending paragraph read: "It was strange—perhaps a writer's conceit—to begin the list of things the Nazis took from Kibort with a reference to his bicycle. Here's why I did it:"

The unnecessary introduction of the writer into the story is bad enough. Even worse it acknowledges something that we are trained to conceal, namely that a newspaper story is constructed by a writer who makes many choices that shape it heavily and who has a lot of discretion over how it turns out. I broke the taboo on purpose, mostly for the sake of breaking it. We don't need to start putting ourselves in every story or explaining our writing devices, but I think it would be healthy to break that rule occasionally.

After my friend's "cringe" remark, I made a point of asking a few others what they thought of that device. The journalists among my sample generally said it was unnecessary and made them uncomfortable. The non-journalists said they hadn't really noticed it. You win some, you lose some, you tie some.

The Anniston Star

Rhea Wessel

Finalist, Covering the World

Rhea Wessel is a feature writer for *The Anniston* (Ala.) *Star* where she writes for the weekly food, entertainment, and lifestyle sections. She began her career in 1995 at the German Press Agency in Hamburg, where she spent two years writing news and features in the northern German port city. She wrote independently from Sarajevo and Bosnia-Herzegovina and reported from the United Nations headquarters in New York. She has a master's degree in international affairs from Columbia University.

In "Alabama Feeds Mother Russia," Wessel tells a fascinating Thanksgiving story about the intersections between American chicken farmers and their Russian customers in a post-Cold War global economy.

Alabama feeds Mother Russia

NOVEMBER 26, 1998

MOSCOW—Families in Alabama gather together today to give thanks for abundant blessings. Russian families crowded around a dinner table 5,500 miles away may also have reason for thanksgiving.

In recent years, Russians have not faced such formidable conditions: an early winter with harsh temperatures, the worst harvest in 45 years and, topping it off, a financial crisis that has caused the ruble to evaporate.

Things look so bleak the West is preparing to ship in food aid. Alabamians' efforts loom large.

Though Russians don't have a harvest festival similar to Thanksgiving, many families are grateful for every night they are able to sit down to a warm dinner. They give thanks that they made it through the day. Hopes for tomorrow are dim.

Many Russian families fret about surviving the winter, feeding their children, persisting on fixed retirement incomes of less than $50 a month.

One answer to Russians' prayers this cold and hungry winter comes out of the foothills of Appalachia. It is Alabama chicken farmers. It is Larry Buckner's Ragland family, among others.

The biggest worry on Buckner's plate today is paying his 13-year-old's tuition at Auburn University in a few years. The worries of Russian families rise and fall with the sun. What will be for dinner tonight? Can more corners be cut? Quick, turn out that light; the electricity bill is going up.

Buckner raises 135,000 chickens every six weeks and some of his birds make their way to Russian dinner tables. They don't fly here, they take a long march to Russia via Gadsden and Blountsville, and on to ports in Mississippi. Much of the poultry crosses the Atlantic by ship, lands in St. Petersburg, traverses the European continent by train and ends its journey in Moscow's outdoor markets.

Some 78,000 Alabamians work in poultry—78,000 Alabamians helping feed Mother Russia and benefiting from the economic trade.

Spanning 11 time zones, Russia is the main export market for U.S. poultry, and Alabama ranks fourth in domestic poultry production.

The U.S. and Russia have a mutually beneficial relationship when it comes to chicken. Americans generally prefer boneless breast meat and Russians like the juicier dark meat of legs and thighs. (And Chinese like the feet.) The chicks grown by Buckner, a supplier for Tyson Foods, are split down the middle. The top half stays in the U.S. and the leg quarters hit the chicken trail to Russia.

Here in Russia, the back ends are fondly called *Nozhki Busha* or "Bush Legs" for the former U.S. president who first promoted the trade.

Far across the Atlantic and on the far side of Europe is Nina Apollonova, a 73-year-old pensioner. The widow lives in eastern Moscow in a high-rise building. Her efficiency apartment is one room that measures roughly 25 feet by 15 feet, plus a small bath. Black-and-white photos of her two sons hang above her sagging bed, which is a few feet from her dinner table, a few inches from her sofa.

Mrs. Apollonova is energetic and excitable. She talks with her hands. When she laughs, a twinkle shows in her eyes and the light catches the gold caps on her lower teeth.

Cooking is an art for Mrs. Apollonova, and she talks zealously about her recipes for Alabama chicken: broiled birds with prunes, chicken Kiev, and her favorite—a spicy blend from Georgia—the country south of her own.

Back in Ragland, Nonna Buckner, Larry's wife, also loves to cook. Once a month, she drives her Dodge Caravan 50 miles to buy bulk groceries from a warehouse grocery in Birmingham. Every day Mrs. Apollonova walks three miles from market to market looking for the lowest prices. Her cupboard and refrigerator space are limited so she bundles up, pulls on her snow boots and straightens her fur *shapka,* the hat so many Russians wear to keep out the biting cold.

The petite, muscular grandmother emerges from the summer-like conditions of her apartment into weather colder than Mrs. Buckner's deep freeze. On this mid-November day, it was already 5 degrees Fahrenheit.

Another household on the receiving end of Alabama's chicken trail is the Ostashevskaya family. Nikolai, an engineer, drives a white minivan for Tysons. Nadya, his wife, used to teach English. Now she does odd jobs such as baby-sitting and housekeeping. Nikolai worked in aeronautics until his job was phased out after the breakup of the Soviet Union in 1991.

Mrs. Ostashevskaya likes to warm up in the evenings by drinking homemade chicken bouillon. When Ostashevskaya gets home from work around 7 p.m., the couple eats her cooking and settles in for the night.

In Ragland, a similar scene is lived out.

Buckner has taken his last shower of the day trying to rid himself of the smell of his source of income. He and his wife eat the supper she cooks and serves while talking about farm jobs they finished and what needs to be done tomorrow. The kids run in, grab a plate. Larry catches the 10 o'clock news.

In western Moscow, sitting in his cloth-covered armchair, wearing an argyle sweater, Ostashevskaya is also watching the tube. Maybe it's a rerun of *ER* or an old French flick. Though the Russian engineer has attended college, Buckner nets more than 100 times his salary of about $1,000 a month. But at the end of the day, it really doesn't matter. They are both dog-tired.

The Cold War officially defrosted long ago. Some Americans may still think of Russians as our recent Communist enemy. A few may also recall Russia was our World War II ally before the Stalinist regime soured relations.

The new global economy that exports Alabama chickens to Russia is recipe for a whole new relationship. The poultry industry is not charity but international trade with considerable monetary benefit to producers.

Instead of "us" and "them," Alabamians and Russians are simply trade partners.

The two peoples have sound economic and social reasons to learn mutual understanding. The process begins by recognizing cultural differences and similarities.

Take shopping as an example. While Americans wait for their Sunday newspaper inserts to scope out the lowest prices on food, Mrs. Apollonova joins other pensioners in a weekday morning shopping crunch. Instead of a frozen food section, all goods come that way. Anything left outside in Russia's frigid winters for any time will begin to crystallize.

As two Americans bump into each other in the produce section of Winn-Dixie, Mrs. Ostashevskaya sees friends and interacts with neighbors at her local *rynok,* or outdoor market. Shopping is a social event—a time to see familiar faces and to find someone to commiserate with about the high prices.

Since Russia's financial system collapsed Aug. 17, some prices have doubled while salaries have generally stayed the same. Many workers are on an unpaid "holiday" as they wait until the economy improves. In some cases, families lost their whole life's savings when the ruble lost its value and banks closed their doors.

At a butcher shop or small grocery store, Mrs. Ostashevskaya shells out her rubles for Alabama Bush legs. No need to stand in line. That's a futile effort. The way to make it to the front is to push your body toward it. The eager but silent mob doesn't seem to vex the lone clerk behind the counter.

Mrs. Ostashevskaya's food has made it past the cashier. She's on her own to pack it into her personal grocery cart, much like luggage wheels with metal tubing and a leather-look sack. She layers her milk, her cabbage and her Alabama chicken legs.

Had she forgotten to bring her own shopping bag, Mrs. Apollonova or Mrs. Ostashevskaya would have to pay a small sum for a plastic one. No freebies here. Many street vendors sell plastic shopping bags decorated with scenes from a fantasy life—fast cars, jet planes and island vacations.

At Wal-Mart SuperCenter in Oxford, cashiers make brief eye contact asking, "How are you today?" Programmed to the greeting, the typical reply is, "Fine. How are you?" As niceties are exchanged, your shampoo, your new radio and your Alabama chicken legs are double bagged.

Since market reforms took hold in Russia, superstores have begun to open.

Unlike American ones, where discounts are the attraction, hypermarkets in Russia have variety and availability as their selling points. Shoppers are usually the upper middle class, newly rich Russians or Americans and Europeans working in Russia.

A blast of hot air welcomes shoppers to Ramstor hypermarket in Western Moscow. Instead of an elderly people-greeter at the door, the shopper first encounters two men holding mops. The moppers are everywhere. Twenty or 30 of them. Following in shoppers' footsteps. Interested in the muddy slush tracked in. A foreigner looks guilty for causing such work. High unemployment eases the conscience.

Perusing the acres of shelves on Sunday morning at the squeaky clean and glimmering 24-hour store, the director of the U.S. Department of Agriculture's Trade Office in Moscow notices the variety of American chicken available. Bob Walker comments that poultry is one of the lowest-priced sources of protein for Russians and before the financial crisis, the U.S. sent 100,000 tons each year. At many shops, beef is twice the price of chicken.

Mrs. Ostashevskaya has done her shopping for the week, and it's time for Sunday-style family activities and Alabama chicken, of course. As Larry and Norma head to Hardin Chapel Bible Church in Ragland, Nadya and Nikolai make for the woods outside Moscow. The couple owns their own cross-country skiing gear and they like getting exercise and fresh air. Speaking for her husband, Nadya says they are Orthodox Christian.

"Nikolai doesn't go to church, but he believes in God in his heart," she says. Married 24 years, with one son, Nadya is the talkative one, and she is clearly in control.

Larry and Norma have been together since she was 14. They operate by consensus, discussing whether their youngest son, Pike, should switch off the television and practice his trumpet. In their 33 years of marriage, they have four children. Two boys, Pike the surprise, and then a girl.

The oldest two are Jeff, 31, and Bradley, 28. Pike, the youngest son, is 13, and Beth is 10. Kira, the dog, joined the family somewhere along the way.

"I wouldn't change a thing. I wouldn't have it any different," says Mrs. Buckner.

Buckner opted for a good job with the phone company and he was sent away for training for a few months.

He missed Norma so much he went home to Ragland and married his sweetheart.

Nadya and Nikolai fell in love when they were a bit older. She was 21, and he was 29. She had introduced another couple and the friends wanted to return her favor. Enter Nikolai and the rest is Russian history.

Together with Riki, a 9-year old Airedale terrier, they have lived in their two-bedroom apartment in Moscow for the past 24 years. Their son, Artem, who is 22, is married and lives with his wife in Moscow.

At the distant dinner tables, both Mrs. Buckner and Mrs. Ostashevskaya serve their husbands the dishes they cooked on their gas stoves. Buckner and Ostashevskaya are seated; the women are scurrying, making sure the chicken doesn't get too brown.

Western pop music by Sting and the Pet Shop Boys plays in the background of the small Moscow apartment that's about 350 square feet of living space. The phone rings as the screen-saver on the family computer kicks in. (Ostashevskaya studies English on the computer.)

At the 140-acre Buckner farm the big screen television and microwave hum in the background of the 2,700-square foot house. Beth has connected to a Beanie Baby Web site to find out which one she wants to add to her collection of 123 just as Pike, the eager concert and marching band member, practices his scales.

Wine or vodka is poured as dinner is served in Moscow. Little chunks of chicken are layered into a salad. In a second dish, cooks combine finely chopped chicken into a smooth recipe somewhat like pate. This precedes a main course of broiled chicken with prunes and cauliflower, something of a Russian standard.

The Buckners are true Southerners, and they take their chicken fried with a glass of iced tea to wash it down. Norma slices breasts lengthwise, dips them in milk and egg, dredges in White Lily self-rising flour and fries in a little bit of corn oil. The fixin's? Mashed potatoes and gravy, macaroni and cheese and a green salad dressed by Paul Newman. Pickled vegetables from the family's *dacha,* or suburban garden house, dress the bird in Moscow.

A toast is made to all present and even to those who aren't. Careful not to set your glass down without drinking or it will bring bad luck. Women, don't sit at the outermost seat or you may not get married for the next seven years. And never leave an empty alcohol bottle on the table. It's a bad sign.

The Ostashevskayas and guests linger at the rectangular lace-covered table in their living room. It is furnished with a long armoire and a framed mirror.

The armoire holds the family's treasures—a flowered china set, pictures and trinkets.

Tea is served Russian style. Leaves are steeped in a small pot and half a teacup of the strong brew is served. Then boiling water from a different kettle is poured on top. The samovar, an ornate container once used for boiling water, is mostly for decoration these days.

Nadya takes a teaspoon full of cranberries in gooey sauce and stirs them into her green tea, called *chai*. "It's better than sugar," she says, spooning out the warmed fruits when she's finished with her tea.

Next come the candies. Individually wrapped and served in a beveled glass dish, the Russian specialties are crisp and rich. A large box of Western European chocolates is opened at the table. The guests' eyes grow large with anticipation. At the Buckners, it's apple pie for those who have any room left.

For some Russian families not as fortunate as the Ostashevskayas, the meal never progresses to dessert. It is chicken—boiled, baked, rolled, stuffed or broiled. It is every last piece, cleaned to the bone, then boiled again to make broth.

And thousands of miles away, Buckner excuses himself from the dinner table. It's time to check on his chicks. The chicks that will soon help nourish a hungry Mother Russia.

Lessons Learned

BY RHEA WESSEL

The fun started a few minutes after landing in icy Moscow. I didn't have any problem spotting the man who was to pick me up. He was a 6-foot-4-inch tall former basketball player named Vadim. We grabbed my things and headed for his snow- and mud-covered Lada, seats draped with carpets. At 5 degrees Fahrenheit, it seemed like eternity before Vadim found his key.

Bending down to his thigh level, Vadim put the key in the lock and gave it a wrench. Frozen shut. He tried the other side. Back to the driver's door. Hunched over, he began to blow from the long depths of his body in hopes of defrosting the lock. I assumed the same position on the other side. Lips puckered on the lock, I blew and blew, hoping those kissing lessons in high school would somehow pay off.

The trip to Moscow to write about Alabama chicken exports was full of other oral experiences. Food. Drink. Laughter. Chapped lips. Suspicious translations and interesting uses of the American language.

In fact, the story started with a dropped jaw, mouth full of an Alabama bagel sandwich. For 10 minutes, my managing editor had been answering all my questions with *da,* the Russian word for yes. I didn't understand why she was insulting me, saying, "Duh, duh. Silly." Our executive editor, Chris Waddle, sat down and said, "Rhea, we want you to go to Russia to write about Alabama chicken exports for our Thanksgiving Day issue."

It was a visionary idea. Chicken links Alabama and Russia, and it is an ideal starting point for translating the cultures.

The majority of my reporting was done before I arrived in Moscow. I had talked chicken with all the relevant associations, visited a chicken plant, and dined with an Alabama chicken-growing family. And I had packed the first three days of the two-week trip full of appointments. I took an expandable folder full of background information, categorized by my story subjects. I had also collected telephone, fax, and cell phone numbers in advance. This was essential, since finding such information in Moscow is cumbersome if not impossible.

I had two weeks' notice before I was to leave for Moscow. I wanted to do a crash course in Russian history and re-read

Crime and Punishment. But getting a visa and shots and learning all about chicken took priority.

Keeping a focus on culture was key in my story. The first two days of my in-country reporting dealt with what happens to Alabama chicken after it crosses the ocean.

More important was shopping, cooking, and dining—the universal and accessible elements of the story. One dinner meeting with a rural family had fallen through. I pushed my sources to help me set up another.

The actual writing of my story came in the wee hours of the morning, after I had downloaded most of the digital photos I took. At my editors' insistence, I had played with a few leads and "nut" graphs before I left. I pulled up that file on my laptop, reread it, and wrote anew. I wrote from memory, inserting question marks on things I wanted to check. I avoided digging in my notes until I had written the full story. I didn't want to disrupt the flow. I had thought through the topics I wanted to cover and which anecdotes would work as transitions, but I didn't formally outline.

Cathi Downing, my editor and our features editor, said the most challenging part for her was communication with me. I had given her a clock set to Moscow time to keep on her desk. But we hadn't agreed on specific times for conference calls. Each morning I was gone was met with the trepidation that e-mail might fail or I could not be reached by phone for questions.

The biggest lesson I learned was that the success of an overseas "parachute" writing trip is all in the preparations. Without thorough research and planning, I could not have written my stories on deadline.

I also learned that despite the cold, the Russian people are warm and friendly. Many a night was spent crowded around a table full of chicken scraps, vodka on the lips, and laughter in the air.

A big thanks to my editors for their commitment and support.

Bringing home lessons learned in distant lands

BY STEPHEN BUCKLEY

On a sparkling afternoon in November 1996, I straddled the Rwanda-Zaire border as nearly 1 million Rwandans shuffled shoulder-to-shoulder, silent and determined, back into their homeland. They carried bundles of clothes, bags of grain, pots and pans, farming tools, and other possessions—sewing machines, homemade children's toys, bicycles. Some were clearly exhausted, having walked as long as 10 hours. Only the shh-shh-shh of their feet against sand and stone broke the quiet.

I'd never seen anything like it, and neither had any of my reporting colleagues. I would spend nearly three and a half years in sub-Saharan Africa, based in Nairobi, Kenya, and I would see lots of extraordinary things, but none more so than this. It came to symbolize for me how utterly surreal covering Africa could be sometimes. I used to tell people that, of all *The Washington Post*'s foreign bureaus, this had to be the most foreign of them all.

Africa was indeed a very different place to do reporting. But the lessons I learned as a reporter in that distant land apply universally. They're lessons that are relevant to reporters at small-town weeklies as well as big metro dailies. It doesn't matter whether you cover city hall or write features, whether you do a couple of projects a year or churn out a couple of stories a day. The lessons still apply.

Time and space prevent me from sharing all the important lessons Africa taught me, but these are among the most crucial: Practice patience. Go deep. Challenge conventional wisdom. Find universal themes. Embrace complexity. These habits will bring depth and richness to your stories. They'll imbue your reporting with vision and creativity and brighten your writing with evocative—and provocative—details and images.

First, a little personal history.

I am an accidental correspondent. I had always dreamed of going overseas, but thought of it as just that—a dream. I had spent five years covering cops, courts, and schools on the metro staff when the paper asked me to go to Africa. I was both elated and frightened; my stomach fluttered with equal parts dread and anticipation. My predecessor told me this would be the toughest job I'd probably ever have. He also said it would be one of the most rewarding.

He warned me that the reporting would consist largely of grappling with logistics. He told me to expect planes that leave hours late, or not at all. He spoke of antiquated phone systems, miles-long moonscapes that passed for roads, and officious, brutish border officials. The actual reporting and writing would be a piece of cake, he said. Getting to the story would be the real feat.

And don't forget, he told me again and again: Be patient. I realized what he meant immediately upon starting my assignment. The rules for time were different in Africa. A government minister who promised to meet me at 10 a.m. might not turn up until 2. An embassy would tell me to return the next morning for a visa; I'd go back and bureaucratic delays might force me to wait the whole day. Using an interpreter during an interview, which I did often, typically doubled its duration. Just getting non-negotiable necessities such as name, age, and occupation, could take 20 minutes.

So I learned patience. I'd never thought of it as a virtue in reporting. In 12 years of writing for newspapers, I had never heard anyone connect patience to getting good interviews or catching critical details. But in Africa I learned that the ability to simply hang in there, to wait an extra 20 minutes or two hours or two days—whatever I could afford—was an invaluable skill. The best reporters and photographers knew this and practiced it until it became an unshakable habit.

This lesson struck me most powerfully during my last full year on the continent. I was working with photographer Carol Guzy on a story about the triumphs and struggles of an Ethiopian midwife. Our goal for the week was to see Tamunie Hegisso deliver a baby. When she told us, through an interpreter, that she typically delivered a couple of babies a week, we thought: Great, maybe we'll actually see two births. We figured we'd have no problem getting back to Ethiopia's capital, Addis Ababa, by mid-morning Saturday to fly back to Nairobi.

But by Thursday, Tamunie hadn't delivered. And our nerves were strained. We had spent four days reporting and now all we could do was wait. We played soccer with the village kids. We played cards. We went on rounds with the midwife. Then we waited some more.

By Friday afternoon, it was clear that one of Tamunie's neighbors was in labor, but it was far from certain that she'd deliver early enough in the evening for us to get back to Addis Ababa. Midnight passed, and then 1 a.m., and still no birth. Finally, finally, at 3:16 a.m., Tamunie helped pull a husky, bright-eyed girl into the world. Tamunie raised her hands to heaven in the darkness of the hut.

Then we caught a couple of hours of sleep and raced back to Addis Ababa, six hours away, to catch our plane. We made it in five and a half, breathing hard when we boarded the flight.

The live birth brought the story to life that reconstructions rarely can. It provided drama, and it helped draw readers into a place most had never been. It had been worth the wait.

We could not have gotten Tamunie's story without the critical help of a great interpreter. I often used interpreters in Africa, especially in rural areas. I always wished I could communicate directly, but I found that a good interpreter could be a fine bridge. I found that the best interpreters would anticipate questions and ask them before I could. Often, those questions were simply, "What happened next?" Or "Can you give another example?"

As an American reporter, I'd become enamored of questions designed to draw emotive responses: "How do you feel?" I discovered in Africa that questions designed to allow a subject's narrative to spool out slowly, in vivid, often painful detail, made good stories lustrous. A great detail can carry more emotion than even the most pathos-laden quote. Listening to someone actually tell the story in their own words lent it a clarity and drama and perspective that I'd rarely known. I learned that three or four in-depth interviews could prove far more helpful than a dozen 10-minute quickies. I learned to go deep.

This was especially helpful when I covered breaking stories. It wasn't unusual for me to leap on a plane from

Nairobi to another country to catch a breaking story—
to Rwanda after a massacre, to Tanzania for a ferry
sinking—hire a driver, find a good interpreter, dash to
the scene, do interviews, check into a hotel, and then
file a piece over some of the world's worst phone lines.
Often I'd have time for three, maybe four, interviews
before having to rush to a hotel to write.

So I had to focus on a few individuals, finding out as
much as possible from them by asking, "What happened next?" again and again. The rewards of such
reporting proved rich. Readers often read the most disturbing stories, simply because the characters portrayed in the pieces compelled them to.

They were people such as a Kenyan woman named
Agnes. This is how her story began:

"After more than 30 years of being threatened,
chased, slapped, thrown, punched, kicked, choked,
whipped and stepped on by her husband, Agnes summoned the strength last winter to take an unusual step
for an abused African wife.

"She left."

That grim list of violent acts came out of a 75-
minute interview with Agnes, who had asked not to be
fully identified, during which I asked her again and
again to detail for me exactly what her husband did to
her during her three decades together. When the interview ended, I went back through my notebook and
highlighted all the verbs she had used to describe the
abuse. Kick. Choke. Punch. Slap. Throw. Whip.

And I knew I had a lead.

And I knew those kinds of details would make
Agnes's pain immediate and real for readers.

Readers connected with this story in a way that I
never expected. The paper received numerous calls,
including some from angry Africans who felt I had
unfairly attacked their continent. But many callers
wanted to know how to help Agnes. A couple of
women's rights activists contacted me directly, seeking
ways to assist the shelter for battered women to which
Agnes had escaped. It was the first of its kind in Kenya.

Stories about ordinary people such as Agnes always
drew a reaction from readers. She represented something larger than just a sad, infuriating tale of a woman
trapped in a violent marriage. She stood for the long suffering and courage that readers, some of whom undoubt-

edly were in similarly brutal relationships, easily identified with.

It's hard to find subjects such as Agnes, people who stand for universal themes—hope, progress, redemption, perseverance, and so on. They're not the types who hold news conferences. They don't hire public relations firms. They tend to be outsiders. And they tend to be people who don't necessarily appear newsworthy at first glance.

Finding a universal theme moves a story from the mundane, or mildly interesting, into the unusual. In late April 1996, for example, I heard of a young man who longed to become the first doctor in his Masai village. A friend invited me to cover a fund-raiser for the student in the village. I decided to go.

Before the fund-raiser, I did a little reading about the Masai. I knew that they were probably Africa's best known tribe. I didn't know that they were one of the continent's most fiercely isolated groups, whose people had shunned education until recently. I didn't know that families and friends of children who had longed to go to school mocked them mercilessly. Now, I was about to do a story about a young man who not only wanted to become a doctor; he was hoping to do it with help from his fellow villagers, few of whom made more than $100 a year.

And suddenly, my nice little story transformed itself into a much more important piece about a young man who symbolized his tribe's newfound determination to move into the modern age. It became a tale that lots of working-class and middle-class Americans could identify with. It became a story about progress and the power of community.

When the village recognized Wilson Naiyomah's brilliance, I wrote, its residents "essentially adopted him. Sometimes neighbors paid his school fees; other times, his teachers helped him earn money by paying him to run errands for them or to work in their fields. Some neighbors provided money for school uniforms and shoes. Others bought his textbooks. Some bought him toiletries. The government nurse in the area's only health clinic treated him for free."

Writing about people such as Agnes and Wilson was easy. They were doing extraordinary things. They were quiet heroes. They were not, journalistically speaking, complicated subjects. But I found that that wasn't always the case in Africa. Sometimes it was hard to tell the innocent from the oppressor, the victim from the villain. I learned that truth is indeed stranger than fiction. It's also usually a lot more complicated.

No story was as complicated as that of the returning Rwandans. On television, it appeared that they were refugees coming home after being chased from their country more than two years earlier. In fact, thousands of those Rwandans had taken part in an unspeakably vicious campaign to exterminate members of the country's minority tribe, the Tutsis. These Rwandans, mostly from the country's Hutu ethnic majority, had massacred at least 500,000 (some estimates run as high as a million) during 100 days in 1994.* When a Tutsi rebel group overwhelmed the Hutu-led government that directed the slaughter, those who had hacked and stabbed and bludgeoned their neighbors to death streamed out of the country in the hundreds of thousands, fearing retribution. A lot of the Hutus who returned in November 1996 hadn't taken part in the genocide. Many others had.

To suggest that this was simply a joyous homecoming ignored the potential for a fresh, years-long chapter of repression, violence, and revenge in a country where such cycles had long ago become a way of life. The return of the Hutus wasn't an ending. It was the beginning of a critical, and very uncertain, phase in that tiny country's fragile life.

And so to write this as a story about innocents returning home would have told just half the story. Which is what many of us do. We leave out facts that contradict our black-and-white rendering of our subject because we're afraid to diminish the story, afraid that readers won't want to navigate the gray. But readers are intelligent. They understand human nature. They don't shy from the contradictions that make up our stories.

*[*Editor's Note: Mark Fritz, a national writer for the Associated Press, won the Jesse Laventhol Prize for Deadline Reporting for his coverage of the ethnic massacre in Rwanda. His articles appear in Best Newspaper Writing 1995.]*

I still recall anguishing over the ending of my story about the Ethiopian midwife. The piece had focused in part on how she had gone from using unsanitary methods of delivery to cleaner, safer methods. She was, for example, not supposed to use razor blades to cut a newborn's umbilical cord anymore. She was to use the scissors the health department had supplied her.

But when Tamunie delivered the baby in the predawn darkness of her neighbor's hut, her scissors didn't work. Maybe they were dull. Maybe she was nervous. Who knows? After several tries, she pulled out a razor blade and used that to snip the cord.

I was horrified. There goes the Progress theme, I thought. But when I sat down to write, I realized that I was wrong. Her resorting to a razor hadn't ruined my story; it had authenticated it. Progress is always one step forward, two steps back. It's herky-jerky, not linear. Progress is complicated. So are people. And our stories should reflect that.

The return of the Rwandans helped teach me one other critical lesson: Always challenge conventional wisdom. Before this extraordinary event, anyone who suggested that the Hutus could indeed return en masse found himself the victim of disdainful sneers and condescending chuckles. No one believed it could happen.

In retrospect, it wasn't so far-fetched. Rwandans had repeatedly moved in enormous groups throughout the country's violent history. In July 1994 they had moved with incredible speed, hundreds of thousands of them, their belongings piled on their backs, their children stumbling to keep up, as they scrambled to leave Rwanda. Why couldn't they return the same way?

We embraced conventional wisdom because we didn't know our history. Or, more accurately, we ignored what we knew.

If we had questioned conventional thinking about the possible return of the Rwandans, we would have asked some difficult questions long before that warm November afternoon. We could have asked how the government would handle the terrible housing crisis that would occur if the Hutus came back en masse. And how would Rwanda's government services, already stretched beyond capacity, handle the overwhelming demand that would accompany such a return? And how would the government, suddenly faced with the return of Rwandans who bludgeoned and hacked their neighbors to death, manage to keep their country from descending into yet another years-long cycle of bloodletting and instability?

But none of us deigned to scoff at conventional wisdom. I wish I had. And I wish more of us would.

Challenging conventional wisdom in Africa requires guts, just as it would in America. And great reporting takes the same skills, no matter where you are. It takes brains and guts and moxie. It takes patience. It takes the vision to see stories that trumpet universal themes. It takes the same discipline to go deep. Employ these lessons wherever you are, and you'll be able to craft stories that connect readers to any world, no matter how familiar or foreign, with freshness, depth, and insight.

[Stephen Buckley opened a Brazil bureau for The Washington Post in 1999 after serving three years as the paper's correspondent in Nairobi, Kenya. For six months in 1998, he was a visiting professional at The Poynter Institute.]

Annual bibliography

BY DAVID B. SHEDDEN

WRITING AND REPORTING BOOKS 1998

Fellow, Anthony R., and Thomas N. Clanin. *Copy Editor's Handbook for Newspapers.* Englewood, Colo.: Morton Publishing, 1998.

Fink, Conrad C. *Introduction to Professional Newswriting.* 2nd ed. New York: Longman, 1998.

Fox, Walter. *Writing the News: A Guide for Print Journalists.* 2nd ed. Ames, Iowa: Iowa State University Press, 1998.

Garlock, David, ed. *Pulitzer Prize Feature Stories.* Ames, Iowa: Iowa State University Press, 1998.

Garrison, Bruce. *Professional Feature Writing.* 3rd ed. Hillsdale, N.J.: Lawrence Erlbaum Associates, 1998.

Goldstein, Norm, ed. *The Associated Press Stylebook and Libel Manual.* New York: Perseus Press, 1998.

Hicks, Wynford. *English for Journalists.* 2nd ed. New York: Routledge, 1998.

Klement, Alice M., and Carolyn B. Matalene. *Telling Stories/Taking Risks: Journalism Writing at the Century's Edge.* Belmont, Calif.: Wadsworth Publishing Company, 1998.

Knight, Robert M. *The Craft of Clarity: A Journalistic Approach to Good Writing.* Ames, Iowa: Iowa State University Press, 1998.

Lehman, Daniel Wayne. *Matters of Fact: Reading Nonfiction over the Edge.* Columbus, Ohio: Ohio State University Press, 1998.

Library of America. *Reporting Vietnam.* (2 Volumes) New York: Library of America, 1998.

Mencher, Melvin. *Basic Media Writing.* 6th ed. New York: McGraw Hill, 1998.

Rystrom, Kenneth. *The Why, Who, and How of the Editorial Page.* 3rd ed. State College, Pa.: Strata Publishing, 1998.

Scanlan, Christopher, ed. *Best Newspaper Writing 1998.* St. Petersburg, Fla.: The Poynter Institute, 1998.

Stewart, James B. *Follow the Story: How to Write Successful Nonfiction.* New York: Touchstone Books, 1998.

Titchener, Campbell B. *Reviewing the Arts.* 2nd ed. Hillsdale, N.J.: Lawrence Erlbaum Associates, 1998.

Yudkin, Marcia. *Writing Articles About the World Around You.* Cincinnati, Ohio: Writers Digest Books, 1998.

CLASSICS

Atchity, Kenneth. *A Writer's Time: A Guide to the Creative Process, from Vision through Revision.* New York: Norton, 1986.

Berg, A. Scott. *Max Perkins: Editor of Genius.* New York: Dutton, 1978.

Bernstein, Theodore M. *The Careful Writer: A Modern Guide to English Usage.* New York: Atheneum Press, 1965.

Biagi, Shirley. *Interviews That Work: A Practical Guide for Journalists.* 2nd edition. Belmont, Calif.: Wadsworth, 1992.

Blundell, William E. *The Art and Craft of Feature Writing: Based on The Wall Street Journal.* New York: New American Library, 1988.

Brady, John. *The Craft of Interviewing.* New York: Vintage Books, 1977.

Brande, Dorothea. *Becoming a Writer.* Los Angeles: J.P. Tarcher; Boston: distributed by Harcourt Brace, reprint of 1934 edition, 1981.

Brown, Karen, Roy Peter Clark, Don Fry, and Christopher Scanlan, eds. *Best Newspaper Writing.* St. Petersburg, Fla.: The Poynter Institute. Published annually since 1979.

Cappon, Rene J. *The Word: An Associated Press Guide to Good News Writing.* New York: The Associated Press, 1982.

Clark, Roy Peter. *Free to Write: A Journalist Teaches Young Writers.* Portsmouth, N.H.: Heinemann Educational Books, 1986.

Clark, Roy Peter, and Don Fry. *Coaching Writers: The Essential Guide for Editors and Reporters.* New York: St. Martin's Press, 1992.

Dillard, Annie. *The Writing Life.* New York: Harper and Row, 1989.

Downie, Leonard, Jr. *The New Muckrakers.* New York: NAL-Dutton, 1978.

Elbow, Peter. *Writing With Power: Techniques for Mastering the Writing Process.* New York: Oxford University Press, 1981.

Follett, Wilson. *Modern American Usage: A Guide.* London: Longmans, 1986.

Franklin, Jon. *Writing for Story: Craft Secrets of Dramatic Nonfiction.* New York: Atheneum, 1986.

Goldstein, Norm, ed. *The Associated Press Stylebook and Libel Manual.* 27th edition. Reading, Mass.: Addison-Wesley, 1992.

Gross, Gerald, ed. *Editors on Editing: An Inside View of What Editors Really Do.* New York: Harper & Row, 1985.

Howarth, William L., ed. *The John McPhee Reader.* New York: Farrar, Straus and Giroux, 1990.

Hugo, Richard. *The Triggering Town: Lectures & Essays on Poetry & Writing.* New York: Norton, 1992.

Mencher, Melvin. *News Reporting and Writing.* 5th ed. Dubuque, Iowa: William C. Brown, 1991.

Metzler, Ken. *Creative Interviewing: The Writer's Guide to Gathering Information by Asking Questions.* 2nd ed. Englewood Cliffs, N.J.: Prentice Hall, 1989.

Mitford, Jessica. *Poison Penmanship: The Gentle Art of Muckraking.* New York: Knopf, 1979.

Murray, Donald. *Shoptalk: Learning to Write With Writers.* Portsmouth, N.H.: Boynton/Cook, 1990.

— *Writing for Your Readers.* Old Saybrook, Conn.: Globe Pequot Press, 1992.

Plimpton, George. *Writers at Work: The Paris Review Interviews.* Series. New York: Viking, 1992.

Ross, Lillian. *Reporting.* New York: Dodd, 1981.

Scanlan, Christopher, ed. *How I Wrote the Story.* Providence Journal Company, 1986.

Sims, Norman, ed. *Literary Journalism in the Twentieth Century.* New York: Oxford University Press, 1990.

Snyder, Louis L., and Richard B. Morris, eds. *A Treasury of Great Reporting.* New York: Simon & Schuster, 1962.

Stafford, William, and Donald Hall, eds. *Writing the Australian Crawl: View on the Writer's Vocation.* Ann Arbor, Mich.: University of Michigan Press, 1978.

Strunk, William, Jr., and E.B. White. *The Elements of Style.* 3rd ed. New York: Macmillan, 1979.

Talese, Gay. *Fame & Obscurity.* New York: Ivy Books, 1971.

Wardlow, Elwood M., ed. *Effective Writing and Editing: A Guidebook for Newspapers.* Reston, Va.: American Press Institute, 1985.

White, E.B. *Essays of E.B. White.* New York: Harper & Row, 1977.

Witt, Leonard. *The Complete Book of Feature Writing.* Cincinnati, Ohio: Writer's Digest Books, 1991.

Wolfe, Tom. *The New Journalism.* New York: Harper & Row, 1973.

Zinsser, William. *On Writing Well.* 4th ed. New York: Harper & Row, 1990.

— *Writing to Learn.* New York: Harper & Row, 1988.

ARTICLES 1998

Auletta, Ken. "Writing In-Depth Profiles." *The IRE Journal* (January/February 1998): pp. 6–7.

Beasley, Berrin. "Journalists' Attitudes Toward Narrative Writing." *Newspaper Research Journal* (Winter 1998): pp. 78–89.

Clark, Roy Peter. "The Tools of Clarity." *The American Editor* (October/November 1998): p. 8.

Franklin, Jon. "The Narrative Tool." *The American Editor* (October/November 1998): p. 6.

French, Tom. "Subversive Storytelling." *The American Editor* (October/November 1998): p. 9.

Fry, Don. "Too Many Ingredients Ruin the Story Stew." *The American Editor* (October/November 1998): p. 10.

Hart, Jack. "Music In the Words." *Editor & Publisher* (Jan. 31, 1998): p. 6.

Kees, Beverly. "Detecting Fiction." *The American Editor* (July/August 1998): pp. 11–15.

Kirtz, Bill. "Tell Me a Story: Narrative Journalism Not New Genre, Just Today's Version of an Age-Old Skill." *Quill* (April 1998): pp. 3–5.

Knight, Robert M. "Brick By Brick: Good Writing Built with Skill by Careful Masters Who Love Language." *Quill* (April 1998): pp. 29–31.

LaRocque, Paula. "It's a True Fact Writing Can Repeat Again What's Been Said Before." *Quill* (December 1998): p. 25.

Long, Kate. "10 Ways to Tune in to Your Best Voice." *The American Editor* (October/November 1998): p. 7.

Masse, Mark H., and Mark N. Popovich. "Assessing Faculty Attitudes Toward the Teaching of Writing." *Journalism & Mass Communication Educator* (Autumn 1998): pp. 50–64.

McGrath, Kevin. "Treasure Your Verbs, For They Are Golden." *The American Editor* (December 1998): p. 28.

Overholser, Geneva. "Editor Inc." *American Journalism Review* (December 1998): pp. 48–65.

Raines, Howell. "A Proud Moment of Outrage." *The American Editor* (July/August 1998): pp. 5 6.

Rowe, Sandy. "Rewarding Good Writing: A Happy ASNE Mission." *The American Editor* (March 1998): p. 2.

Russial, John. "Goodbye Copy Desks, Hello Trouble." *Newspaper Research Journal* (Spring 1998): pp. 2–17.

Stepp, Carl Sessions. "This Magic Moment." *American Journalism Review* (July/August 1998): pp. 38–41.

Weinberg, Steve. "Tell it Long, Take Your Time, Go in Depth." *Columbia Journalism Review* (January/February 1998): pp. 56–61.

To the reader

Peter St. Onge wrote a prize-worthy account of the courtroom hearing in Jonesboro, Ark., at which two boys were adjudicated delinquent for murdering four girls and a teacher and wounding 10 others in 1998.

Unfortunately, that's not the account in this book. We hope there is an additional lesson learned.

Mr. St. Onge's story in *The Huntsville Times* was a finalist in Deadline News Reporting. When it came time to incorporate the story in this book, we simplified the production process by acquiring the electronic copy of the story in the Nexis database. That version turns out to have been edited after being distributed by the Newhouse News Service.

Every newspaper writer dreads picking up the paper to find the story was altered. We regret doing that to Mr. St. Onge, to *The Huntsville Times,* and to our readers. We apologize. We also will be determined in the future to make sure that the electronic record of fine journalism is the same as the original.

For Jonesboro families, 'There's no justice'

AUGUST 12, 1998

JONESBORO, Ark.—They rose slowly, one by one, shuffling through the silence to the front of the courtroom, wearing white ribbons, carrying statements written on looseleaf that shook as they spoke. Mostly, the families of the Westside school shootings brought questions, soon to be unanswered, because as most parents understand, children have difficulty explaining the most benign of wrongdoings, never mind the most horrific.

On Tuesday, at the Craighead County Courthouse, 12-year-old Andrew Golden and 14-year-old Mitchell Johnson answered legally, at least, for their crimes. In an unusual public juvenile hearing, each was adjudicated delinquent for the acts of murdering four girls and a teacher and wounding 10 others at Westside Middle School, just outside Jonesboro.

The boys were sentenced to a youth detention center near Little Rock, where they will begin a confinement that should last at least until their 18th birthday, their 21st if the state builds an adequate facility as promised.

All of which could have been decided months ago, in a closed courtroom as is the case with most every juvenile proceeding. But Circuit Chancery Judge Ralph Wilson, not usually known around the courthouse as a big-picture guy, decided his community needed more than a whispered conclusion to the killings.

And so, an extraordinary incident spawned an extraordinary event. Wilson shooed precedent aside, moving the juvenile hearing to the large courtroom in the building and reserving 130 seats for victims' families, shooters' families, and Westside students and staff.

He allowed the boys to wear civilian clothes instead of the mandatory blue-and-white striped uniforms for accused male delinquents. Andrew Golden wore a green polo shirt, jeans and the new $120 Doc Martin boots he had put in the getaway van before the shootings. Mitchell Johnson, on his 14th birthday, got to wear a collarless cotton shirt with jeans and hiking shoes.

The boys entered the courtroom just after 10 a.m., their eyes swiveling to look at the people looking at them. This was part of Wilson's purpose for the hearing, for the victims and families to see the boys, for the boys to see the victims and families, for the chance that some thread of understanding could pass one way or another.

Or if not, for the chance at least to vent.

That came after lunch, after Johnson had pleaded guilty and Golden was declared the same in the face of quick and overwhelming evidence.

Mitchell Wright, husband of slain teacher Shannon Wright, was first to speak for the families. Each had been mailed a victim's impact statement form, which contained questions like, "How has this affected you" to help keep grief focused. But when Wright sat at the witness stand, he absently set his statement aside.

"I not only lost a wife, I lost a best friend, thanks to you two," he said, looking at the boys. "My son looks for his mother to come back. I have to explain to him that his mother's in heaven. I have to explain what you two did."

Johnson rocked back and forth at the words, nodding his head and wiping his eyes. Golden stared blankly, expressionless as he had been all hearing. When Golden's attorney, Val Price, objected and the judge cautioned Wright not to speak directly to the boys, Wright smiled wryly and continued.

He talked about how his wife had helped Golden work through a difficult class puppet project this year. He talked about how his wife had nothing but praise for Johnson when he was in her class a year ago.

He said, finally, that he wished he could sit and talk with the boys someday and find out why.

"That's what everyone wants to know," he said.

And everyone who followed asked it again.

Debbie Amer, mother of wounded child Christina Amer, said her daughter now wishes she were dead along with her two friends and teacher.

Lloyd Brooks, uncle of murder victim Natalie Brooks, quaked as he said, "I don't know where to start," then finished: "I know these two will be leaving a little while, but I hope they never return."

Regina Kaut, aunt of murder victim Britthney Verner, read a statement from the girl's mother, Suzann Wilson. "It's like living in a world without color," the words said.

Finally, when the victims were done, Mitchell Johnson stood with his own sheet of paper. "As I have sat during the last four months, I have had the opportunity to think about what happened on March 24, 1998."

He read haltingly, rocking back and forth, crying through the words.

"I am sorry," he said. "I understand that it may be impossible for some of you to forgive me."

And: "I never really felt anyone would be hurt. I thought we would shoot over everyone's heads."

And: "I hope that anyone who will listen to these words will know how sorry I am."

Minutes later, he and Golden were escorted out of the courtroom, the hearing over, the audience stunned at Johnson's statement, angry at his explanation.

Said Wright later: "When I looked at that boy in the eyes, he didn't look very sorry to me."

So the pain continues, as it will through birthdays, anniversaries and the inevitable appeals. Val Price quickly promised to fight Wilson's refusal to consider insanity or incompetence arguments that he raised Tuesday. Price argued that the boy was too young to understand the crime or the hearing. Wilson ruled that insanity or incompetence pleas do not apply to juvenile cases.

"Those are issues that will come up," Price said later. He expects the motion to take a year to file.

But Tuesday wasn't only about that kind of justice. It was a day made public for the Westside families, a chance to see the too-young killers, to talk to them, to empty out the last of the emptiness.

"I'm relieved it's over," Mitchell Wright said. "But there's no satisfaction. For any of these families, there's no justice."